Andrea Colli has written a splendid history of the multinational enterprise from medieval Europe to present day business. Practically every chapter has a case study illustrating the theme of the chapter. These case studies accent the evolving forms of multinational enterprise through the centuries. Colli shows with great skill how the organizational and administrative forms of multinational enterprise have altered through time. His book puts the multinational enterprise into the context of the changing world order.

Mira Wilkins, Professor, *Florida International University, USA*

A convincing presentation of the historical roots of today's most dynamic economic actor: International business. Colli understood to combine major trends with illustrative detail. A masterpiece on economic history.

Harm G. Schröter, *Professor, University of Bergen, Norway*

This is the textbook I was looking for when I set up a new history course on International Business and Nation States. It gives the students a much needed long-term perspective on the development of international business.

Ben Wubs, Associate Professor, *Erasmus University Rotterdam, the Netherlands*

Andrea Colli has skilfully produced an innovative book which brings together the role of markets, firms and entrepreneurs to explain the past and current challenges and dynamics of international business in the global economy. It will be of great interest to those studying or teaching international business and its history.

Teresa da Silva Lopes, *Professor, University of York, UK*

This is a very personal, fresh new narrative that intelligently integrates theories of international studies, and organization, in the historical description of key periods of change in world business history from medieval times to the present day. There are vivid case studies that will appeal to readers with an appetite for real history, as well as are synthetic integration of many debates and theories for audiences that want analysis and concepts. A welcome, much needed contribution that should be required reading in any international business history course.

Paloma Fernández Pérez, *Senior Lecturer, University of Barcelona, Spain*

Dynamics of International Business

Dynamics of International Business offers a comparative, chronological overview of the strategic and structural evolution of international firms.

Organised around eras of global economic development, the text synthesises research on the internationalisation of firms, highlighting crucial turning-points in the evolution of the international economy. A particular emphasis is placed on the relationship between historical evidence and the theoretical frameworks available for its interpretation. Each period is illustrated by a selection of short case studies from a variety of industry sectors, including the Levant Company, Nestlé, Singer, Saint-Gobain and NEC.

An essential textbook for courses in business and economic history, this book will also be a valuable resource for scholars and students of international business more generally.

Andrea Colli is Professor in Economic History at the Bocconi University, Italy.

Dynamics of International Business

Comparative perspectives of firms, markets and entrepreneurship

Andrea Colli

Routledge
Taylor & Francis Group

LONDON AND NEW YORK

First published 2016
by Routledge
2 Park Square, Milton Park, Abingdon, Oxon OX14 4RN

and by Routledge
711 Third Avenue, New York, NY 10017

Routledge is an imprint of the Taylor & Francis Group, an informa business

© 2016 Andrea Colli

British Library Cataloguing in Publication Data
A catalogue record for this book is available from the British Library

Library of Congress Cataloging in Publication Data
Colli, Andrea, 1966–
  Dynamics of international business : comparative perspectives of firms, markets and entrepreneurship / Andrea Colli. – 1 Edition.
    pages cm
  Includes bibliographical references and index.
  1. International business enterprises–History. I. Title.
    HD62.4.C625 2016
    338.8'8–dc23
            2015028347

ISBN: 978-0-415-55916-4 (hbk)
ISBN: 978-0-415-55917-1 (pbk)
ISBN: 978-1-315-84839-6 (ebk)

Typeset in Bembo
by Taylor & Francis Books

Contents

List of illustrations

Boxes

Acknowledgements

This book has been written under very special conditions, determined by the pressure of necessity. I have been teaching business history at graduate level at the Bocconi University in Milan since the beginning of my career in the 1990s. In 2006, I was asked to design and implement a course on themes relating to the evolution of the forms of the business enterprise for the students of a very demanding M.Sc. programme entitled International Management. In a (maybe sharper) way, I had to face the not-so-easy challenges that professors of history who teach in schools of economics and management are continuously confronted with. First, to make students who are normally trained in "hard", sometimes very hard, subjects which are characterised by very intense formalisation methods, interested in more "soft" approaches, at the same time maintaining a good level of intellectual stimulation. Second, to teach them "history" – something I am supposed to do, under my contractual obligations – at the same time trying to convince them that a course of history is neither a purely cultural exercise, nor a waste of time, and that the acquisition of some "historical sensitivity" (that is, the capacity to look at the present while keeping the fact that "not *everything* is new under the sun" firmly in mind,[1] and that a knowledge of the past is a powerful instrument to evaluate the status of the present) is an essential characteristic of well-trained and well-educated managers. Needless to say, this is something at which I, myself, am only sometimes successful. This urgency impacted, of course, both on the syllabus of the course as well as on the necessity to propose appropriate and suitable teaching materials. Furthermore, external constraints compelled me to transform a teaching style largely based upon frontal, traditional lectures – which I was used to, first as a student and then as an instructor – into a much more interactive one, based upon an intensive use of class participation and case discussion. This considerably reduced the "room for manoeuvre" that I had at my disposition; and it soon became clear that the students did not like the use of materials such as articles or papers at all. Many of them had started their graduate experience with no, or little, historical background. Many students are non-Europeans, an increasing number, and they bring very different experiences, points of view and comprehension to those of their fellow classmates into the discussions. Other external constraints included the quantity of pages: the course was going to include intensive class discussion activity; thus, this did not allow other textbooks, written by prominent colleagues, and already in use in other business schools and universities, to be used. These books, which one can find cited in this book, remain a key reference for everyone interested in international business history and international business in general: this book aims much more modestly to provide both students and the instructors of courses on global entrepreneurship with a learning tool which is simultaneously both flexible and provocative.

Therefore, while writing this book, I kept in mind some of the basic elements necessary to make it a useful companion for courses on the history of international business.

First, the book is intended to convey quite simple and precise concepts. Given that the realm of international business is extremely complex, in terms of the actors involved and elements which mutually influence one other, an effort to simplify and to provide a synthesis was extremely important. Because this is a textbook, the volume had to take into account the fact that, as stated above, the majority of its potential readers may have little or no historical knowledge, as they may be used to more synthetic approaches. The search for synthesis does, however, come at a price: reality is, in fact, full of nuances and cannot be easily simplified and reduced to its basic components. I am perfectly conscious of this. Each chapter conveys, beyond the narrative, a few, maybe just one or two, very simple messages that can provide generalisations: for instance, messages about risk and uncertainty, about the role of governments and political economy in international business, about the impact of technological change or of institutional constraints on the behaviour of internationally active entrepreneurs. A consequence of all this is that, while there is much included in each chapter, there is also a lot left out. For instance, one may criticise the fact that there is no detailed analysis of the role of joint ventures and other contractual agreements in international business in the volume. Others may find the (perhaps excessive) space devoted to cartels in the interwar period to be unmerited. Others will find a bit provincial the excessive use of examples derived from Italian business history, which is, however, rich in interesting and very instructive cases. But this is again an issue which regards the selection of the messages to be delivered – and of the freedom left to colleagues who will be free to choose to emphasise some messages instead of others.

The teaching methods that I have employed in this and other courses – methods which are increasingly becoming diffused at international level – call for a textbook which provides a ready-to-go framework for class discussion, in order to offer an effective mixture of case histories and frontal lectures. In principle, the book is composed of very broad "frames" (the chapters), in which it should be easy to insert the analysis and discussion of one case or more. Each chapter is more or less equally divided into the analysis of the micro-structures at work in the realm of global entrepreneurship. For the same reason, I decided to add text boxes to each chapter, which could form the basis for additional discussion or simply for further in-depth analysis through structured concrete examples. These text boxes have a different origin. Some are syntheses of cases written by the instructors on the course over the years; others have been specifically written for this volume by the author and/or some of his colleagues; still others are the synthesis of valuable research already published by other colleagues. Responsibility for the selection of the topics and for the text boxes rests exclusively with the author.

Theories of international business are implicitly discussed in each chapter, but I have consciously avoided framing them in a separate section of the book. In the end, this is a *history* book, and a specific section dedicated to theories would probably have been inappropriate. However, interpretative frameworks are very much relevant, given the fact that, as stated above, this book is (also) for students in schools of economics and management, who are used to theories and abstractions. In this book, theories are contextualised and associated with the different phases, in order to make them more understandable and effective in explaining the variance in the real world. The main interpretative paradigms are thus discussed as the products of the specific historical phase which influenced and/or determined their creation and diffusion.

A third hazardous choice made was the decision to avoid an excess of emphasis and of detail in the description of the most recent trends. The final chapter, which contains in its title the word "Epilogue", is, in fact, an attempt to summarise in a few pages the momentous transformations in the framework of international entrepreneurship which have taken place during the last twenty-five years. The underlying reason for this, perhaps, "excessive" endeavour to synthesise is twofold. First, the process of transformation within the new framework of globalisation that we have witnessed in recent years is still under way. One of the privileges afforded to a historian is the fact that, in principle, he or she can (and, to my mind, definitely should) avoid using the past to forecast the future, and, given the complexity of the transformations under way, I fully intend to exploit this privilege. Second, it would probably reveal an excess of confidence for a historian to attempt to explore the current dynamics of the strategies and the structures of multinational firms, something which, again, I am happy to leave to my colleagues in the field of international strategy. What I have, instead, tried to do is to use the last chapter as an example of how historical sensitivity can help to evaluate the present in the light of the past, distinguishing what is genuinely new from what has already happened before.

This book has, unfortunately, taken me a long time to write, given that it is some years since I drafted the original project – which, in the end, has not been greatly changed or revised. In a sense, this has probably been for the best, for, during these years, I have had the opportunity to accumulate further research and teaching experience which has been transposed to the pages which follow this introduction. However, at a certain point, it was *really* necessary to conclude, and in this the gentle but firm pressure of my editor, Sinead Waldron of Routledge, has been essential, as have the flexible professional skills of Chris Engert in transforming my English into something acceptable. Many people have, in one way or another, willingly or less willingly, collaborated in this project, without *any* responsibility, and they deserve full recognition: the "team" of international business history courses, that is, Veronica Binda, Katja Girschik, Marina Nicoli, Alexandra Papadopoulou; Marco Bertilorenzi and Mario Perugini, authors of some of the text boxes. Stephanie Decker and Christina Lubinski, Valeria Giacomin, Pavida Pananond, Teresa Da Silva-Lopes, Mira Wilkins, Geoffrey Jones, Matthias Kipping and Lucia Piscitello, with whom I discussed some aspects of the story recounted in the book; Maria Fusaro and Isabella Cecchini, who gave me invaluable suggestions concerning historical periods with which I am less familiar; and, last, but not least, Fabrizio Perretti and Markus Venzin, the present and past Directors of the International Management programme. My students, too, deserve a mention: they have been ruthless judges, and their sharp, incisive evaluations have continuously forced me to fine-tune my arguments. All this said, the usual *caveat* applies. Finally, while writing this book I greatly benefited from periods of study and visiting professorships at the Harvard Business School, the European University Institute in Florence and the Fondazione Cini in Venice.

Finally, this book is dedicated in equal measure to Franco Amatori and to our never-ending friendship; and to my daughters, Anna, Caterina and Maddalena, who, I hope (and not without some foreboding and apprehension), will live happily in a peaceful and truly "global" world.

Note

1 Apologies to Ecclesiastes, Chapter 1, Verse 9: "What has been will be again, what has been done will be done again; there is nothing new under the sun."

List of abbreviations

AFC	*Alais, Froges et Camargue*
AIAG	*Aluminium Industry Aktien-Gesellschaft – Alusuisse*
ALCAN	*Aluminum Company of Canada*
ALCOA	*Aluminum Company of America*
ALTED	*Aluminium Co. Ltd. of Canada*
ARKK	*Awaji Rennyu KK* or *Awaji Condensed Milk*
BACO	*British Aluminium Company*
BRIC	Brazil, Russia, India and China
C&C	Computers and Communications
CGN	*China General Nuclear Power Group*
CIA	*Convention Internationale de l'Azote*
CMI	Capital Mobility Index
DEN	Deutschland, England and Norway
EDF	*Électricité de France*
EIC	*East India Company* (British East India Company)
FDI	Foreign Direct Investment
GCC	Global Commodity Chains
GDP	Gross Domestic Product
GNP	Gross National Product
GVC	Global Value Chains
HSBC	*Hong-Kong and Shanghai Banking Corporation*
IDP	Investment Development Path
IMF	International Monetary Fund
IRI	*Istituto per la Ricostruzione Industriale*
ISE	*International Standard Electric*
ITT	*International Telephone & Telegraph*
MITI	Ministry of International Trade and Industry (Japan)
NATO	North Atlantic Treaty Organization
NEC	Nippon Electric Company
NITREX	*Nitrogen Chemical Fertilizer Export Cartel*
OECD	Organisation for Economic Co-operation and Development
OLI	Ownership, Location, Internalisation advantages
PCAC	*Produits Chimiques d'Alais et de la Camargue*
R&D	Research and Development
SASAC	State-owned Assets Supervision and Administration Committee (PRC)
SEMF	*Société Electrométallurgique Française*

SKF	*Svenska Kullagerfabriken*
SME	Small- and Medium-Sized Enterprise
SOE	State-owned Enterprise
SS	Steamship
UFC	United Fruit Company
UK	United Kingdom
UN	United Nations
UNCTAD	United Nations Conference on Trade and Development
US	United States of America
USD	United States Dollars
VAW	*Vereinigte Aluminium Werke*
VOC	*Verenigde Oostindische Compagnie* (Dutch East India Company)
WTO	World Trade Organization

Introduction

1. Key factors in the global economy

Multinational firms and global companies are key actors in the present global economy. If we adhere to the standard definition of a multinational as a company controlling income-generating assets in at least two different countries, very many (if not all) of the largest companies in the world belong to this category.

Some companies are so international, in terms of sales, production, and distribution facilities, that they proudly define themselves as "global", that is to say, present, active and competitive throughout the entire world. "A Global Company" is the subtitle most frequently found when browsing corporate websites and brochures.

The world's largest multinational corporations are sometimes *incredibly* large. Rankings are abundant, depending on the measure of the size – in terms of turnover, sales, employees, and market value. According to one such ranking, one which identified the world's largest "economic entities" in 2009 – according to their size in terms of gross domestic product (GDP) (if countries) or revenues (if companies) – there were forty-four corporations among the top one hundred entities. Almost all of them correspond to the standard definition of "multinational corporation". The largest and wealthiest countries are clearly at the top of the ranking. However, in twenty-second place one finds *Wal-Mart*, the chain of department stores which is internationally present in more than fifteen countries with around 600,000 employees. *Wal-Mart* precedes countries such as Sweden, Norway, Austria and Taiwan in the ranking. *Shell* and *Exxon Mobil* (thirty-fourth and thirty-fifth) are bigger economic entities than Finland. This may not tell us much about how these companies are shaped and run, but it does tell us a lot about their economic relevance. The companies listed in the same ranking accounted for around 10 per cent of the total world GDP – about 6.6 trillion United States dollars (USD) – in 2009.

However, today, and much more so than in the past, it is not just large companies that invest abroad. A growing number of small- and medium-sized enterprises (SMEs), almost always family-owned or individually owned, also invest abroad. They are much smaller than the giant global companies in the top rankings, unless they cross their respective national borders and operate production facilities abroad, thanks to a number of favourable conditions which allow them to act globally with a relatively reduced financial, organisational and managerial effort.

A notion strictly associated to the multinational (actually, a synonym) is that of foreign direct investment (FDI), a concept which indicates the willingness of investors (be they companies or individuals) to exert a direct influence on the management and strategies of the companies in which they invest. However, the relevance of foreign direct investment activity in today's global economy is not easy to estimate. Data are often extremely accurate for some countries, but less so for others, and the distinction between the specific *purpose* of the investment (control or a simple financial investment) is often subtle and subjective. There are, however, enough sufficiently accurate statistics available to allow us at least to estimate the relevance of foreign direct investments in the global economy.

The International Monetary Fund (IMF), the Organisation for Economic Co-operation and Development (OECD) and the United Nations Conference on Trade and Development (UNCTAD), for instance, all produce in-depth statistical measurements of foreign investment activity both in the developed and in the developing economies. According to the UN 2013 World Investment Report, which continuously monitors the status of foreign investment activity throughout the world, in 2012, the total stock of foreign investments abroad (measured by the amount of outward foreign investments, that is, the investments held in countries different from that of the origin of the investor) amounted to nearly 23.6 trillion dollars, almost 33 per cent of world GDP. Outflows (that is, the amount of foreign investments on a yearly base) amounted to 1.4 trillion dollars − actually signalling a slow recovery after the financial crisis that hit the world economy in 2008 and 2009. The foreign affiliates of domestic companies held assets to the tune of 86.5 trillion USD, produced an added value of 6.6 trillion USD, and employed about 71.6 million people.

Although these numbers are astonishing *per se*, they become even more impressive when they are viewed from a long-term perspective. If we just consider outward stocks, the UNCTAD statistical databases report that, if their total amount in world GDP was around 33 per cent in 2012, this percentage was 24.8 per cent in the year 2000, 9.4 per cent in 1990, and only 4.7 per cent in 1980. No previous data are available in the databases. However, from other existing quantitative and qualitative research, it is possible to argue that even the figure for 1980 was a peak in foreign investment activity which began in the years following the Second World War. Since 1945, in sum, the trend in foreign investment growth as a percentage of world GDP went on almost uninterrupted, albeit with two relevant exceptions: 2002 (the year following the terrorist attacks against the United States of America on 11 September 2001), and 2008, when the stock of outward investments decreased after the diffusion of the global sub-prime financial crisis.

At a less aggregate level, qualitative evidence also reveals the pervasiveness of multinational activity among the largest companies in the world. The lists of the world's top leading companies, independent of the indicator chosen, include companies which, with very few exceptions, all engage in multinational activity. It is hard to find non-multinational firms among the global ranking of the largest companies in the world (by market value) as compiled yearly by the *Financial Times*, or in similar rankings published by economic periodicals such as *Forbes* or *Fortune*.

In sum, both at aggregate level and at the level of individual companies, there is clear evidence of the growing relevance of foreign investments and multinational activity. This, however, is only one of the sides of a multi-faceted coin.

Another relevant, and much debated, issue today is that of the geographical diffusion of multinationals. According to the UNCTAD statistical databases, in the year 2000, the total of inward investments stock (which allows us to identify the distribution of investments by looking at the countries of destination) was unequally distributed. 75.6 per cent was directed to developed countries (almost exclusively Europe and North America).

During the following decade, the situation quickly changed, and today the percentage of total foreign investments directed to the developed economies has declined to 62.5 per cent. One might be surprised by the fact that, in 1980, the amount of foreign investments was even more equally distributed than today. The developed economies were hosting 57.5 per cent of total investments abroad, and the developing countries 42.5 per cent.

While developed countries steadily decline in relevance for foreign investors, they are also increasingly less relevant as the *sources* of foreign investments. In 1990, developed countries were the origin of 93 per cent of the world's total *outward* investments. By 2012, this percentage had declined to 79.1 per cent, mirroring a rise in developing economies as sources of investments abroad. And now, without the "Hong Kong effect", the rise in the rate of outward investments has, as one might expect, been mainly located in Asia (South and Eastern), and specifically in Singapore, China and Hong Kong, which became an active investor abroad immediately before its return to China.

The evidence at "micro" level is straightforward here. If one considers the companies among the largest 500 by revenue, and looks at the companies present in the list of the so-called BRIC countries – Brazil, Russia, India and China – that is, the economies considered to be the future protagonists in the world economic scenario – one will find seventy-three companies: eight Brazilian, seven Russian, eight Indian and fifty Chinese. Most of them are multinationals with a large number of operations abroad. In 2005, there were three from Brazil, three from Russia, five from India and sixteen from China. In 1992, Brazil had one (*Petrobras*), Russia none, India six and China none (*Fortune Global 500*, various years).

It is, in sum, not a one-way road. But the road is becoming increasingly busy. For different reasons (ranging from technology and knowledge seeking, to the quest for the necessary natural resources, to the exploitation of specific and particular advantages in other markets), companies from developing countries have become active investors abroad to such an extent that, in Western countries – the US included – governments and public opinion have started to worry about a sort of counter-colonisation. An effective symbol can be seen in the acquisition in 2008 of two "icons" of the British motor industry, *Jaguar* and *Land Rover*, by the Indian leader *Tata Motors*. Indian "global powerhouses" (after the title of a famous Harvard Business School bestseller) are now flanked by other powerhouses from the rest of the developing world, China first and foremost.

2. Old and new debates

This intensive (and growing in intensity) traffic across the world's borders has renewed long-standing debates concerning multinational enterprises, such as agents, brokers and, in general, the "symbols" of globalisation, and has attracted – for the multinational enterprise – the same criticism and support that the process of globalisation attracted. To put it quite simply, multinationals can be considered to be the "micro components" of the macro phenomenon of globalisation – or, alternatively, globalisation is something which travels around the world on the shoulders of multinational investments and global products.

The idea of multinationals and, in general, *all* companies internationally active as the agents of globalisation (or, in the words of Vladimir Ilyich Lenin, of imperialism and exploitation), is certainly not new. The dramatic diffusion of the multinational enterprise after 1960 coincided with a parallel wave of debates, both in the academic world and in the popular press, on the good and the bad of multinational activity. As one might expect, these debates have been intensifying in the period of the "new globalisation", and multinationals have – not surprisingly – been identified as the primary targets of anti-globalisation movements. While, quite generically, multinationals were seen, in the past, alternatively as agents of exploitation and imperialism, or as supranational organisations which threatened both the sovereignty and the power of the state, today, the sources of criticism are more detailed and articulated. "Corporate social responsibility" issues, for instance, are a core component of the polemic against multinational enterprises, criticised for not applying the same standards in the various countries in which they are present. Today, they are also blamed for the damage that they do to the environment, and/or for spreading corruption and bad business practices, particularly in under-developed countries. These criticisms have often been so strong that it is now very common practice among the largest multinationals to engage in philanthropic and humanitarian projects, sponsoring foundations and charities, especially in poor countries. There are countless examples of this: for instance, one of the most criticised and scrutinised multinationals in the world, *Nestlé*, runs six different development programmes, in areas such as nutrition, human rights, water supply, the environment, rural development and the sourcing of raw materials.

Public opinion in Western countries, particularly in periods of economic crisis and downturn, tends to see foreign investment activity in a quite ambiguous way. While outward investments (that is, those made by domestic firms abroad) are seen as threatening the internal economy and ultimately resulting in a loss of jobs, inward investments are also seen as threatening, as foreigners are seen as doing "easy shopping" – with possible dangerous consequences in terms of lay-offs.

Today, this criticism is extended even to the multinationals and to the foreign direct investments from the emerging economies or the recently developed countries. As suggested above, both public opinion and the politicians in developed countries have recently been seriously worried by the tendency shown by the newly industrialised countries to acquire companies abroad, especially in advanced countries. In some cases, the tensions have merely nationalistic origins. In others, they are motivated by the necessity to protect strategic knowledge, resources, and technology. In other cases again, more delicate issues are at stake, as, for instance, in the case of Chinese acquisitions and direct investments in Western countries. Here, again, examples are multiplying at a fast pace. A particularly telling example is that of the *China General Nuclear Power Group* (CGN), an international company constructing nuclear plants, which, around 2012, joined *Électricité de France* (EDF) in a joint-venture project to build nuclear plants in the United Kingdom. According to the *Financial Times*, this is creating a "national security headache for the government".[1] The reason is quite obvious: a foreign firm is going to control a strategic resource, in this case, energy. To make things worse, CGN is not only foreign, but Chinese, and openly describes itself in its website as a "colossal state-owned enterprise", being directly controlled by the State-owned Assets Supervision and Administration Committee (SASAC), in its turn directly responsible to the Communist government. Ironically, EDF is also a state-owned enterprise (with nearly 85 per cent of its shares in the hands of the French government), but this seems to have raised less concern in British public opinion, although the irony has been noted.[2] In the end, and again ironically, a substantial section of the British fully liberalised energy sector will be supplied by plants directly under the control of two (foreign) state-owned enterprises.

Global companies often see themselves as truly global, and less and less as "national champions", that is, as the carriers of the interests of their countries of origin, a vision which was once extremely popular. Nonetheless, their actions abroad are often interpreted, and managed, as a mixture of economic and political motives. The Chinese appetite for natural resources, from oil to rare earth elements, has led to Chinese (mainly state-owned) multinationals setting up exploitation projects throughout the underdeveloped countries of Asia, Africa and South America, buying concessions and establishing joint ventures with local firms, together with programmes of local development agreed with the national governments. The aggressiveness of Chinese companies is openly supported by the Chinese government, through visits by top officials, in a joint effort which concerns other foreign companies – mainly Western – which are not supported by their respective governments. An instructive story here concerns the successful penetration of the Chinese state-owned company *Sino-U*, a producer of uranium for nuclear energy plants, in Niger, one of the poorest African countries (with 665 dollars *per capita*, Niger is 176th out of 180 countries in the World Bank ranking of *per capita* GDP). The Niger uranium market used to be completely at the disposal of *Areva*, a French state-owned multinational, which exploited the local mines in order to supply fuel for France's nuclear production plants (curiously, Niger's second main export after uranium is onions, which might also generate French interest). In 2010, *Sino-U* successfully broke what was technically a monopsony, agreeing to partner the Nigerien government in a new production plant, and to build a hydro-electric plant and other bonuses. Moreover, breaking the French monopsony meant that *Areva* had to agree to better conditions more favourable to the Nigerien government in order to maintain its concessions (and obtain new ones).

And China is not alone. Many global companies are a direct expression of the governments of emerging countries – often authoritarian regimes – which are both willing and able to invest abroad by leveraging on a considerable amount of financial resources managed through investment vehicles such as sovereign wealth funds, which often perform their investment(s) through controlled companies (or sovereign wealth enterprises) which actually make the direct investment(s) abroad.

As the Niger case shows, the border between the bad and the good side of foreign investment activity is extremely vague. A foreign investment brought about the elimination of monopsonistic power enjoyed by another foreign investor, and ultimately resulted in major benefits for the country of investment (hopefully, the Chinese and French money will not be embezzled by government officials and politicians).

But there are many reasons on the good side. There is consolidated literature (and evidence) which stresses how foreign investments are constantly generating positive spillovers, both for the countries generating and for those receiving the investment. Multinational investments have been seen as the agents of the diffusion of knowledge, technological progress and expertise. They have taken innovations, knowledge, capital, and employment around the world. An updated version of this view is one which considers international investments as a key agent in the process of the globalisation of the world economy. In particular, in the case of emerging countries and of developing economies, inward investments (those coming from outside the country) are considered not only to be key elements in providing access to the international economy and to global markets, but also to standard international business practices. In some cases, foreign acquisitions act as the drivers of modernisation, promoting imitation by local entrepreneurs who face new competitive threats and introducing them to innovative business practices. In others, governments that are willing to modernise their countries' industrial apparatus have turned heavily to foreign investors, attracted through privatisations and sales, as happened in some Western European countries during the 1980s and in the former members of the Soviet Communist *bloc* after 1989.

In sum, and from a particular point of view, the renewal of the criticism and of the debates about multinational firms and cross-border investment activity is witness to the growing relevance of the issue in a phase in which the global economy is constantly expanding its borders, notwithstanding temporary downturns. And, in such an inter-connected world, it is characterised by growing entropy, in which companies expanding their activities abroad are increasingly relevant protagonists.

3. A new phenomenon?

According to *Etymonline* (http://www.etymonline.com), the adjective "multinational", referring to a corporation, became common usage during the 1960s, while its abridged version, the noun "multinational", has been in use since the early 1970s, less than fifty years ago. Etymologically speaking, multinationals are thus a quite recent phenomenon.

Even the theoretical apparatus currently in use to interpret the existence of the mul-tinational corporation and its strategies and structures is not that "old". The first attempts to systematise the phenomenon go back to the 1950s, while the most relevant field-specific interpretative framework, the Ownership Location Internalisation (OLI) framework, was provided by John Dunning at the end of the 1970s. Although multinationals, as a topic of academic interest, may be relatively young creatures, they may, nonetheless, be fully mature. The relative "novelty" of this research field is also reflected in the dominant approach in the literature, which tends to consider multinationals and international business activity in general as a contemporary phenomenon, and focus basically on the phase of intense globalisation which followed the fall of the Berlin Wall in 1989.

Historians, however, and economic and business historians in particular, have a more complex and less linear view, which derives from in-depth research into the individual cases of companies, which, in turn, has led to the establishment of patterns of con-tinuity and change in international business activity. In particular, the added value(s) of historical research on multinationals, and, more generally, internationally active firms, functions at two levels.

The first concerns the internal structure, or "form", of the multinational corporation, or of the international activity of business firms. From a historical point of view, multinational corporations existed long before the noun was coined. If one adheres to the standard definition of the multinational enterprise, companies that controlled income-generating assets in more than one country existed in considerable numbers long before the 1960s.

The US sewing-machine producer *Singer*, for example, which is credited with being the world's first modern multinational, had already opened a production facility in Glasgow in 1867, followed by a similar investment in Russia in 1897; the German electro-mechanical companies were key agents in the electrification of Europe and South America, opening branches and directly engaging in the creation and management of electricity providers. The French glassmaker *Saint-Gobain* adopted an aggressive strategy of acquisitions and foreign investments throughout Europe, becoming the leading com-pany in the industry in Spain and Italy. The German steelmaker *Mannesmann*, leader in the production of seamless tubes, invested in several European countries, including the United Kingdom in 1897, and Italy in 1908. Recent historical research has demonstrated how, before the Second World War and even during the years of the Great Depression, a great deal of foreign investment went to European countries.

As the following chapters will show in greater detail, the standard "modern" multi-national started to spread as a dominant form of enterprise in international business activities during the second half of the nineteenth century, coinciding with a technological revolution which made the transfer of people, goods, information, and money much easier, and with the consolidation of favourable conditions for international trade and entrepreneurship, mainly of a cultural and institutional nature. Historians know well, however, that the "modern" multinational was only *another form* of enterprise through which the international activity of entrepreneurs in manufacturing and services was taking place; *another form*, since entrepreneurs and their enterprises had been engaging in doing business abroad, even in different countries and locations simultaneously, confronting themselves with similar problems and strategic choices, just like their more "modern" counterparts, long before. According to a much less restrictive, but much more realistic, definition of multinationals, there has always been "business operating across borders".

A great deal of historical research into international business activity, starting from a detailed analysis of the complex operations of medieval merchants and bankers, to the initiatives of privileged trading companies which enjoyed the protection of their own national governments in order to consolidate their economic and political power overseas, has shown the huge variety of the forms of international business which succeeded one another over time in line with the evolution in the general context provided by markets, institutions and technology.

History stresses, in sum, the huge variety of forms which international business activity assumed both over time and in the long run. In doing this, it also provides another valuable assessment, that is, that something which is normally considered as a "new" phenomenon, generated by the current process of globalisation, is, in reality, *anything but* new, and that the strategies of the enterprises and entrepreneurs active in the present complex framework of the international market have been anticipated in the past by other, no less creative, economic actors that had to cope with similar, or even greater, conditions of uncertainty.

A second area in which the historical approach can provide high added value to the research on international business lies beyond the internal structure of the company and concerns the investigation of the relationship between the *forms* of international entrepreneurship and the process of economic globalisation.

Economic historians have dealt with the concept of globalisation for a long time. If one defines economic globalisation as the increase – at an unprecedented speed – in the rate of economic interactions across the globe thanks to technological and institutional innovations, it becomes clear how the present globalisation is the latest in a series of episodes which have punctuated the history of the world economy during the last ten centuries.

The fascinating history of the medieval international land routes and sea-trade routes linking the North and the South of Christian Europe to the Islamic North African coast, and, through the silk and spices road, to the flourishing economic systems of India and China, is a tale of globalisation which was made possible by technological and institutional innovations, a globalisation which was not so very different in its internal structure from that brought about by the rise of empires during the nineteenth century.

At a certain point in history, around the second half of the nineteenth century, the world was divided into empires, some of which had significant developments overseas. European countries had created their empires and protectorates in Africa, while China and Japan fought to consolidate their dominance in East Asia. The Russian Empire was the largest in the world, at least in terms of surface territory, and pushed to extend its influence into Indian regions. The "symbol" of imperialism was, however, that of the British influence throughout the world. Phileas Fogg, Jules Verne's fictional globetrotter, travelled, in eighty days, around a world which was – directly or indirectly – mainly under British rule, or culturally close to the United Kingdom. To a different extent and with different degrees of authoritarianism, empires acted as the powerful agents of integration, albeit often on an unequal basis, and of cultures and markets. At the same time, starting from the 1860s, technological innovations (which included such audacious initiatives as the building of canals such as the one at Suez or the realisation of transatlantic telegraph connections through underwater cables) made the interconnection of individuals and economies, embodied in a revolution in transport and communications, both faster and easier, in a way which is comparable only to that which took place with the diffusion of the Internet and satellite communications, of mass air transport and high-speed trains.

Besides this notion of "multiple globalisations" (which, again, shows how historical analysis allows the present to be put into a more realistic perspective) historians have also stressed how the globalisation process is far from being a linear one. The phases of globalisation are, in fact, separated by phases of disintegration, in which the previous achievements dissolve and in which separation prevails. Borders suddenly become less permeable, people travel and transfer financial resources more slowly, and protectionist policies, tariffs, and trade barriers serve to encourage *autarkic* behaviour. "De-globalisation" begins.

Business and economic historians clearly agree about the fact that an intensification in the process of globalisation normally coincides with an intensification of international business activity, international investments, and with increasing opportunities for entrepreneurs willing to tap into enlarging and increasingly dynamic markets.

As this book will show, the different waves of globalisation have been characterised by different examples, or forms, of international business firms, each one emerging as particularly efficient within the general framework conditions. Across time and phases of globalisation, entrepreneurs and enterprises have found endless opportunities, ways, forms and strategies to expand their initiatives beyond the borders of the local and national markets. In some ways, this is a further confirmation of the ultimately "global" nature of capitalism, and the historical approach to the internationalisation of business allows us to appreciate this complexity further.

4. The dynamics of international business

This book is exactly about the *long-term* forms of international business enterprises, and about the challenges and choices which they have to face in their process of international growth. Explicitly, the book will not focus on the history of multinationals "*strictu sensu*", but, more generally, on a broader concept of international business activity, of which, as stated above, the modern multinational is only one of the possible forms.

The conceptual framework proposed here is both chronological and thematic. In the very long run (roughly, the last 800 years), the succession of the phases of globalisation and the phases of de-globalisation has generated significant business opportunities for enterprises and entrepreneurs, as well as for entire countries and national systems. In their turn, these processes of globalisation have been determined, incentivised or hindered by a set of variables, and, in particular, by *technology*, which allows us to transfer goods, information, people, and capital in faster and safer ways than in the past; but it is *institutions* (conventions), intended as regulations, at national and, above all, at international level, which facilitate or hinder the globalisation of business activities. Examples of institutional devices range from the standardisation of business practices and of commercial laws and codes, to the creation of practical standards which eliminate information asymmetries in different markets, from a shared system of measures, to the elimination of the gold standard, from apparently less "exciting" things, such as the gauge of trains, to the invention of other standards as the container and bar codes. A third variable, in part overlapping with the second, is the role played by national governments.

Despite a very diffused perception of globalisation as being incompatible with the role of national governments, the latter played and continue to play a pivotal role in the process of the internationalisation of enterprises and entrepreneurs. Governments historically play a relevant role as both the facilitators and the supporters of the internationalisation of domestic firms, both directly and indirectly, and through the use of different instruments, which include a good deal of violence, military power and diplomatic manoeuvring. From the centrally coordinated protection of mercantile ventures in Medieval Europe to the governmental ownership and involvement in trading companies, to the Japanese coordinated internationalisation policy of the 1970s and 1980s, to the aggressive investment policies of Chinese state-owned enterprises today, governments actively pushed for the internationalisation of domestic firms, thus providing further incentives in the process of international expansion. The attitudes of governments towards inward foreign investments are the other side of the process, as we can see, for instance, in the case of the above-mentioned privatisation programmes which explicitly allow the intervention of foreign capital and investors, or in the case of governments which explicitly oppose the activity of foreign investors, or subordinate the possibility of investing to certain conditions – for instance, the compulsory involvement of a local partner.

A last, relevant, and often under-estimated variable is found in the *cultural* and *political attitudes* towards globalisation processes, which help to explain a great deal of the market opportunities for international companies. Positive attitudes towards foreign products and culture can serve to explain the incentives that spurred both the international medieval merchants investing in and exporting spices which were highly fashionable and in great demand in Europe, and the opportunities enjoyed by American companies in Europe during the 1950s and 1960s, at the apex of the process of cultural homogenisation known as "Americanisation".

This book is, in sum, a book of international business history. It depicts firms and entrepreneurs doing business across borders and designing their strategies and making their choices within the framework of the waves or phases of globalisation and de-globalisation, which, in their turn, are the result of the continuous interaction among forms of technology, institutional devices facilitating trade and investment, and government attitudes and cultures. The results of this dynamic interaction are to be found in the changing forms of international business enterprises over space and time.

Notes

1 http://on.ft.com/1ahgkjM.
2 www.theguardian.com/environment/2013/oct/21/china-nuclear-power-britain-outdated-technology.

1 International business before the Industrial Revolution

Introduction

This chapter addresses the nature and structure of "international business" before the Industrial Revolution. As we will see later in greater detail, the First Industrial Revolution, which, from the beginning of the nineteenth century, radically changed the physiognomy of both the world economy and society, was also at the basis of a radical change in the very forms in which business was carried out internationally. A deep discontinuity with the past was created by the diffusion of new means of production and of the factory as a way of organising capital and labour in an increasing number of industries. Together with this, the presence of institutional devices able to foster the globalisation of markets was of paramount relevance. This has often induced scholars of international business to focus their attention on the historical period which followed this epochal watershed, when the embryonic precursors of the modern multinationals appeared. Right or wrong, this approach has had the consequence that very few studies which focus on the history and the economics of international business take the variety of activities present in the so-called pre-industrial age into account.

However, from another point of view, scholars interested in the history of the international economy in the centuries preceding the First and Second Industrial Revolutions are familiar with the diverse and variegated forms of international activity. Clearly, before industrialisation, international business activities took a very different shape from in the decades and centuries which followed the First Industrial Revolution and the appearance of the factory as the principal way of assembling the factors of production, as this chapter will show. However, this does not mean that international trade played a negligible role, relative to the size of the global economy, both at "national" and at global level. This perception has a lot to do with one of the paradoxes of modern thinking, which is to consider the present as being characterised by a degree of complexity which is, in all respects, much higher than in the past – and, consequently, considers contemporary human beings as more intelligent and more alert to new ideas than their predecessors. The degree of sophistication of international business activities in the pre-industrial period, which will be addressed in this chapter, militates, however, in the opposite direction. It bears witness to the fact that, before the Industrial Revolution, the activity of trading and doing business in general beyond "local" borders was not only normal and intensive, but was also characterised both by a range of solutions for complex and uncertain situations, and by a variety of organisational devices which were able to cope with "environmental complexity", both of which were, at the very least, just as elaborate as those which we possess today, and which we analyse in advanced courses on international corporate strategy.

The aim of this chapter is thus twofold. The first is to assess the very general framework of the international economy before the First Industrial Revolution, before what historians label as the "great divergence", to wit, the rise of the West over the rest of the world, and the consequent disruption in the overall economic and political structure of the Ancient World. Clearly, it is not necessary to stress the fact that the data and, in general, the quantitative evidence which can be put forward in this respect, are both scarce and neither reliable nor comparable with those available today. This chapter will thus be largely based upon the qualitative evidence derived from the existing research, and quantitative data will be used only for the sake of exemplification and descriptive purposes.

The second purpose of the present chapter is to describe, at a more "micro" level, the dominant forms of entrepreneurial activity which could be found in the pre-industrial economy, and also to analyse their structural characteristics in the light of some of the dominant theoretical frameworks in use in the field of international business.

1. The adventures of Pietro Querini

At the beginning of October 1432 – just some decades before the great geographic discoveries which opened up the phase of European expansion abroad – Pietro (or Piero) Querini – a Venetian nobleman, member of the *Maggior Consiglio* (the main governmental body of the *Serenissima*, or the Venetian Republic) and *"capitano da mar"*, as a sea captain was called in Venice – finally returned to his home town. He had been away – actually, he had been considered missing, lost at sea, or dead – since the summer of the year before, when his galley, called the *Querina*, left Finisterre in Spain destined for Flanders. The *Querina* – which had been loaded in Crete (or Candia, as it was then called), where this Venetian nobleman and merchant held some of his family possessions – was carrying a variety of merchandise which Pietro wished to sell abroad, which included a huge quantity of wine (a kind of fortified *Malvasia*), and spices, wax, cotton, alum and many other items which had a huge market in the northern regions of Europe. What happened to Pietro is narrated in his diary. The *Querina* left Crete in the spring of 1431, sailing close to the coast of the north of Africa, – and carefully avoiding Genoese vessels, given the war that had, in the meantime, begun between the two sea Republics. It first called at the port of Cádiz and then at Lisbon, before heading north at the end of the summer. Then something happened. The vessel was set off course due to a very severe storm, and started drifting, borne by the current of the Gulf Stream, which took it first to the coast of Ireland, and then to the North Sea, where it was shipwrecked around mid-December of that year. Abandoning the ship, Pietro and the remaining crew took to the two life-boats, which continued to drift in the storm. On 4 January 1432, a few survivors, all that remained of the *Querina*'s crew, landed on a rock near Røst, a small island in the Lofoten archipelago in Norway, well within the Arctic Circle and thousands of miles away from the original destination of the voyage. They managed to survive on this tiny island for another month, when the locals finally succeeded in rescuing them. After some months, Pietro and his fellow survivors had recovered sufficiently to start their journey home, which brought them first to Bergen and then to London, where Pietro was hosted by the powerful Venetian community. He eventually reached Venice by land, after crossing the Channel. The legend built around Pietro's adventurous journey credits him with being the first person to import the dried white codfish known as *stockfish* in Norway, and as *baccalà* in the Venetian dialect, into the Venetian region, where it remains, to this day, a vital ingredient of some typical local dishes which continue to be based upon this totally imported ingredient.

Even if the diffusion of *bacalhau* (Portuguese) or *baccalà* in Southern Europe is attested to have occurred in the fifteenth century, the trade of *stockfish* between the Norwegian coast and Britain actually goes back to the ninth century; dried fish was a suitable merchandise for long-distance trade, particularly in those European countries where it was also a fundamental ingredient in the "religious" diet for lean days, typically Friday, or during the period of Lent, when meat was prohibited. It is therefore quite difficult to believe this part of the story in its entirety; there are, however, a number of elements which allow us to understand the characteristics of international business before the First Industrial Revolution in greater detail.[1]

One out of thousands, in Europe, Scandinavia, the Middle East, India, South East Asia and China, Pietro was regularly producing and trading wine and other commodities from his family's estates in Crete with the rest of the Mediterranean. However, the most profitable areas for running these commercial activities were in Flanders, already a fairly rich region that had no vineyards but had to be supplied with wine, which was a basic ingredient of daily life as well as of religious practices. Pietro was thus travelling regularly from the shores of Asia and Africa to the colder regions of North Europe, and close to what could be rightly seen as the "frontier of civilisation", connecting physically different markets, different supplies, and different, yet complementary, needs.

Pietro's adventurous travelling is, however, also relevant for another important reason. The following section of this chapter will, in fact, depict a very general and impressionistic story of international business activities before the Industrial Revolution. The focus will be on the geographic extension of long-distance trade, its progressive articulation into a unique global system, and its overall complexity, the strategies and the forms of behaviour of merchants and entrepreneurs, and the main devices which made such a delicate mechanism function in such a surprisingly smooth way. However, such complexity could be interpreted as something involving the consumption propensity (and the purchasing power) of a handful of the happy few belonging to an *élite*. Economic and social historians have, however, demonstrated that the demand and consumption of exotic merchandise, or simply of goods produced in distant lands, was by no means confined to a limited number of consumers. The hundreds of tonnes of pepper, nutmeg, cloves and other spices consumed yearly by Europeans, then replaced by other mass-consumption products from coffee to tea, from cocoa to tobacco to sugar, all demonstrate how long-distance trade was able to revolutionise the day-to-day lives of people, *ordinary* people. The average Chinese citizen needed silver for his payments, his taxes, or as a savings fund (value storage), just like his emperor, while, in Acapulco, the descendants of Spanish expatriates were dressing their Indian *mestizos* (persons of mixed race, especially the offspring of a Spaniard and an American Indian), or Spanish wives in silks which came from China, across the Pacific, via Manila, or eating out of and drinking from *Ming* porcelain. But ambiguity and contradictions are, at the same time, part and parcel of the very nature of the pre-industrial world, in which one part is trapped in small local universes submerged in the immense ocean of the countryside, while another part is able to frame complicated networks of exchanges over long distances, making unknown and exotic items available to those who demanded them, desired them, and had the wherewithal to pay for them.

2. Long-distance trade before the industrial revolution: relevance

One of the first important elements which impresses the reader of Querini's adventures is the actual extent and coverage of international trade and business activities in the pre-industrial period. The general argument is quite delicate here. As economic historians have clearly demonstrated, before the Industrial Revolution, self-sufficiency based upon the primary sector, agriculture, was the norm. The low *per capita* income of individuals, and the gross national product of countries and regions, were overwhelmingly based upon the rural production and the *autarkic* practices dominant in the countryside, which accounted for 90 per cent of all production. The rest was divided into manufacturing, services, and, of course, trading – as part of services. Intuitively, manufacturing occupied a relevant proportion of the non-peasant activities, and was mainly concentrated in the very rare – when compared to today – urban concentrations, with a sort of appendix in the rural-based putting-out system, a medieval sub-contracting system which temporarily included large sections of peasant society within the manufacturing sphere. Services were also mainly concentrated in urban settings, where self-production and consumption was less pervasive, and trading, too, had, in proportion, greater relevance in the towns than in the countryside. Trading was, in its turn, to be divided between short- and long-distance trade, two concepts which are largely relative – and intuitive. Today, this distinction is easier, since long-distance trade and international trade tend to overlap; but, in an age in which national states simply did not exist, the same distinction was far from being intuitive. Long-distance trade was better identified with the trading of commodities at a distance which was so great that all the information embodied in the commodity itself – its price at origin above all – vanished, provided, of course, that the same commodity was unavailable in the area of destination. The most intuitive example can be found in the history of spices. But spices – consumed in great quantities in the Europe of the Middle Ages – are just a symbol. Along the "silk route" and other routes travelled an endless variety of exotic items for which there were few or no substitutes at all (not to mention precious metals, such as gold and, above all, silver, which were going in the opposite direction). There was always something which was not immediately available, or which was tremendously scarce, or almost non-existent, but, by chance or fortune, was nonetheless deemed to be absolutely necessary, from wine to spices, from wood to silk, from dried fish to ivory, and even slaves. Historians have demonstrated – and continue to demonstrate – that long-distance trade activities have been less irrelevant, and less trivial, than was once estimated and than the sense of the superiority of present times allows us to imagine. And if, before the end of the sixteenth century, a solid, articulated and non-episodic system of Eurasian long-distance (in this case, *intercontinental*) trade was already in place, which had originated at least as far back as the thirteenth century, commerce steadily expanded like a sort of plague or contagion – with the irony that the trade routes and ships which regularly served to connect continents also served to diffuse plagues and diseases from continent to continent (see Map 1.1).

It is, of course, impossible to offer even an approximate account of the quantitative relevance of intra-European trade (the one in which Pietro Querini was just one of the countless actors), or of the intra-Asian trade and Eurasian trade, in the period preceding the Industrial Revolution, given the absence of trade statistics of any kind. However, given their relevance as a consumption item, some rough estimates are available for spices. Some calculations estimate the quantity of pepper imported to Europe every year at the beginning of the fifteenth century to be around 1,000 tonnes per year, accompanied

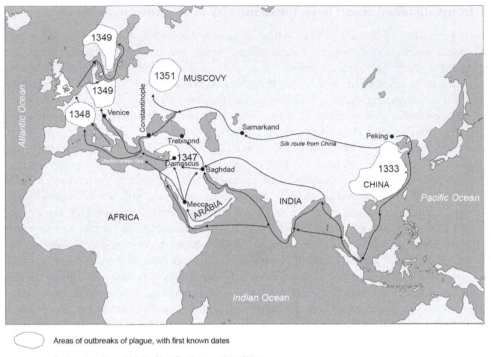

Areas of outbreaks of plague, with first known dates

Trade routes along which the Black Death spread from China

Map 1.1 The spread of the Black Death in Europe and Asia, fourteenth century

by another 400–500 tonnes of other spices. If one considers the usually (in the absence of artificial barriers) linear relationship between *per capita* GDP and the consumption of both domestic and foreign goods, the fact that the absolute majority of the world's riches was probably concentrated in Asia (and basically in India and China) at the beginning of the sixteenth century, (according to some calculations, the distribution of world GDP in the year 1500 was as follows: Europe 18 per cent, India 24 per cent, China 25 per cent, Africa 8 per cent) confirms the impression that an overwhelming part of the world's foreign trade in all kinds of merchandise was concentrated in Asia. Furthermore, after the Black Death (the devastating plague which affected Europe in the middle of the fourteenth century (1346–1353)), the increase in the *per capita* income of the survivors was translated into higher living standards, and hence into an increase in consumption levels. According to some estimates, pepper consumption in fifteenth-century Europe had risen to 1,200 tonnes per year, while that of other exotic spices more than doubled, reaching 1,300 tonnes per year.

3. Long-distance trade before the industrial revolution: geographies

The integration of trade on a global scale went on during the early modern period (1500–1800), from the beginning of the sixteenth century up to the eve of the First Industrial Revolution, giving origin to a multi-layered system of long-distance trade divided into regional/national, continental and intercontinental clusters of exchange.

Here, too, it is again impossible to calculate, even approximately, the total volume of trade, which, on the eve of the First Industrial Revolution, was no longer confined to Europe and Asia. After the (heroic) phase of the great geographic discoveries and of the opening of the sea routes across the Atlantic and the Pacific Ocean, the domain of world trade had, in fact, extended to the rest of the globe. If we define the presence of multiple, stable, long-distance (for instance, those linking the Scandinavian countries to Southern Europe, or those established between the Italian ports of Genoa and Venice and the Black Sea or Azov region), even intercontinental trade relationships as "clusters" of exchange, then, we can affirm that at least three main "clusters" existed during the seventeenth century.

The first cluster (and the oldest, most articulated and complex) was the already mentioned Eurasian trade relationship, which was established between the Middle Ages and the early modern period, and resulted, in its turn, from the progressive integration of two already existing continental exchange systems, the European one (in its turn, a very complex array of trade sub-systems, including the Baltic, the North Sea, the Mediterranean, the continental European and the Black Sea markets) and the Asian one (largely clustered in the Indian Ocean, the Bay of Bengal and the South China Sea). During the Early Middle Ages (the twelfth to fifteenth centuries), these were initially integrated by a complex system of land routes crowded by caravans, largely monopolised and controlled by Muslim merchants, which flourished and prospered until the first half of the fourteenth century, thanks to the so-called *Pax Mongolica* (the establishment of stable political control by the Mongols of Genghis and Kublai Khan on a vast mass of lands stretching basically from the Black Sea – that is, the door to the European trade system – to Beijing). After a phase of harsh and ferocious conquests, from the beginning of the fourteen century, the Mongols began to establish safe trade routes across the territories which they controlled to such an extent that European merchants could travel safely across Asia, with or without the intermediation of local middlemen. The *Pax* disintegrated by the middle of the fourteenth century, and with it the temporary safety of the trade routes across Asia. This served to stimulate the invention of alternative routes, mostly by sea. These offered quicker, cheaper and, to some extent, safer transport for Europeans to reach India and its riches. They included the discovery by Vasco da Gama of the passage to the East Indies around the Cape of Good Hope (1488), which basically allowed Europeans to skip the intermediation of Muslim middlemen.

Vasco da Gama's journey (1498) was preceded by a series of progressive discoveries along the Atlantic coast of Africa by Portuguese seamen, and ended in the establishment of a stable presence of Portuguese traders on the west coast of India, one of the world's main commercial hubs, whose ports were already crowded with ships and merchants from Asia Minor, Persia, and from the East African coast, importing all kinds of merchandise, from Arab horses to ivory, from carpets to gold, from ebony to pearls, slaves, and dyestuffs in exchange for cotton cloth, which also constituted the main item in Indian trade towards South East Asia and China, which, in its turn, sent spices, tea and porcelain to India. Thanks to the Portuguese initiatives, Europe, coming from outside and in a latecomer position, became increasingly integrated in the Asian system of exchange by means of the sea routes, which progressively substituted (but never completely replaced) the traditional, but riskier, caravan trade by land. At the same time, ethnic groups of merchants increasingly benefited from the exchange opportunities emerging in specific contexts. But how can we categorise, for instance, the behaviour of Armenian merchant communities based in Madras on the Coromandel Coast in south-east India,

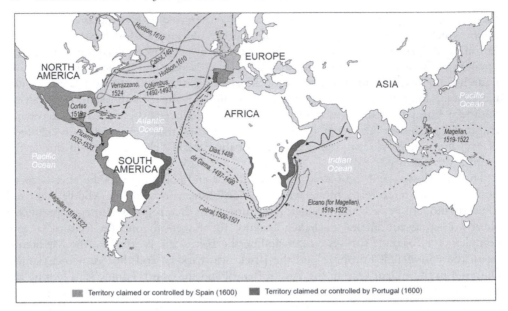

Map 1.2 European explorations and colonisation, fifteenth–seventeenth centuries

which sold local cloth and textiles in Manila's markets in exchange for the silver coming from Peru?

A second system started to consolidate after the establishment of the first permanent European settlements in both South and North America. This cluster of trade and commercial routes, known under various labels as the Columbian or Atlantic Trade System, linked the new continent to the Atlantic side of Europe. In principle, the opportunities provided by the geographical expansion of trade routes through sea exploration were available to all the Atlantic countries, especially "first movers", such as Spain and Portugal. This was undoubtedly true, at least at the very beginning, particularly for Spain. The decades following Christopher Columbus' voyages, and the Spanish *de facto* occupation of the Caribbean Islands, and of Central and South America, saw a growing trade through the transatlantic link called the *Carrera de Indias*, which continued until the beginning of the seventeenth century. Clearly, in its formative stage, this exchange was heavily asymmetrical. Until the mid-seventeenth century, New Spain (the Mexico of today) basically "exported" precious metals, through plundering at first, and then mining, while importing very little apart from a growing number of human beings, through the profitable slave trade, amounting to around one million people between the sixteenth and seventeenth centuries. According to some conservative estimates, between 1500 and 1800, Latin America alone produced about 150,000 tonnes of silver, roughly 80 per cent of the total world production in that period. It was an astounding quantity of precious metal, which dwarfed the production capacity of the two most important areas of silver production at the time, namely, South Germany and East Japan. Most of this silver travelled to Asia, as we shall see, moving both eastward and westward across the Pacific.

Brazil entered the domain of international trade at the beginning of the sixteenth century, when the Portuguese started to exploit local natural resources. Soon increasing flows of African slaves were landing on its coasts, as the workforce for the sugar-cane plantations which spread throughout the country in order to meet the growing demand for sugar coming from Europe, which, in its turn, exported manufactured goods to the New World, goods which increasingly came from continental and northern Europe, and progressively less from the Iberian peninsula.

A third system, or cluster, of exchanges and trade routes followed in the last quarter of the sixteenth century, when the Spaniards took control of the Pacific and seized Manila in 1571, moving westward to reach the same location that the Portuguese had reached by moving eastward exactly sixty years before, when they had permanently settled in Malacca (Malaysia) and, in 1557, in Macao. Both Manila and Macao became key components of intra-Asian trade. An interesting example can be found in the role played by Portuguese merchants during the late-sixteenth to early seventeenth centuries in connecting the Chinese demand for silver and supply of raw silk with Japanese silver production (which, at the beginning of the seventeenth century accounted for a good 20 per cent of the world total) and demand for silk; two countries were hostile towards each other and hence direct trade between the two was impossible. The Portuguese were so successful in the region that they were allowed to settle in the port of Nagasaki in 1571, at precisely the same period that Spain took control of Manila. And if the Portuguese successfully exploited their Japanese connections, the Spaniards applied leverage on their Manila outpost to set up a unique creation in international trade, namely, the bilateral trade relationship between China and the New World. Manila, which at the beginning of the seventeenth century had a population that was similar in size to the main Mediterranean ports of Barcelona or Venice, became a frenetic hive of activity in which growing quantities of American silver were exchanged for Chinese merchandise, above all, silk. The "Silver Galleons" or "Manila Galleons", as the ships were known, started to cross the Pacific regularly, bringing huge quantities (in size, millions of *pesos*, smuggling well over the official limit of 500,000 *pesos* set by the Crown) of precious metal, in response to the demand from China as a result of the collapse of the paper-money system in the middle of the fifteenth century and the conversion of its whole tributary system to silver, and bringing Mexican merchandise, above all, exotic silk, back to the beautiful natural bay of Acapulco, where local merchants sold it in the domestic market, without the expensive costs of intermediaries travelling westward, from China to Europe and across the Atlantic. The Pacific Trade, or, as it has been nicknamed, the Magellan Trade, heavily damaged the monopolies granted by the Spanish Crown to the Atlantic trade, as well as the local Mexican and the Spanish home-based textile industries. Officially, the authorities tried to cap the volume of exports from the Philippines, but without great success. Thus, the Magellan Trade continued for decades, with traders amassing and accumulating enormous fortunes, and allowing the Philippines to remain a prosperous outpost of the Spanish presence in the Pacific.

Box 1.1: The Manila Galleon or *"Nao de China"* (the China Ship)

On 21 November 1564, after the repeated failures of the Spanish to reach East Asia from the Spanish American colonies, a new expedition under the command of Miguel López de Legazpi, a Spanish-born Mexican navigator who had been granted the title of *Adelantado* by the King, sailed from the port of Natividad, on the island of Natividad, off the north-west coast of Mexico, to reach the Philippines. One year later, on 27 April, the expedition reached the port of Cebu in the Philippines, and seized a number of islands in the name of King Philip II. The discovery of the return route by one of the ships of the expedition initiated the connection between New Spain and the Philippine islands and allowed the Castilian Crown to penetrate East Asian commerce. The Manila galleon trade, the Spanish trade monopoly between New Spain and the Philippine islands, was established a few years later, in 1571, with the founding of the city of Manila on the island of Luzon as the capital of the Spanish colony, and the luxurious trade continued until it had to be abandoned in 1815, on the outbreak of the Mexican War of Independence.

From the beginning of this trade, the Spanish galleons reached the port of Manila, to be loaded with the commodities coming from the orient (China, Japan, Borneo and Malaysia), in particular, silk, but also porcelain items, spices and other commodities, all destined for New Spain. On the return journey, between October and April, the galleons were loaded with a growing amount of bullion extracted from the mines in New Spain and the Potosí mines in Peru, and stored in the port of Acapulco to be transported to Manila, only to be re-exported to China and other Asian markets. The annual galleon cargo of silver destined for Manila served not only to cover the costs of the merchandise contracted by merchant groups, but also to provide the "*situado*", the salary sent by the authorities in New Spain to pay for the costs of the Spanish administration in the Philippines.

The Manila galleon trade grew into an increasingly monopolistic structure formed by a series of restrictions and royal policies, caused by the increasing central pressures to reduce the portion of trans-Pacific trade. Unfortunately for the growth of Manila, this excessively profitable trade exchange met with protests in Madrid, from both the Council of Portugal and the guild of the Sevillian merchants, who saw the Chinese silk not only as a threat to the Spanish silk industry, but also as a drain on New Spain's silver production. Conflicting interests between the merchant and industrial groups in both Spain and the colonies, along with their rivalry with the Portuguese in the Asian markets, partially explains the reluctance of the Spanish Crown to establish other outposts beyond Manila. In 1593, a royal decree put an end to this undisciplined trade, and limited the freight value of the galleon cargoes to 250,000 *pesos* for Manila, and to 500,000 *pesos* for Acapulco. Investment in the galleon cargoes was regulated by the *boleta* system, which was based upon the issue of shares of equally divided cargo space on the galleon for the colonists, officials and clergy of Manila, in an effort to protect them from competition from New Spain. Every year, only two galleons, whose cargoes were not to exceed 300 tonnes, were allowed to sail from Manila to New Spain. Furthermore, direct exports from Manila to Lima (Peru), Tierra Firme (Ecuador) and Guatemala, and any other region except Japan, were prohibited, and Chinese goods could only be imported to New Spain.

Despite the increasing royal restrictions imposed on this trade, the development of Manila continued to accelerate as a part of the emerging multi-faceted global silver economy; it functioned as a pivotal port of the Pacific Rim maritime zone, while the powerful *Ming* Empire lay at its centre. The silverisation of China during the sixteenth century, caused by domestic monetary and fiscal events, generated the demand and impetus which increased trans-Pacific trade. However, although the Spanish dominated the Atlantic routes of the silver trade, they failed to do so with regard to other segments of this transport chain, especially with regard to the trading networks that linked the European *entrepôts* to the prosperous Chinese markets. The Portuguese, the Dutch and the British all had a strong grip on the eastern route with secure outposts in India and Malaysia (Goa, Malacca), and China (Macao), and Japan (Nagasaki).

Thus, finding itself excluded from intra-Asiatic trade, the Spanish Empire saw its only prospect of a direct link to silver-hungry China in Manila. High silver prices in China, in conjunction with low production costs in Japan and Spanish America, made the Manila–Acapulco trade extremely profitable for the Spaniards.

The inter-regional scale of the Manila galleon trade corresponded to the global-reach scale of the silver trade in which it was embedded, with backward and forward linkages to all four continents: the Americas, Asia, Africa and Europe. The port of Manila functioned as a linchpin for different entrepreneurial groups engaged in specialised trading networks. Notwithstanding the official restrictions, merchants from different ethnic and cultural backgrounds provided the cargoes of the Spanish galleons. The inter-mingling between Chinese, Muslim, Japanese, Armenian, Mexican, and European merchant groups reflects the dynamics of trans-Pacific trade, with the port of Manila as a nexus of cross-cultural exchange. Nonetheless, the Manila galleon trade exploited the interactions between networks of Muslim, Malay, Overseas Chinese, and inhabitants of the Ryukyu Islands south of Japan, all of whom connected *entrepôts* such as Malacca, Brunei and Chinese coastal centres, such as Quanzhou, which had existed and flourished prior to the arrival of the Europeans.

This box was written by Alexandra Papadopoulou.

★ ★ ★ ★ ★

By the middle of the seventeenth century, in sum, the three intercontinental, long-distance trade systems had consolidated and taken a definitive shape. As stated above, the Eurasian trade system was by far the most complex of these, because it resulted from the integration of two pre-existing long-distance trade systems which had developed enormously since the Middle Ages, that is, the kaleidoscopic European trade system – which, in its turn, had its centres of gravity in the Mediterranean, the North Sea, the Baltic and the Black Sea, and the Asian Sea, roughly divided into the Indian Ocean and the vast area extending from the Bay of Bengal to the South China Sea. The fortuitous discovery of the New World had radically transformed this scenario, with the introduction of two new intercontinental systems, to wit, the Atlantic trade system, from the end of the fifteenth century, followed by the Pacific trade system. In principle, these three systems could be considered as being independent of each other. However, from 1571, the year after the Battle of Manila, in which the city was razed to the ground, they can also be considered as being increasingly integrated. There was, in fact, one single, very specific and particular kind of merchandise which was both exchanged and transported across all the three trade clusters, an item which was, until the first quarter of the seventeenth century, the most expensive and sought after in one of the largest economies of that epoch, the Chinese *Ming* Empire, while remaining the cheapest in the common core of the Atlantic and the Pacific trade systems: silver. Silver was, as described above, being transported both eastwards and westwards, the item covering probably the longest distances from *Cerro Rico* near Potosí in the Peruvian mountains to the Chinese mainland. It was transported either directly to China through Manila, or, more tortuously, by crossing the Atlantic and the Indian Ocean, in exchange for an astonishing variety of countless exotic items of merchandise which Asia was providing to Europe.

An intense debate among scholars of globalisation concerns the fact that the integration of world trade, and world economies due to the interconnection of these main trading

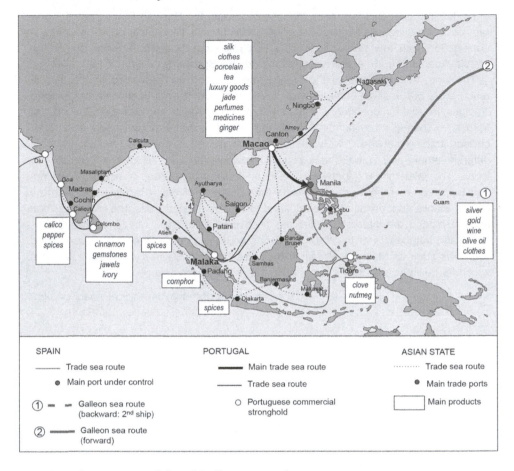

Map 1.3 Trade routes to and from Manila, seventeenth century

areas after 1571 effectively led to the first real globalisation, something about which not everybody agrees. In any case, by the beginning of the seventeenth century, and thanks to the self-interest-driven efforts of Iberian governments, mariners, priests, *conquistadores*, middlemen, and a vast array of others all in search of fortune, the basis for the further integration of the world economy into one single entity had been established. And in this more and more intensely global world, silver was, and was going to be for many decades, the most important commodity of exchange, acting as blood in the veins of commerce. Upon this basis, other domestic economies built their fortune, linking their destiny to prosperity, which, in its turn, was closely related to their participation in intercontinental, long-distance trade, even though it was to rely on a different set of actors and strategies.

However, before examining what happened to international business activities during the seventeenth century and before the First Industrial Revolution, it is worth turning to two issues of high relevance for this book. The first concerns the nature of the exchanges that took place in international markets, and the general conditions in which they took place, exchanges which were the basic building blocks of long-distance trade. Surprisingly, while the available literature has examined relevant issues such as the extension and directions of international trade routes – as summarised in the previous sections – and the quantities of merchandise (precious metals included) delivered, and the prices, along with their upward and downward movements, in depth, far less attention has been devoted to the micro-structures and the overall conditions of mercantile activity. Quite generally, "high levels of risk" are normally mentioned, something that is somewhat connected to the high levels of remuneration. However, few detailed analyses of the nature of the risk(s) involved in long-term trade activity are available, and one purpose of this chapter is to analyse these aspects in greater depth.

4. Risk management in pre-industrial international business

Pre-industrial merchants, in whatever trade they were involved, were basically "re-sellers". In contrast to those who simply supervised the transfer of a good from one owner to another, as a norm the merchants in this period actually obtained full possession of the items which they traded, sometimes only for the relatively short period during which the goods were transferred from the outlets of, say, the Black Sea to the market towns in Central Europe. This means that merchants, and international merchants in particular, were assuming a considerable share of the risks involved in the process of the international transfer of resources.

In order to understand the second crucial issue to this chapter, it is both necessary and relevant to assess the actual nature of the risks involved in long-distance trade, that is to say, the ways in which merchants tried to place limits, or exert some control, on the level of the risk involved in making transactions in conditions of extreme uncertainty. The theoretical issue here is quite simple. One basic concept in current economic theory is that market exchanges are internalised into organisations when the cost of transacting is higher than the cost of internalising the transactions and creating bureaucratic organisations. At a very general level, this is true for all business organisations, and also lies at the heart of a relevant section of transaction-cost theory, as applied to international business, which explains the rise of multinationals as the necessary consequence of the internalisation of transactions in markets which are, by definition, imperfect and uncertain. The theoretical reasoning implies that, if internalisation does not occur, one or more of the following conditions will apply: a) markets are efficient and certain; b) the cost of the creation of bureaucratic organisations is excessive; and/or c) there are alternative devices to bureaucratic structures which can be used to control risk.

The economic actors who were active in the international economy in the age of merchant expansion faced multiple risks and difficult situations, which made transacting and trading an extremely complex task. Schematically, risks could be divided into objective risks (the control of which does *not* depend on the actor's learning capability), and subjective risks (the intensity of which can be reduced through learning, once one has started a certain activity). A typical example of a subjective risk which can be solved through learning can be found in language/communication difficulties, or, for instance, in risks relating to the quality of the items involved in the exchange, and, in general, in those connected to the familiarity of the merchants with local conditions – all of which can, in fact, be reduced through learning. Objective risks are much more differentiated in their nature. There are risks which relate to the physical, institutional and political environment, or which derive from the local social conditions and market conditions (including financial markets). These kinds of risks are, to some extent, subject to a certain level of learning by economic actors – for instance, knowledge of typical (local) behaviour in a certain social environment can make a transaction, and the concomitant risks connected to it, to some extent predictable. However, in other respects, these risks can only very rarely be controlled, and remain largely unpredictable (for instance, in the case of major political upheavals, or financial disruptions). The main examples of objective risks, which are only to a minimal extent subject to learning and control, are those which relate to natural events, which may seriously cause perturbation to the activity of economic actors, and thus remain, to a large extent, unpredictable.

In principle, the risk categories listed above are present everywhere, and concern every type of economic actors. In practice, there are some conditions which further amplify or augment the impact of these risks. The first one is, of course, the extension of trade simply in geographical terms. Long-distance trade and economic activity which takes place in locations which are, by definition, distant and relatively unknown increase the objective risks enormously, also making it more difficult to manage the subjective risks. It was one thing to sell Candia wine in the Flanders, where local communities of Venetian merchants already existed in a relatively stable and predictable institutional environment; it was quite another to set up an exchange network which extended from Alexandria, in Egypt, to the Eastern coast of Africa, which was characterised by much more complex political and institutional conditions. The incidence of objective risks increased proportionally with distance: for instance, in the case of land transport, the longer the journey or distance, the higher the probability of encountering difficulties, such as in negotiating political risks in unstable territories, as the end of the *Pax Mongolica* (see above) made evident for European traders. Moreover, not surprisingly, long-distance trade and economic activity involved not just one type of risk, but multiple types of risks, both subjective and objective, simultaneously. Merchants such as Pietro Querini, for instance, while sailing around the Mediterranean, faced not only the subjective risks pertaining to the local market conditions, but also the objective political risks, the risk of expropriation and theft by pirates, the problems deriving from temporary religious upheavals, plagues and diseases, not to mention the inherent and sempiternal risks posed by the uncertainty of the weather and the sailing conditions – as befell the unlucky Venetian merchant, who was shipwrecked in the North Sea.

The spectrum of risks – and thus the strategies to bring or keep them under control, or at least to reduce them to an acceptable level – also included a number of other threats or risks which affected the goods exchanged, and not only the activity of the agents, or their physical integrity, involved in the trade. Long-distance trade did not involve perishable goods, given the average time of transport, in the order of months or even years in the case of very distant locations. But even in the case of non-perishables as the increasingly required nutmeg, for instance, there were some risks of deterioration. And, above all, the risks which involved finished, semi-finished and raw materials included those derived from sudden or unexpected shortages. Yet another risk which should also be taken into consideration derived from the fact that, sometimes, the supply of a certain item could exceed the demand of the traders, with the resultant fall in price.

Independently of the taxonomy that one wants to use, risks were of an extremely variegated nature, increasing with distance and the probability of operating in very different environments. One common characteristic was, however, that, with very few exceptions, all the risks, both those relating to people and those relating to goods, could, in some way, be more or less successfully managed through a number of risk-management devices which could be put in place simultaneously.

The case of pre-industrial long-distance trade is particularly interesting in this respect. Some of the strategies put in place to manage the risks involved in long-distance trade by medieval merchants are still commonly used to this day, while technological and institutional revolutions have, of course, enormously affected both the nature of risks and their incidence, as well as our ability to manage them.

Box 1.2: Andrea Barbarigo, merchant of Venice

Andrea Barbarigo was born to a noble Venetian family in 1399. But, when he started his business activity, aged nineteen, he was almost poor, possessing only a couple of hundred *Ducati* which his mother had put at his disposal. His father, Nicolò, had commanded a fleet of mercantile ships in 1417, one of which was shipwrecked on the way back from Egypt. Under pressure to reach Venice as soon as possible because of the valuable goods that the vessels were carrying, he left a ship that had run into trouble to its destiny, for which the senate tribunal found him guilty of negligence, and fined him 10,000 *Ducati*, a sum which was sufficient to destroy the family wealth. Soon after the trial, Nicolò left the family and retired to a monastery.

When Andrea died, in the summer of 1449, he was one of the most dynamic members of the small and clubby Venetian merchant élite. His wealth was noteworthy, even though he was not among the wealthiest men in the city. His assets were estimated to be worth around 15,000 *Ducati*, a considerable sum, when one considers that an average *bourgeois* family could live very well with a mere fifty *Ducati* per year. Yet, what his wife Cristina and two young sons Nicolò and Alvise could rely on was not safeguarded in one of the banks, nor stored in the form of real estate property. Even the luxurious palace on the *Canal Grande* in which the Barbarigo family lived, was rented. His cousin, Andrea da Mosto, put a small sum of money at the disposal of the widow in order for her to cover the funeral expenses, simply because Andrea's huge assets, which he had accumulated in over thirty years of commerce, speculation and business, were travelling around Europe and the Mediterranean, from Crete to London, from Bruges to Asia, in the form of pepper, silk, raw cotton, purple dyestuff, and other high-added-value merchandise. It had taken Andrea nearly three decades of hard work to restore his family's wealth and make it even greater, starting basically from scratch. Such an outstanding success was made possible undoubtedly by his intelligence, sense of business, and ability to exploit the opportunities that presented themselves, but also by the institutions underpinning the *Serenissima* – as the oligarchic Republic of Venice loved to define itself – which, at the beginning of the fifteenth century was reaching the apex of its power.

The Republic of Venice was built on commerce and lived through trade. Trade had been the very reason for its own existence for at least 500 years. Generation after generation of Venice's ruling class counted trading (of all kinds) as its main activity. Before massively investing their fortunes in real estate at the beginning of the sixteenth century and becoming landowners, mercantile families identified themselves with the oligarchy which ruled the state. In the fourteenth and fifteenth centuries, Venice had approximately 100,000 inhabitants, of which 1 or 2 per cent were nobles, male, and of sufficient age to be involved at various levels in the political and economic life of the Republic, which was governed through a complicated, but, in the end, efficient, oligarchical institutional structure. The *Doge* was the head of the state, but had an essentially formal role. The real power was managed by the *Maggior Consiglio*, composed, when Andrea Barbarigo was in business, of around 1,000 people, in effect the (adult male) representatives of the noble families. Both nobles and non-nobles could, however, share the same privilege or right, that is, to trade "under the flag of St. Mark", one of the writers of the four Gospels in the Christian Bible, symbolised by a lion. His body was buried in the splendid Church of Saint Mark's at the heart of the city, which was, in its turn, the heart of the Venetian Empire. Venice's merchants were thus at the top of the economic, social and political hierarchy of the Republic. And this ruling class was fully aware of the fact that both its power and the stability of the state itself resided in a flourishing trading activity, especially over long distances. Long-distance trade was, in sum, the blood that flowed in Venice's veins. Venetian merchants, or their agents, could be found almost everywhere in Europe and Asia, and even far from the colonial empire, which extended from the Alpine passes controlled by Venice with their roads to the German territories, to the Dalmatian coast, to Crete, Cyprus and the Aegean archipelago, and included some strategic Greek ports.

While Venetian merchants were everywhere, foreigners were travelling to the "Pearl of the Laguna", in many cases, covering very long distances, for instance, from the Baltic and German regions, in order to sell their merchandise in the biggest market in the world at that time. This made Venice exactly like the central section of an hourglass: in this small and relatively unhealthy coastal town, all kinds of rich and precious merchandise converged, to be sold for huge profits everywhere in Europe, Asia, and Northern Africa.

Given their relevance for the survival of the state itself, commercial techniques were developed at the highest level over time. The "physical" infrastructure for trade was essentially ships, and at the time of Andrea Barbarigo, these were built and crafted in a state-owned shipyard, the *Arsenale* of Venice, in order to maximise their efficiency and storage capacity. The *galea grossa da merchado* (the big galley for trade or big merchant galley) was employed throughout the Mediterranean, and was about 50 metres long and 7 metres wide. The merchandise was stored in the bow and in the stern of the ship, while the central part was occupied by the rowers, masts and sails. Battleships were also manufactured in the *Arsenale*, the *galee sottili* (small, or "thin" galleys), which were used to patrol the trade routes. Thus, the *Arsenale* was efficiently organised to build ships of all kinds using the best techniques available.

More than ships and innovative navigation techniques, it was the very complicated and sophisticated way in which long-distance trade was organised and carried out which made the Republic's fortune. First of all, commerce over long distances was strictly regulated in its timing. The *galee* (galleys) – that is to say, their cargoes – were grouped into "*mude*", naval caravans or convoys, each with a specific destination. Even if, in principle, each cargo vessel was free to travel autonomously, this never happened, and, in the Mediterranean at least, the "*mude*" almost always included some battleships. Each *muda*, or naval caravan, was headed by a Captain – representing the state, which was often renting or leasing even the *galee* (galleys) – and by an Admiral. The *mude*, or naval caravans, left Venice according to a calendar which took into account the seasonal weather conditions and the commercial cycle of the destination. Whatever their destination, the *galee* left Venice with a full payload of merchandise, returning, hopefully, after several months, with another full load. Ships were expected to return roughly in two periods: one in the autumn, the other in June, when market activity intensified.

The "skilled", or sometimes "lucky", merchants were those who were able to make all, or at least a part, of their capital circulate at least twice a year, exploiting to the maximum the trade cycles of the *mude* as best they could, brokering the merchandise and exotic goods coming from the East, such as spices, pigments, perfumes, silk and cotton, with those produced in Northern and Central Europe: silver, wood, and woollen goods.

This intense flow of commerce did not mean that the merchants physically had to follow the merchandise in which they invested in person. The "Age of Marco Polo", who had personally borne all the risks of a dangerous journey, had ended roughly one century before Barbarigo was born. As commerce expanded, it became impossible for individual merchants to travel such long distances several times a year. Venetian commerce was, thus, at the beginning of the fifteenth century, flowing more intensely than ever before, while merchants carried out their business sitting at their desks.

The agency contract linked the merchant resident in Venice to an agent located overseas. The agent acted on behalf of the merchant – often on behalf of several merchants – who basically gave him some very general directives about the nature and quantity of the merchandise which they wanted to be bought or sold, leaving the agent to buy or sell at the best price. In order to provide the necessary information to his agents, Andrea Barbarigo regularly sent letters to them. Letters between the merchant and the agent were often encrypted; in order to be able to read them, the agent had to use a code with which the merchant had provided him. Letters were usually sent in several copies, through different routes in order to minimise risk, or to maximise the probability that they reach the recipient on time. Agency contracts were strictly regulated, even if their enforcement was not always easy. The agent was paid a fee by the merchant, which was calculated as a small percentage of the whole sum. Another important duty of the agent was to take care of the shipping of the merchandise, making sure that it was delivered in good condition. In many cases, agents were allowed to operate freely by their principals, in order to profit from the best opportunities offered by the market.

In the course of his professional life, Andrea Barbarigo relied on the services of several agents. Alberto Dolceto, a good friend, took care of his affairs in Syria. In Valencia, there was Bertuccio Zorzi, the son-in-law of Francesco Balbi, a banker with whom Andrea had a long-standing business relationship. In London, Andrea relied on his brothers-in-law, the Cappello brothers, while, in Bruges, he was in contact with two other Venetians, Alvise and Gerolamo Bembo.

Agents would, however, have been almost useless without a specific legal arrangement, and it was here that the *consortium* evolved. This legal device had many varieties and nuances, but its basic structure was as follows: a group of merchants formed an association – each with a share, which could be different from those of the others – in order to buy a given amount of merchandise, to be shipped and sold abroad. One of them could also act as the agent of the others – or put his own agents at their disposal – for the purchase and shipping.

As already established, Venice's life and blood was trade, and safe trade was the basis of the Republic's existence. Even if formally free and independent, the merchants of Venice did their business under the protection and the authority of the government, which did everything it could to make business safer and easier. For example, during the thirteenth century, the "*Serenissima*" waged several wars in order both to establish and to maintain its control over the Mediterranean.

Merchants endeavoured to do business in distant places where the direct influence of the Venetian state was strong and where their rights could be easily enforced by law; St. Mark's Lion would appear in its usual shape, holding the open Gospel – representing not just the "Word" of God, but also order.

But, in other cases, something different was needed. When trade was done beyond the direct control of the state, the Senate assumed control, deciding upon a yearly basis which foreign destinations would receive the protection of the Navy, the flag of which was once again the Lion of Venice, but in a very different form, with the Bible closed and a dazzling sword drawn and at the ready.

The Senate not only decided upon the destinations, but also fixed a conventional freight charge or fee, in an attempt to afford to every merchant the possibility of joining the convoy under its protection. Clearly, it is possible that some members of the Senate were acting or taking their decisions on the basis of their own personal interests or for their personal advantage, applying insider-trading practices. Collectively, however, the Senate was an institution that granted relatively equal treatment both to the big wealthy merchants and to those who had no alternative but to carry out their international business with the protection of the state.

As stated, Venice was governed by an oligarchy, but one which knew well how to use, and not to abuse, its power, and was thus able to perpetuate itself for over 400 years, until 1797, when Napoleon triumphantly entered Venice at the head of the French Army.

Adapted from Fredrick C. Lane, *Andrea Barbarigo, Merchant of Venice, 1418–1449*, Baltimore MD, 1944.

★ ★ ★ ★ ★

Naturally, such a risky activity as international trade involved a great inclination towards risk-taking, or, if one prefers, a low level of risk aversion. However, it has also to be considered that, in order to deal with this high level of risk, a number of strategies were available to international traders, as we shall see.

5. Avoiding, preventing and mitigating risk

Looking at the existing research in the field, four very broad categories of risk management can be identified.[2] *Avoidance*, which occurs when the actors simply avoid entering a market, both for trading and producing, because the level of risk involved, whatever its nature, is too high. The Japanese *Tokugawa* policy of closure to external influence in place at the end of the sixteenth century, reinforced by religious pogroms and persecution, is a clear example of a practice which resulted in the country's *de facto* commercial seclusion for centuries. Even if smuggling, particularly from and to the Chinese coast, was always in place, for legitimate merchants, the sole option to avoid major risks there was simply to avoid operating in that market.

A variation of avoidance is *withdrawal*, which occurs when once-established favourable conditions turn into problematical ones. Frequently, withdrawals are connected to political and institutional overturns and changes which suddenly turn favourable environments into unfavourable ones. In the previous pages, we have already mentioned the collapse of the *Pax Mongolica* as an example, but the waves of piracy both within and outside the Mediterranean which coincided with the cyclical difficulties in establishing military control over the sea routes by land powers constituted another. The probability of withdrawal was thus inversely proportional to the ability of merchants to locate their businesses in political environments which were characterised by stable institutional conditions, thereby reducing the (always present) level of risk.

While *avoidance* and *withdrawal* can be classified as "passive" risk management strategies, other forms of behaviour aim at a more active form of risk management on the part of individuals. The theoretical literature identifies two further risk-management strategies. The first one is *prevention*, which involves all the efforts which can be put in place *before* a specific investment decision is taken in order to make the environment more stable, or to lower the probability of unforeseen situations. As one may imagine, the probability of success in risk prevention for merchants active internationally was directly proportional to the ability which they had in influencing the local business and political environment, for instance, through pressure, lobbying or corruption. This was the norm for influential houses in international banking, which traded in assets (money and finance) which were absolutely strategic and vital to governments, but not to merchants of the size of Pietro Querini. In this respect, a relevant role in prevention strategies was thus played by merchants' associations in foreign locations. The communities of traders, diffused in all the major centres of commerce and business in the global trading world, assumed a role to ensure their mutual protection and, frequently, took on the function of a pressure group or lobby with regard to the local authorities, which, in their turn, were inclined to listen to the requests of the foreign merchants in proportion to the revenues that they themselves could obtain from international trade activities. One interesting example in this respect can be found in the formation and expansion of the Hanseatic League, which started in Lübeck during the second half of the twelfth century as an alliance among merchants and, above all, merchant towns, active in the Baltic region. The alliance, which expanded progressively during the fourteenth and fifteenth centuries, came to cover almost all the Baltic region. The purposes of the alliance were many, but two of them fit quite well with the concept of prevention discussed here.

The first strategy enacted by the Hanseatic League was to set up a mutual defence force which travelled on commercial ships in order to protect merchants and traders from hostile behaviour and piracy, a typical strategy of prevention against risk situations. The second strategy of prevention was carried out through lobbying local authorities and even imperial powers in order to obtain favourable treatment (for instance, in fiscal terms) for all merchants belonging to the league.

Prevention strategies included those which aimed at embedding merchant activity into the local environment and into local society, which, for instance, could be carried out through a strategy of local networking and through connections, for example, through marriage into the local economic and political élites.

The strategies of prevention described here are, of course, strategies which go beyond the most classical instruments of risk prevention and risk sharing, and, with the increasing intensification of risk, which required the creation of institutional devices in order to prevent and to reduce it, progressively began to be used together in the expansion of long-distance international trade. For the sake of clarity and synthesis, we will focus on two of these devices here: insurance, and the creation of limited liability partnerships, the aim of which was to share or divide the risk among the different participants. Both insurance contracts and partnerships are quite complex institutional artefacts which are

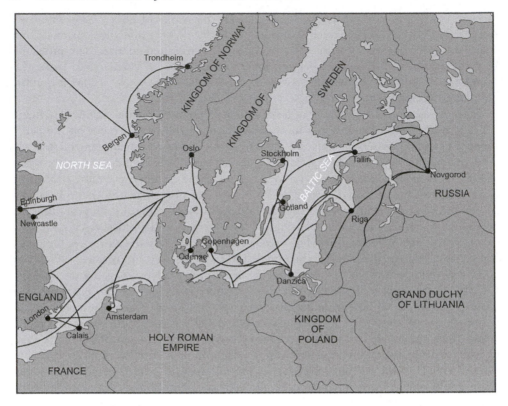

Map 1.4 The Baltic Exchange

not easy to synthesise. It is not by mere chance that modern insurance contracts developed in maritime trade at the end of the fifteenth century and the beginning of the sixteenth century, progressively developing into more sophisticated forms in the different merchant communities. While insurance tended to reduce the level of risk through a process of partial or total compensation in the case of unexpected events, partnerships were based upon another principle, which was the distribution of risk among the various participants. Trade partnerships, in whatever form, were based upon the principle of risk-sharing among the participants, or, from the perspective of the single merchant, of the diversification of risk through the diversification of investments. For instance, for a Venetian merchant who was somewhat more sophisticated, endowed and structured than Pietro Querini, one who was not travelling with his merchandise, but was sitting at his desk in a beautiful house on the *Grand Canal*, it was absolutely normal to participate in a huge number of trading initiatives carried out with others of his peer group. A standard device, for instance, in use in Venice from the eleventh century onwards, was the *colleganza*, elsewhere known as the *commenda*, a kind of contract which was also in use in the Muslim world and probably elsewhere in trading communities from Europe to Asia. It was fundamentally a partnership between somebody who basically provided resources (mainly financial, but sometimes also in kind) to be invested, and somebody who provided far less (or no) capital, but accepted to bear the risk of trading, getting his capital back at the end of the transaction, plus a major part of profits, from the main investor, and keeping the remaining revenues as the price both of his services and for his physically or financially accepting the risk. As one may imagine, the variety of such devices was almost infinite, while the substance always remained the same: somebody was investing financial resources in somebody else who had some trading capabilities and expertise – or, to put it bluntly, one part of the contract bore the risk of losing his or their resources, while the other risked losing his life. This was, in its simplest form, a sort of risk management device which could be multiplied, allowing a multiplication of profits as well as a reduction of the probability of risk. For instance, the same Venetian merchant mentioned above could simultaneously be involved in multiple contracts of *colleganza*, or consortia, with different partners trading in different ports of the Mediterranean.

Clearly, the efficiency of these (and other) institutional devices for risk management and prevention was largely linked to the efficiency of the legal system in which they were developed and embedded, in terms of regulation and, above all, enforcement. In this perspective, the absence of formal international trade agreements and, above all, of a sort of international business law or code made prevention devices such as the above-mentioned Hanseatic League absolutely vital for the existence of long-distance international trade.

A fourth, proactive strategy of risk management is that of *mitigation*, which occurs once the decision to set up a trading activity in a certain location has been taken. In this case, risk and uncertainty is an endemic situation. The aim of mitigation strategies is *not* to reduce the probability of managing a risky situation, but to reduce the impact of the risky situation itself when it is encountered or when a transaction takes place in a risky environment. The difference between prevention and mitigation is, of course, not always clear-cut. A good example can be found in the military intervention of governments in support of mercantile activities, which took place in probably the most sophisticated way in the case of the Venetian Republic during the Golden Age of the *Serenissima*, that is, from the second half of the fourteenth century to the sixteenth century. Among the other institutional devices in support of commercial activities, the Venetian government put in place a system of protection of mercantile activities. This was based firstly upon the systematic control of sea routes against piracy *within* the borders of the Venetian Empire – which extended from the coasts of the Adriatic Sea to the Ionian Sea – by following a sort of prevention strategy; and secondly upon the protection afforded to mercantile convoys travelling *outside* the borders of the Empire itself by the Republic's Navy, by resorting to violence, or rather, the deterrent of violence, as a way of mitigating the risks to which merchants operating abroad were exposed – see Box 1.2. However, domestic governments were not always ready and/or prepared to back merchants and traders. Venice was almost an exception, at least with regard to the efficiency with which she employed force in order to maintain a safe environment in the Adriatic, and to her willingness to protect her own citizens doing business abroad. Other states and cities were not so efficient, nor so interested. Moreover, this protection was afforded only to some convoys, taking place on specific, designated routes and in certain periods of the year, but not to everybody. Pietro Querini could, in fact, enjoy the protection of the state of Venice while travelling from Crete through the Ionian Sea. Thereafter, sailing westward, the direct protection of Venice ceased, and Pietro had to be very careful to avoid the risks of piracy, both from the North (Genoa) and the South (the north African coast), at least until he and his crew reached Gibraltar, where the risks turned out to be of a very different nature.

One well-known variation of risk mitigation in use among international merchants both before and after the First Industrial Revolution was diversification of investments, both in terms of the number of ventures in which each was participating and investing, but also in terms of the specific items which were traded. The diversification of investments in terms of the number of ventures was, of course, necessary when objective and subjective risks remained of some relevance, particularly in the course of the transport of items from distant locations on both sea and land routes. Thus, merchants used to invest in different locations simultaneously through their connections with multiple agents (see below). In contrast, diversification in terms of the items traded was necessary for two different reasons. The first was the simple reason that, even if the items shipped were normally durable goods, some damage could occur during their transport. Spices travelling from Aleppo in Syria to the Spanish coast in the Mediterranean could deteriorate, as well as the dried cod mentioned above or Pietro's wine, or the cane sugar sailing across the Atlantic, or the coffee or tea shipped from Africa and India to Europe. Second, and most relevant, as we shall see in the following section, was the fact that information was not only the most strategic item, it was also the most fragile item in this global world of trade. And information was fragile because it was uncertain. Let us make the virtual case of a merchant in Venice committed to selling to a wealthy customer in, say, Augsburg, a consistent quantity of nutmeg at a certain price. Nutmeg was, around the second half of the fifteenth century, arriving at the Mediterranean coast, where this merchant could count on the services of a Venetian agent/correspondent based in Aleppo, through the caravan trade, which, in its turn, travelled from Mecca to Syria (and, in its turn, the nutmeg destined for Germany was arriving at Mecca through both land and sea transport from India). The agent – in theory, something very close to the notion of a *broker*, i.e. somebody acting on behalf of one or more principals who invested their money, and who hence did not bear any of the risks of ownership and were remunerated by the agent's intermediation capabilities – had, upon the basis of his previous experience, informed the merchant (by letter sent from Aleppo to Venice via sea, thus taking about one month to cover the distance) that nutmeg usually came to Aleppo in a certain quantity (variable, but, to some extent, predictable) at a certain price. The merchant could thus calculate very roughly the profit that he could make out of the business. According to the information collected by the agent, information travelling by word of mouth, the agent learns that the caravan is carrying a large number of chests of nutmeg of good/medium quality – something that is, in part, going to affect the price of the spice on the Syrian market, and, of course, the return forecasting in Venice. However, week after week, as the caravan approaches Aleppo, the information travelling on the grapevine becomes more and more detailed: first of all, the nutmeg is of low quality, but, more importantly, the quantity arriving is small. Thus, a prospectively very profitable business transaction is turning into a zero-profit or even a loss-making one. This, of course, would not be the case with other forms of merchandise, such as amber and coral, or cinnamon; business diversification was thus a logical consequence of the necessity of keeping the overall profit acceptable or above average, by investing in various businesses of which some, from time to time and from case to case, turned out either to be very profitable or to be loss-making ventures.

At this point, one may question whether part of the diversification strategies of international traders also included investments in fixed assets and not just in working capital. The purchase of and the investment in fixed assets and capital were, in fact, common practice in many cases, particularly in the case of wealthy merchants who invested in land ownership, in real estate, or even in the purchase of expensive *objets d'art*. This, however, was part of a strategy which was different from that of diversification in trade, and aspired more to the sphere of social status than to that of mercantile activities. Investing in real estate could, to some extent, be a sort of diversification of risk, but it was usually considered to be the apex of a successful career in business, as it was an acquisition by which one obtained the status of nobleman. In some cases, even integration into shipping was not uncommon, and merchants accepted the additional risk of having their merchandise – even though it was insured – shipped by somebody who was *not* under their direct control. The Venetian case, again, is an exemplary one in this respect. The actual ownership of the ships which were used in the seasonal, regular convoys (the so-called *mude*; see Box 1.2 above) which connected Venice with the Levant and with the Western Mediterranean ports during the fourteenth and fifteenth centuries belonged to the state, which, in its turn, sub-contracted the management of the voyages to private enterprises but maintained close supervision of the whole enterprise through the presence of a civil servant, the *Capitano da Mar* on board the ship (see Map 1.5). The public ownership, and, to some extent, the management of the shipping was an ingenious way which allowed the merchants – independently of the volume of their trade – to increase the level of security of trading without the necessity of investing in the ownership of ships, be it on their own or with others.

Last, but not least, risk-mitigation strategies could involve the adoption of technological innovations in trading. Institutional innovations have been discussed above, and

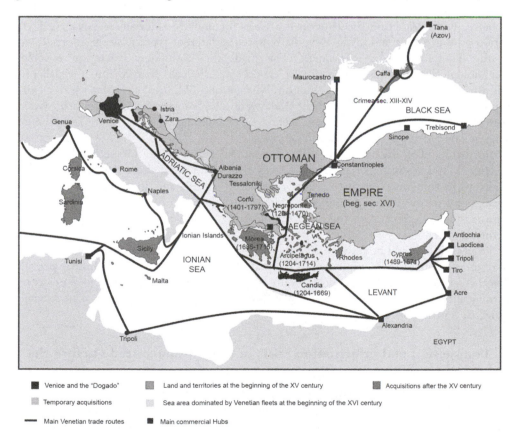

Map 1.5 The "*mude* system"

here it is worth concentrating on technological innovations, first of all, in sea transport, including navigation techniques. A long process of risk mitigation due to better communication and transport techniques had begun by the mid-thirteenth century, from the time of the increase in the use of the compass and other instruments, which allowed faster and safer navigation (enabling mariners partially to avoid coastal navigation, although open sea navigation increased the risks of piracy); this was to continue steadily in the following centuries. At the same time, shipbuilding techniques allowed risks to be mitigated from other perspectives. If we return to the history of Venice, for instance, it was the adoption of a new, bigger (and armed) ship, the *Galea Grossa* – the key instrument of the complex system of convoys (*mude*) which travelled partially under the protection of the Venetian government – from the fourteenth century onwards which determined a sharp reduction in risk for the merchandise being transported from the Eastern Mediterranean ports to Venice.

It was, of course, the same evolution in shipbuilding, sailing and navigation techniques that allowed the establishment first of Atlantic, and then of Pacific, trade routes, which could, more or less regularly (still largely dependent on the prevailing weather conditions) connect the various areas involved in the global exchange of merchandise. First the Portuguese, and then the Dutch, made substantial progress in this sense, advancing both shipbuilding and sailing techniques by increasing the size and volume of the vessels (thereby reducing transport costs per item) and by improving the reliability of the ships. For instance, while Venetians relied upon the *Galea* for their Mediterranean voyages, navigation around Africa and in the Atlantic required a different type of vessel, more suited to the different sailing environment. This made the Portuguese expansion possible. Technologically, they relied first on the carrack (which later evolved into the galleon) and the caravel (in Christopher Columbus' voyage of 1492, the *Santa Maria* was a 100-tonne carrack, while the *Pinta* and the *Niña* were 60–75-tonne caravels), both of which were improvements on the Genoese technique of building agile but quite large sailing ships suitable for open sea navigation.

Notwithstanding the strategies put in place in order to limit the inherent risks, trading activity over long distances remained a heavily risky business for those who engaged in it. Risks were sometimes of an extremely concrete nature, and involved not only the damage to, or the loss of, goods and merchandise, but also of the capital invested, of personal fortunes in cases of unlimited responsibility, and even the lives of those directly involved in trading.

However, it should be recalled that the issue of risk and uncertainty was only one of the components of the complexity of international trading in the pre-industrial period. Another element, which is just as relevant as risk and uncertainty, relates to issues concerning information asymmetry and imperfect knowledge in the activity of trading: in short, to transaction costs.

6. Transaction and information costs in long–distance trade before the industrial revolution

The notion and concept of transaction costs is often closely connected to that of risk and uncertainty. However, for the purpose of this chapter (and the volume in general), it is probably worth keeping the two concepts distinct. Risk, both objective and subjective, has to do mainly with conditions maturing in the external environment, which can, of course, affect transactions, but are nonetheless of a general nature. Transaction costs only affect the act of transacting, and, in principle, can be quite independent of the general level of risk and uncertainty present in the environment. In other words, costly transactions are possible in safe environments, from the legal, environmental, and also "physical" points of view, and, conversely, exchanges can take place with transaction costs that are low or even close to zero in highly risky environments.

There is a vast amount of literature which dissects and examines the notion of transaction costs. The concept, formally developed from the 1930s onwards, has undoubtedly been one of the most powerful concepts in the field of economics, and has been widely borrowed by economic and business historians, as well as by many other social scientists, in order to interpret many phenomena, including those connected to international business. The cost of transacting, that is, of participating in a market exchange, involves at least three sub-categories of the costs which traders incur. The first is the cost of obtaining reliable information about the object of the transaction, its availability, quantity, quality and price; in sum, everything connected with the good or service traded. This type of cost was particularly common in the case of pre-industrial trade. Prices, quantities and qualities were rarely known in advance, particularly when the parts involved were located in very distant areas, and, in this case, the incidence of another component in the process, namely, *information asymmetries*, was particularly high – and was, of course, also the basis of the huge profits that could be gained in this kind of trade.

The second component of transaction costs is the cost of bargaining. Together with the cost of obtaining information, the main efforts in pre-industrial trade were linked to the problem of attaining sufficient familiarity with the other parts involved in the exchange. The cost of bargaining was (and, of course, is) clearly inversely related to the frequency of the transaction, or to whether the transaction is a once-and-for-all one or a repeated transaction.

Finally, the third relevant component of transaction costs, labelled sometimes as the cost of enforcement or the monitoring cost, refers to the efforts to ensure that the other party/parties respect(s) the agreement(s), and to the efforts to take counter-measures when free-riding, or inappropriate behaviour, takes place.

Intuitively, all three of the components of the transaction costs listed above are, to a large degree, present in the long-distance trade transactions which we are considering in this chapter. The physical, cultural, institutional distance between the producers and the final consumers of the goods traded over long, often very long, distances was enormous, and merchants offered themselves as specialised, indispensable intermediaries in these exchanges. Even if they were skilled, specialised and, to some extent, able to control the risks, the merchants were, nonetheless, in some sense largely assuming the burden of the costs implicit in the exchange themselves, a burden for which they were consistently remunerated.

As demonstrated above, information was difficult to acquire and was also rarely completely reliable due to poor means of communication and slow diffusion across space. Merchants were, to some extent, repositories or virtual stores of information; however, the process of building this expertise was time-consuming and complex, given the scarcity of information at their disposal. Bargaining was expensive as well. Transactions were, in fact, rarely codified and repeated, even if they took place in given periods of the year: in sum, the exchange was certain, but not the actors of the exchange, and this left a great deal of room for free-riding and other inappropriate practices. Finally, enforcement was difficult in a context in which elementary notions of international commercial law were still absent, and the enforcement power was frequently left in the hands of local powers that were not bound to any sort of international agreements.

Two questions, which are mutually connected in part, arise at this point. The first one relates to the fact that long-distance trade was not only affected by the high levels of subjective and objective risks examined above, but was also taking place in a context in which transaction costs and hazard were considerably high. However, both of these conditions were *not* sufficient either to stop international trade (which simply slowed down in cases of substantial turmoil and perturbations, but never ceased) or to generate what transaction-cost theory applied to international trade predicts, that is, the transfer of risky, uncertain and costly transactions from the market to a bureaucratic organisation, to wit, to a cross-border operating firm. In sum, international merchants continued to act as intermediaries between the buyers and the sellers, creating markets for exchange, and making money from their trading specialisation even under extremely unstable conditions, but never attempting, on their part, to integrate into a single organisation, for instance, the purchase of the raw materials or exotic goods that they were selling in distant markets. They accepted playing the role of temporary, very temporary in some cases, owners of "circulating capital", namely, the merchandise travelling on camels' backs or in the holds of ships across seas and oceans, solely for the period necessary to transfer the capital from the production sites to the places where it was sold, but resisted all temptation to internalise trade into a single organisation, an organisation, which, in theory, could lower the risks and costs implicit to transactions over long distances.

The second issue, partially related to this, is that if merchants continued to accept the burden (and, I stress, the remuneration) of transaction costs, this means that their activity was able to rely on a series of devices which partially, but substantially, reduced one or more of the components of the transaction costs, thereby allowing them to trade without opting for some kind of transaction internalisation. Or, to put it another way, merchants were able to rely on instruments and practices which allowed them to afford a marginal cost of transacting which was lower than the marginal cost implied in setting up an investment in fixed capital or in some form of bureaucratic organisation. The marginal cost of transacting was, of course, in itself, a direct function both of the volume of the transactions (even if repeated) and of the efficiency of the arrangements, thus giving them control of the transaction costs.

In theory, a reseller maximises his profits when he is able to buy at the most convenient price and sell at the highest price. This, in turn, as stated above, makes the ability to handle crucial information about, for instance, the quality, quantity, availability, and price of goods probably *the* most strategic asset in managing long-distance trade. Thus, the merchants must have had at their disposal several tactics which enabled them to improve the retrieval of such crucial information.

The first of these was the physical concentration of trading activities in the areas in which exchanges took place both regularly and frequently. Merchant cities and ports had precisely this function, that is, they were not only (and probably, to a minor extent) the locations in which the exchange of merchandise took place physically, but were also the places in which information circulated and was efficiently exchanged. And, on the basis of a quite intuitive effect, and in the absence of distortions (such as religious persecutions or pogroms, for example), there is a cumulative, aggregative effect in the circulation of information, which leads to the formation of "hubs", that is, areas in which the information is collected and distributed. Hubs, in sum, are strategic locations in which the cumulative effect of the circulation of information takes place, and where − to put it another way − the marginal cost of obtaining information is lower than elsewhere, that is to say, in minor or peripheral hubs. Hubs were (and, to a large extent, still are to this day, when we think of financial, fashion, or high-tech hubs) very often specialised in certain types of information about certain kinds of trade. Hubs could coincide with urban areas or with entire regions. For instance, an evident case in this respect can be found in the Baltic Sea area, which was characterised by the presence of the Hansa merchant cities (as mentioned above), which were linked together by mutual exchange of both merchandise and information, and in the Black Sea area, where port cities which specialised in the grain trade between the eighteenth and nineteenth centuries created a sort of coastal trade community (see Map 1.4). Hubs were normally strategically located across the main commercial routes where merchants and their wares travelled regularly. The above-mentioned agent in Aleppo was located in a hub, which, in its turn, was connected to another hub, Mecca, by means of a caravan land trail. He was acting, as stated above, as a broker, but, above all, as a provider of information about the conditions of local trade, of real and expected prices, of quantities and types of merchandise, and even of the political conditions, diplomatic relations and all the external factors which could, in some way or another, influence, both directly and indirectly, the trade activity both locally and in Venice.

The Republic of Venice, strategically placed in the convergence between continental land routes and the Adriatic sea paths leading to Asia Minor and the north of Africa, is probably the most suggestive example of both what a "hub" is and of its effects. The strategic position of Venice made it a sort of natural "hourglass" in which merchandise was exchanged and through which the Levant was connected with the north of Europe through a complex system of land and sea routes. Above all, it was a place which was characterised by the unique combination of dense and specific, sometimes invaluable, flows of information, which accompanied the goods themselves in this sophisticated institutional environment.

And what was happening in Venice was, to a similar extent, happening elsewhere in Europe and Asia, where more or less sophisticated "hubs" allowed regional trade networks to intersect, amplifying the range of local trade. Decades of Euro-centric historical literature about international trade has privileged the analysis of the activity of European merchants and European commercial cities, as well as the achievements of European merchants around the world. But it has also, however, largely ignored the non-European, but nonetheless sophisticated, merchant networks and activities which already existed outside Europe.

For a (sufficiently smart, on the ball) entrepreneur, the very fact of being in an information hub, or connected to one by means of somebody else, was a key asset. There were, however, other tactics which made it possible to lower some of the components of the transaction costs – and not just those relating to information costs. Scholars of pre-industrial trade – and of pre-industrial societies, in general – have long stressed the relevance of the role played by "minorities" in long-distance trade, or, to be more specific, ethnic and/or religious groups, more normally cited as, "nations". Everywhere where trade was taking place – in cities, ports or simply along trade routes – merchants tended to cluster according to some "common" denominator. On his way back to Venice after the adventurous voyage which had led to his being shipwrecked, Pietro Querini enjoyed the hospitality of the powerful Venetian community in London. Merchant communities were disseminated almost everywhere, even in the remotest parts of the world: there were prosperous Chinese merchant communities in Manila at the end of the sixteenth century, Armenian groups everywhere from the Philippines to India and Europe, while Greeks were located throughout the Eastern Mediterranean. Of these examples, a particularly significant one can be found in the Sephardic Jews, who, since their expulsion from Spain at the end of the fifteenth century and the Diaspora that followed, created a sort of global mercantile network. In sum, independently of the aggregating factor, when active abroad, and particularly over very long distances, merchants and traders tended to cluster and group themselves into more or less cohesive and homogeneous communities. The clustering of merchants was associated with another informal institutional arrangement that was essential in mercantile international trade, that is, the network structure of the relationships among traders within the same "community". In theory, clusters and networks are not the same thing: clusters stress the closeness of relationships, while, in networks, the relationship takes place not only locally, but also over very long distances. However, the two concepts are useful to stress their effects on trade relationships and on the costs implied in their transactions. In both cases, mutual "trust" acted as the fundamental device which allowed the participants to handle information asymmetries, to manage not only the transfer and diffusion of crucial information, but also other very concrete inputs such as credit and even cash. Thus, belonging to a network meant access to strategic information and other inputs at a relatively low cost – and concomitantly represented a threat for all those excluded from the community. Trust also acted as a moderator in the case of bargaining costs: members of the network were used to trading upon a fairly regular basis (even if not exclusively) among themselves, something which allowed them to skip the time-consuming and expensive procedures involved in selecting appropriate partners and ascertaining their reliability and loyalty. Finally, networks and communities served – to a certain degree – to mitigate the costs of enforcement and monitoring. Being part of a network not only guaranteed access to the network benefits, it also imposed serious constraints in cases of free-riding. The risk of loss of reputation was, in fact, both very high and very serious in a system based more upon trust than on written contractual agreements. And, as stated above, the cost of permanent exclusion from one, or from more than one, network or community, was very high, far higher than the temporary advantage offered by cheating. In some cases, networks were at the basis of more structured organisations which provided a sort of institutional identity to informal relations. The *Levant Company*, for instance, an English chartered trading company doing business in the East Mediterranean, was *de facto* an "umbrella" organisation under which, in reality, a network of private traders and merchants was operating, not a formalised, bureaucratic structure like other British companies such as the *East India Company* (see Chapter 2).

Rarely, if ever, were merchants connected to international networks alone. The family dimension had key relevance in building the trust necessary for running businesses in an environment that was characterised by very poor means of communication, and in which the principal was substantially unable to monitor the agent upon a frequent and objective basis. Family and, more broadly, kinship ties acted as moderators of transaction costs at at least two levels. The first was that of access to the broader community of the mercantile network or networks: in this case, the family name acted as a sort of "mediator", providing the individual with the necessary connections. In other cases, the family name was an indispensable form of collateral when the individual had need of credit and/or other resources. A second, and more important level was that the family directly provided the resources that were employed in the specific trade, both human and financial. Close or more distant relatives were, in fact, employed as local agents in distant and strategic locations, and belonging to a trusted family was the indispensable pre-requisite for starting an apprenticeship in trading activities. The strategies of merchant families could even attain a certain degree of sophistication, particularly when the extension of the family network was proportional to the dimension of the family itself, and *vice versa*, while the financing of relatives involved a minor degree of risk, at the same time it allowed the consolidation and the further extension of the family's overall network of activity.

Finally, belonging to a network was also indispensable when merchants wanted to engage in complex and exotic trade activities. As scholars of pre-industrial international trade have demonstrated, and debated in depth, if it is true that many transactions took place *inside* religious and/or ethnic networks, a relevant section of international trade involved transactions among different groups and networks. This configured a sort of cross-cultural exchange that was at the core of the global economy in the centuries preceding the First Industrial Revolution.

7. The persistence of market exchange in the pre-industrial period

International trade activities were thus characterised by a considerable degree of risk and uncertainty, which were at a high level in all the components of transaction costs. However, it is hard to find, with very few exceptions, normally in the business of banking and finance, cases in which the result of this uncertainty culminated in the integration of market exchange into a single, bureaucratic organisation. Cases such as the *Medici*, the *Peruzzi*, and the *Acciaiuoli* (just to mention some famous cases in pre-industrial international banking) were as sophisticated as they were rare, and were mostly confined to a specific activity in the financial sector. The rest of international trade activities continued to take place outside bureaucratic organisations and continued to rely on market exchanges which took place both inside and outside networks that were determined by kinship, religion or ethnicity. The two steps which normally followed trading activities when the uncertainty levels were too high, that is, integration into shipping and the production of goods, hardly took place at all before the seventeenth century, when other forms of international organisations started to become progressively diffused alongside mercantile trade. The persistence of market exchange, rather than internalisation, in the pre-industrial period is normally taken for granted, even though transaction-cost theory would, in principle, predict an incentive to internalise transactions, particularly in the two crucial stages of the procurement and the transfer of goods. One may, in fact, ask why a merchant would continue to accept the high level of uncertainty linked to poor information about the volume and the quality of goods on the market, about the state of the caravans and of the ships, and why he would continue to rely on the services of agents who could sometimes be poorly monitored. Why should he accept buying through a broker (someone who might not treat him badly, but would undoubtedly treat him worse than a fellow merchant) and rely on an independent shipowner to transfer his goods or property from, say, Tripoli to Bergen? Although it might not be the case for all goods, it might be more convenient to control the production of a "staple" form of merchandise directly, as, in fact, happened in the case of Pietro Querini, who travelled with the ship loaded with wine coming from his family's possessions on the island of Crete. And, without doubt, integration in shipping would probably have served to avoid a lot of additional issues relating to entrusting somebody with the temporary possession of the goods transferred, even with the guarantee of insurance contracts which allowed the uncertainty to be controlled or held in check. The fact that international long-distance trade and commercial activities were run by on the whole relying on the market could be explained by a number of factors.

One of the first factors is quite intuitively connected to the cost of internalising transactions, which in essence means the establishment of bureaucratic organisations characterised by internal procedures and by delegation to professionals – something which was very close to the permanent investment in fixed assets already discussed above.

A second factor which hindered the creation of stable integrated organisations was undoubtedly linked to the volume of the transactions and their geographic location. Individual merchants, even those running large businesses, were simultaneously dealing with a high number of transactions, but in different locations. The above-mentioned agent located in Aleppo was, in his turn, running simultaneously transactions on behalf of several merchants, who, in their turn, were connected to other agents in other geographic locations. This means that the volume of the single transaction made in a single market by a single merchant was only a small fraction of the merchant's activity – which is perfectly coherent with the concept of risk diversification. As a consequence, however, the incentive for the single merchant to integrate in shipping remained low, leaving the transaction to the market. This was, to some extent, true also for production, which additionally implied a great deal of capital immobilisation in every single investment.

The volume of transactions played a role also from another aspect which is connected to overall demand from the market. Merchants were incentivised to rely more on the market, and not to internalise transactions, since the volume of demand was probably not sufficiently high to justify integration and the costs involved in the process.

A further element which explains the absence of integration relates to what is called "asset specificity". Asset specificity, that is, the fact that a firm controls unique assets, such as technological innovations, for instance, explains the tendency to protect this specificity through the direct control of the foreign activity. For international merchants, however, the crucial asset which could make the difference was information – which was so crucial that sometimes, as already noted, the letters exchanged between the merchant and his agents were actually encrypted. Information knowledge was embodied essentially in individuals. The solution to this problem of specificity was thus, as stated above, to employ members of the family as agents and brokers (which was a sort of implicit integration). One may also imagine appropriating *all* the information and transforming the agent into an employee, that is, hiring him on an exclusive and permanent basis. But this again contrasted with the problem of the volume of transactions handled by a single merchant in a single market, which was, again, too low to justify the investment.

Finally, one may also mention something which was more or less suggested in the previous section. On the one hand, as discussed above, there were high costs and good reasons to avoid the risky and expensive metamorphosis of working capital into a rigid investment. On the other hand, however, one must admit that the tactics available to international traders, which allowed them to control risks and reduce transaction costs, were quite effective, to say the very least.

This situation, which lasted for centuries, would, however, change when volumes of trade and demand sharply changed, deeply affecting the structures of international exchange and creating new forms of exchange.

Notes

1   The etymological origins of the modern word "carnival", the period of festivities that precedes Lent, and the modern Italian word *Carnevale* (Shrove Tuesday), come from the Milanese

"*carnelevamen*", composed of *carn* (flesh) and *levare* (put away), as meat is not supposed to be eaten during Lent.
2 Here, I draw extensively on Teresa Da Silva Lopes and Mark Casson, "Foreign Direct Investment in High-risk Environments: A Historical Perspective", *Business History*, 55(3), 2013, pp. 375–404.

Bibliography

Bernstein, William J., *A Splendid Exchange: How Trade Shaped the World*, New York: Grove Atlantic, 2008.
Findlay, Ronald and O'Rourke, Kevin, *Power and Plenty: Trade, War and the World Economy in the Second Millennium*, Princeton, NJ: Princeton University Press, 2008.
Fusaro, Maria *Political Economies of Empire in the Early Modern Mediterranean The Decline of Venice and the Rise of England 1450–1700*, Cambridge: Cambridge University Press, 2015.
Pomeranz, Kenneth, *The Great Divergence: China, Europe, and the Making of the Modern World Economy*, Princeton, NJ: Princeton University Press, 2000.
Tracy, James D. (ed.), *The Rise of Merchant Empires: Long Distance Trade in the Early Modern World, 1350–1750*, Cambridge: Cambridge University Press, 1990.

2 The age of companies

Introduction

On 16 December 1773, at dusk, a group of around one hundred people, some symbolically disguised as American Indians, assaulted three ships at Griffin's Wharf, in Boston, Massachusetts. Divided into three groups, they boarded the ships, and, without any damage or injury to the three crews, in three hours of intense work, took some 340 chests of tea from the holds of the ships and threw them into the water. As is widely known, this event, the Boston Tea Party, was the first in a series, which soon escalated into a war that ended with the independence of the British colonies in America from the motherland.

What is less widely known, however, is that the tea, as well as the ships that were attacked by the "Patriots", belonged to a powerful, yet declining, British trading firm, the *East India Company*. The tea which was thrown into the waters of Boston harbour had crossed the Atlantic via the company's warehouses, where it had been delivered from East Asia, travelling duty-free, thanks to the British Tea Act of 1773. The Act was, in itself, intended as (and really was) an advantage for everyone. It allowed the *East India Company* (in serious financial difficulties at the time), which already enjoyed a monopoly on the tea market in the colonies, to make additional profits by avoiding export duties. Customers across the Atlantic would have cheaper tea at their disposal (something which would have defeated a flourishing smuggling activity), albeit in a monopoly regime. This was in exchange for a small tax levy imposed by the British Parliament as a contribution to the expense of the French and Indian Wars, in which the *East India Company* had both directly taken part and played a major role (the Seven Years War, 1756–1763). As is well known, however, the case in point was precisely this: independently of whether the tea was cheap or dear, the people in the colonies did not want to pay *any* tax, irrespective of the amount, at least not without a right to representation in the British Parliament.

Needless to say, the episode is a cornerstone in American history, but it is also useful to introduce the main topic of this chapter, which is the role of privileged, or chartered, trading companies in international business. The company involved (against its wishes) in the Boston "Tea Party" was one of the largest and probably the best known at the time. Yet, it constituted, in some way, a sort of standard model in a very variegated panorama.

This chapter will address the very nature of these companies, their diffusion and relevance, but, above all, it will discuss the motives underlying their existence, as well as their structural features, and their impact on international business activities. In many ways, these companies ran their operations in a way which was acutely different from even the sophisticated international merchants of the Middle Ages. In a way, they represented a new form of organisation in international business and trade, which provided an answer to the opportunities and constraints that were emerging from new conditions in the external environment, conditions which included, as we shall see, a new role for states and governments, which had an impact on the way in which business was conducted across borders.

1. New organisational devices

When its ships were boarded in Boston harbour, the *East India Company* was already an old established institution, having been founded on 31 December 1600. Its story is a relatively standard one, and can help to highlight the main characteristics of this kind of institution, which started to become diffused in the sixteenth century, but expanded during the seventeenth and eighteenth centuries. The genesis of the company dated back to before its official birthdate, when London merchants started to associate themselves in companies with the aim of trading directly over long distances, and in particular in the East Indies. In 1600, a group of them, committing a capital of nearly 70,000 pounds partially invested in the acquisition of ships, requested and obtained the Crown's approval under the form of a charter. This granted to their company (the *Company of Merchants of London Trading with the East Indies*) a fifteen-year monopoly on all trade in the area between the Cape of Good Hope and the Straits of Magellan. The *John Company*, as it was nicknamed, was not the first, nor the last. When it was created, other similar institutions already existed, both in the British Isles and abroad. In Britain, for instance, the headquarters of the *Muscovy Company*, which traded with Russia, the *Eastland Company* (Baltic trade), the *Turkey Company*, the *Morocco Company* and others had already been established. After 1600, other European countries started the practice of granting charters and monopolies to domestic companies of merchants almost everywhere in America, Asia and Africa, all active in areas and places in which there were opportunities for trade. Between the sixteenth and the seventeenth centuries more than fifty such companies were founded in Europe, in Britain, Portugal, Germany, France, the Low Countries and Scandinavia.

It is almost impossible to evaluate the share of international trade which was performed by chartered companies, or the size of the individual companies. The data available, however, do show a considerable and steady growth in size of what we can define as "chartered trade" starting from the beginning of the seventeenth century on a scale that was surely unattainable by individual merchants. During the almost 200 years of its existence, the Dutch *East India Company* (*Verenigde Oostindische Compagnie* (*VOC*)), established in 1602, was able to make *circa* 5,000 voyages to the East Indies (an average of slightly less than twenty-five per year, basically two per month), twice the (still considerable) number of the voyages managed by its rival, the British *East India Company*. Although this is, of course, an average, it nonetheless bears witness to the increase in the volume of international transactions, which far exceeded the activities of even the most prosperous merchant houses described in the previous chapter. Clearly, international merchants continued to be active and prosperous in some cases, but, in the decades preceding the First Industrial Revolution, the majority of long-distance trade was intermediated by these companies. Among themselves, they maintained relations of a very different nature from those largely based upon co-operation, which were the norm in the international mercantile networks described in Chapter 1.

One may, in fact, be tempted to consider chartered companies as a sharp discontinuity with the past, which, in certain sense, they were. However, on closer inspection, they

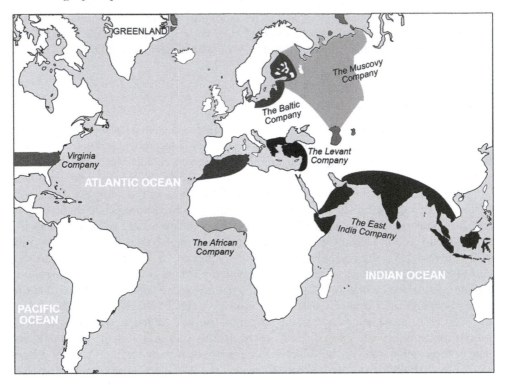

Map 2.1 Spheres of influence of some English commercial companies (beginning of seventeenth
century)

can be seen as an organisational form which progressively emerged from the evolution of
market-based or network-based trade of a mercantile nature. The pre-existing organisation of world trade was put under pressure by external factors, among which the most
important was a sharp increase in the actual *volume* of international trade, which began
from the second half of the sixteenth century onwards. At the basis of this rise in the
volume of transactions, there were many structural and contingent factors, of which two
are worth mentioning here. The first was a consequence of the age of geographic discoveries in conjunction with the technological evolution in sea transport routes and
shipping techniques. There were, simply, larger and more accessible sources of supply for
a global-market demand which was growing in terms both of volume and of purchasing
power, particularly in Europe, and especially in the Western part of the continent. On
average, in Western Europe, the GDP *per capita* (at constant prices) almost doubled
between the years 1500 and 1800, as did the population; in Asia and India, *per capita*
GDP remained relatively stagnant, while the population more than tripled. Europe had
invested an enormous amount of resources, human, physical and financial, in enlarging
potential supply markets. However, the European penetration in Asia in particular, both
westward (through the Straits of Magellan) and eastward (via the Cape of Good Hope)
had, as we have seen above, intensified trade activity that was already present in the area,
resulting in a further increase to the total volume of global trade. It had also greatly
enlarged the geographic span, and hence the duration, of travel and voyages, with a quite
obvious effect on the size of both the fixed and variable costs involved, and hence on the

capital needed. According to recent calculations, the cost of an expedition to Asia at the beginning of the fourteenth century was nearly four times that of one to Africa, or even to the Caribbean. Even though technology progressed, the average level of risk involved in each expedition was in a perfect linear relationship with geographic distance. Ships had to be bigger, as well as their crews, with a direct impact on the volume of the costs of maintenance and wages. In normal situations, the cost of the crews could fluctuate between 30 and 50 per cent of the total capital invested in the venture. In addition, the growing duration of journeys meant another thing. To wit, when the expected return voyages occurred once or twice a year, as in the case of Pietro Querini and his fellow mariners, or once every ten or fifteen years, as in the case of the first Asian voyages, capital was no longer working or circulating: it was transformed into an investment of a fixed nature. In addition, and much more than in the case of intra-European trade, these voyages needed some form of stable presence abroad, which required investments in the form of storage facilities, ports and fortifications, particularly in areas characterised by high levels of objective risks. Chartered companies were thus a necessary organisational and institutional response to the changes in the structural conditions of international trade. Indeed, it was these companies that, *de facto*, made possible the real (even if on a relatively unequal basis) integration of the economic regions in which trade took place before industrialisation.

A second element which has to be remembered is that, while markets naturally enlarged through the combined effect of a rise not only in demand but also in the supply opportunities, there was, as emphasised in the previous chapter, an additional factor which played a relevant role, one which acted as a sort of lubricant, or, if one prefers, as a catalyst for the whole process. Silver – the availability of which increased by chance after the discovery of the New World – was both a good in itself (as we have seen, particularly appreciated in Asia, and, above all, in China), and a device which facilitated exchanges among different areas and across different cultures. In a counterfactual way, even if bullion had not been present in New Spain in the quantities in which it was, the increase in the volume of the exchanges in the global economy would, nonetheless, probably have taken place anyway (in the end, people actually *wanted* spices, cocoa, coffee, tea, porcelain, jewels, silk, pearls, coral, and thousands of other items and goods for their own pleasure), but it would have occurred at a much slower pace than actually happened. And, as we will see, this would probably have had a negative effect on the diffusion and the consolidation of chartered companies, possibly even on their existence.

As anticipated above, the intensification in the extent and volume of trade, and the progressive emergence of new business opportunities in remote regions of the world, put the existing structure of international trade, which was based upon market exchange, and which took place both outside and, more often, within mercantile networks, under serious pressure. As shown in the previous chapter, merchants had been used to associating among themselves, through various legal artefacts, long before chartered companies came into existence. Various kinds of partnerships were created and dissolved, and the merchants were often simultaneously engaged in different partnerships with other fellow merchants. But chartered companies were different.

2. Nature and rationales

Chartered companies, also known as privileged companies, were very diverse, in purpose, size, and geographic coverage. There were enormous variances in their structure and organisation as can be seen, for instance, between the *Levant Company* (see Box 2.2), which functioned mostly as a flexible umbrella organisation for the operations of British merchants in the Ottoman Empire, and the *Hudson Bay Company*, which is, instead, considered an early example of a multinational, vertically integrated bureaucratic organisation. Despite these differences, these companies shared some common characteristics, which deserve further examination.

First, they tended to exist for a long time. The British *East India Company* was officially dismantled in 1874. Its Dutch rival lasted about two centuries, as did the *Levant Company*. The *Royal African Company*, established in 1660, was dismantled in 1821. The *Muscovy Company*, founded in the middle of the sixteenth century, was dissolved as late as 1917. And the *Hudson Bay Company*, founded in 1670, still exists to this very day as a trading company based in Toronto. Other companies, alas, did not survive so long; however, their duration was always considerable and multi-generational. Partnerships among individual merchants, which could, at times, last quite some time, were normally dissolved after a few years, and generally expired when one of the partners ceased to do business. Companies were thus created, at least in principle, with the intention of lasting in time and running a stable business activity.

A second relevant characteristic (which was, however, not exclusive to chartered companies) was their geographic focus, which was sometimes determined by a sort of business specialisation. Many of these companies were created in order to exploit the resources available in a specific location, either a geographically very large area or one more focused in size. In the case of the British *East India Company*, the geographic area involved basically coincided with the Indian Ocean and the Pacific; its geographic focus was thus much wider than, say, the *Greenland Company* (established in 1693) or the *Barbary Company*, also known as the *Morocco Company* (chartered by Queen Elizabeth in 1588). Differences concerned the scope of the activity, which, in some cases, was not specified (the trade included all possible types of merchandise), while, in others, it was much more focused. The *Royal African Company* was originally established to allow Britain to exploit the gold mines in what is now The Gambia. However, it soon diversified its activities, basically taking a leading role in the slave trade across the Atlantic until the early decades of the eighteenth century. The aforementioned *Hudson Bay Company* specialised in fur trading between Canada and Britain from the very beginning, and maintained this business focus for a long time. The various *East India Companies*, established in many European countries, were mainly making their profits from the Western appetite for Asian products, which included spices, tea, silk, pottery, porcelain and various other disparate items. The companies were also different in terms of their operations. Some of them were fundamentally established in order to exploit and transfer natural resources from one part of the world to another (again, this was the case with the British *Royal African Company*). Others (the majority) were trade mediators between the country of origin and the world outside. They exchanged domestically produced items for local resources. The *Hudson Bay Company* traded various items that were indispensable for the survival of both the settlers and the Indians, from knives to woollen fabrics, in exchange for furs. Over time, companies became skilled agents of trade in general, and started to connect exchanges among foreign areas with no involvement from the country of origin, in which they continued to maintain their headquarters. The case of the British *East India Company*, which managed the trade of opium, produced in India and sold in China, where the drug had seen an increasing recreational use, provides a quite famous, but by no means isolated, case. The *Royal Philippines Company*, a short-lived company established in Spain in 1785, made profits managing a tri-lateral trade based upon the "Magellan Trade", importing – in a monopoly regime – Indian and Chinese goods to the Philippines (under Spanish control), to be exchanged for the silver from the Manila Galleons (see Chapter 1), and exporting (always under monopoly) Asian merchandise to Spain, via the Indian Ocean and the Cape of Good Hope.

A third, quite obvious, common characteristic is that they operated as monopolies. The "charter" was *de facto* a right granted by a superior authority (the Crown or the government) to the body of associated merchants, authorising the right to trade in a certain area (say, between the Muscovy area and Britain), under a monopoly regime. It was illegal for anyone else to do business in the assigned area. Those trading outside the monopoly regime were called "privateers" – the plain form for "pirates" – and interlopers, and ran the risk of seizure of goods or other forms of punishment by the authorities. Charters were normally issued for a limited period of time (for instance, the first charter of the *Muscovy Company* was issued for the duration of fifteen years), or even more restrictively concerned some kind of merchandise subject to the monopoly from one area to another, while others remained in the domain of free trade. The *Levant Company*'s charter, for instance, allowed the merchants operating between Venice and England to be the sole importers of currants, wines, cotton and silk, while other goods could be freely traded. Above all, charters were subject to renewal, something that involved a great deal of lobbying by the companies themselves. This, of course, made these companies very much subject to political fluctuations and change, which could easily result in the suspension or even the revocation of the charter. The charter was the necessary premise to obtain a monopolistic position. However, this was a very sensitive and much-debated issue, one which soon attracted criticism from liberal economists such as Adam Smith, to give but one example.

Box 2.1: Exploiting Africa's riches: the *Royal African Company*

The rivalry of European countries in West Africa had probably reached one of its higher levels in the second half of the seventeenth century. In contrast to the imperialism of the nineteenth century, the struggle for Africa in the seventeenth century was aimed more at trade than at territory, and focused mainly on the west coast of the continent. The rise in international competition for trade in Africa was mainly due to developments on the other side of the Atlantic. Even though the purchase of slaves in Africa had begun two centuries earlier with the Portuguese explorations, it was the spread of sugar cultivation to the English and French islands of the Caribbean that exerted a notably strong influence upon European trade in Africa, and the cultivation of sugar was, from its inception, inextricably bound to slave labour.

When King Charles II granted a charter to the *Royal African Company of England* (originally the *Company of Royal Adventurers Trading to Africa*) in 1672, he granted it the lands and trade between Cape Blanco (now Ras Nouadhibou, Mauritania/Morocco) in the north and the Cape of Good Hope in the south for one thousand years. Gold, silver and slaves were mentioned as the company's objectives, and the company was authorised to establish and oversee fortresses, factories (meaning trading centres) and plantations in Africa, to make war and peace with any nation there, to raise troops and to enact martial law. The charter also established the creation of a court of judicature to sit on the African coast to hear and determine cases of interlopers and other mercantile suits. Establishing such a monopolistic joint-stock company made sense, as the *Royal African Company*'s propagandist Charles D'Avenant was to say in 1709, since England's trade with Africa would be most profitable and best protected from foreign competitors if it were organised "under one entire Interest and uniform exclusive management".

The shareholders of the *Royal African Company* included a number of very prominent ministers and courtiers, who were clearly assets of great value. Their presence reassured other potential shareholders who wished to enter the business; moreover, they could, for instance, facilitate the granting of the charter. However, after the first few years, these men were generally either unable or unwilling to dedicate time to the day-to-day problems of the company and their number gradually decreased. Below this group of prominent shareholders came such men as Sir George Carteret, Sir Peter Colleton, Thomas Povey, John Locke, Sir Edmund Andros and Ferdinando Gorges. With the exception of Povey, none of these men were merchants, but all had experience or interests in the colonies. Colleton, for instance, owned a large plantation in Barbados. This group, too, diminished day by day through death or withdrawal. A few holders of minor civil offices, a small number of country gentlemen, and a few widows completed the non-mercantile element in the stock. Even though the ownership of the *Royal African Company*'s shares was continually changing hands, since, apart from questions of indebtedness to the company or infringements of its monopoly, there were few restrictions on the transfer of shares, we can assume that at no time did all the shareholders from outside the business world, ministers of the Crown, courtiers, peers, officials, widows, and gentry, hold more than about one-quarter of the company's stocks. The remainder of the shares were in the hands of men who, even if, in some cases, were not "merchants" within the traditional definition of the term, made their livings by buying and selling, banking and money-lending, and importing and exporting. In a mercantile community such as that of London in the seventeenth century, it was, in the main, the non-specialists who continued to perform these functions. For example, it was not rare for bankers to be dealing in commodities or for merchants to be moneylenders. Beyond and above these practising merchants, the other major shareholders were the great figures of the City, older merchants whose riches and wealth were derived mainly from trade, and bankers and revenue-farmers, who formed the mercantile aristocracy. The *Royal African Company* relied heavily upon them both, the practising merchants and the older merchants, for its capital and for the management of its complicated business. Such notable figures as Sir John Banks, Sir Gabriel Roberts, Sir John Moore, Sir Josiah Childe, Sir Robert Clayton, Sir Samuel Dashwood and Sir William Prichard gave the company more solid support than the ephemeral enthusiasm of prominent ministers and courtiers. At least two-thirds of the capital, and probably more, was thus in the hands of businessmen, of whom the majority were, or had been, overseas traders.

As far as the internal organisation of the company is concerned, the constitution of the *Royal African Company*, as defined by its charter, conformed to the customary pattern of the seventeenth-century joint-stock company. A Governor, Sub-Governor and Deputy Governor were named as the chief officers, with a Court of twenty-four Assistants, all to be chosen by election every year at the General Courts of the whole body of shareholders. Supreme power over the company's business was – at least in theory – completely held by the General Court, but, as long as the company's affairs were fundamentally in order, the General Courts played only a formal role. On average, the full Court of Assistants met once a week, more frequently when it was necessary.

The sub-committees of the Court met almost as often. Many different subjects were considered and discussed by the Court of Assistants. First of all, they read and discussed the letters that had been received since the last meeting of the Court. Immediately following this, any necessary action was decided upon, or, if a problem was complex, it was remitted to an appropriate sub-committee. Next, reports from committees were examined and usually approved. The Court then examined candidates for the frequent vacancies in Africa, and proceeded with the scrutiny and sealing of charter parties. Finally, transfers in the stock and warrants for all money paid by the company were approved. In addition to these usual items of discussion, many others, such as the disposal of goods imported from Africa and the West Indies, the conduct of lawsuits, the organising of pressure on Members of Parliament, interviewing men back from the Coast, the drafting of petitions, and examining samples of exports, appeared frequently on the agenda of the meetings of the Court of Assistants.

The trading activity of the *Royal African Company* can be divided essentially into two branches: the purchase of African products for distribution in England, and the buying of slaves in Africa for sale in the West Indies. The provision of goods for export to Africa was primary amongst the several functions of the Court of Assistants. Unless a sufficient volume of appropriate products was pumped into Africa every year, trade from Africa to England and the West Indies would fade. About half of the company's exports were foreign goods. Chief amongst the *Royal African Company*'s re-exports were East Indian cottons, calicoes and prints, which commanded a ready sale in Africa thanks to their cheapness and bright colours. They were normally bought at the British *East India Company*'s sales, but also were also bought from private traders. Iron and copper from Sweden and Germany were next in importance, followed by two other commodities imported from the Baltic, amber and *sletias* (a German textile). The remaining products re-exported from Europe to Africa were basically brandy and glass and other types of beads. On top of this, a wide range of goods of English manufacture was also exported, including knives, woollen goods, jugs, tankards, brass basins, pans, kettles, small quantities of carpets, spirits, trumpets, scissors, mirrors and other similar merchandise.

The company's imports, though much less heterogeneous than its exports, were still numerous. Gold, ivory, dyewood, wax, hides, gum, malaguetta and palm oil all came from Africa, while sugar, tobacco, cotton, indigo, cocoa, ginger, logwood and silver all came from the West Indies. Both the sale of these commodities and the provision of goods for export were under the management of the Sub-committee of Goods and were supervised by the Court of Assistants. The *Royal African Company* derived a large proportion, probably about two-fifths, of its income from the sale of goods. For the first thirty years of the company's existence, all gold obtained in West Africa was delivered to the Mint in England, where it was coined into guineas. The African goods planned for England were generally shipped home directly, while the slaves were distributed amongst the English West Indian islands of Jamaica, Barbados, St. Christopher's, Nevis, Antigua and Montserrat, with small shipments also being made to Virginia. In these colonies, the company employed agents who managed the sales of slaves, collected the proceeds and arranged for the remittances to England.

Before the Glorious Revolution (1688), the company owned few of the vessels that transported its goods. Even after 1700, when company-owned ships predominated, many of the largest vessels employed were hired. The overall duration of the London–Africa–West Indies–London voyage is best exemplified by the history of the

Falconbergh, one of the company-owned vessels. Between 1691 and 1704, she performed the round trip eight times, more than any other ship that ever sailed in the service of the *Royal African Company*.

Despite having the advantage of enjoying monopoly conditions, the *Royal African Company* had to face several challenges and organisational problems. It had to raise money, buy goods, hire vessels, recruit men for Africa, build fortresses, make agreements with the natives, negotiate with representatives of other European nations, defend its monopoly and account for its actions to the Crown and Parliament. These were tasks which would try a modern corporation: the *Royal African Company* had to face them without modern means of transport or communication. On top of this, like all monopolies based upon royal prerogative, the *Royal African Company* provoked hostility, criticism which became even harsher after the Glorious Revolution. The company was actually attacked by the West Indian colonists for failing to deliver sufficient slaves, by English manufacturers for artificially limiting their markets, and by English merchants who wanted to trade to Africa. Despite its royal support, the company never really succeeded in checking infringements of its monopoly by interlopers. In 1698, twenty-six years after the granting of the charter and after several years of intensive lobbying by both the *Royal African Company* and its opponents, Parliament passed legislation which opened the African market to all English subjects who paid a levy of 10 per cent to the *Royal African Company* for the maintenance of its trading posts, from which all English traders benefited. When the "Ten Percent Act" (1698) expired in 1712, the *Company* produced advertisements warning potential interlopers that, just as before, they would "be duly prosecuted for the Trespasses, Wrongs, and Injuries by them committed, and done to such the Company's Legal Property". But this was pure bluff. The *Company* was in no position to attempt any real enforcement of its charter. The independent merchants and traders, now free of the required contribution to the maintenance of the *Royal African Company* posts, made the most of this cost advantage in the ensuing atmosphere of the *de facto* open trade.

This box was written by Veronica Binda. Based on K.G. Davies, *The Royal African Company*, London: Longman, 1957.

★ ★ ★ ★ ★

It is, however, worth examining in greater depth the structure of the incentives of the most important actors involved, namely, the government (in most cases, the Crown) and the groups of associated merchants. For these actors, the charter – and the monopolistic position attached to it – was, of course, a major incentive. It allowed them to operate in a relatively "safe" environment, which meant lack of competition in the home market and the possibility, to some extent, of deciding the prices of imports, and thus exploiting huge monopoly rents. According to some scholars, this rent-seeking behaviour was *the* main motivation behind the creation of chartered companies, which involved both merchants and members of the Crown and of the government who were in a position to influence the concession of the trade monopoly. Monopolistic positions, held, in some cases, for a long time, allowed these companies to consolidate their power (and also their political influence, with consequent episodes of corruption and bribery at political level); in many cases, the dominant position lasted even after these privileges were abolished, as a result of pressure both from politics and from the demand side of the market. The British *East India Company*, for example, lost a substantial part of its privileges in 1819, but remained a dominant institution for a further sixty years. The *Hudson Bay Company*'s monopoly was also progressively relaxed from the last quarter of the eighteenth century.

Rents apart, merchants were also incentivised to lobby for charters for the quite obvious reason that the increasing flow of merchandise from distant to the domestic markets, run by several independent companies, was acting in the direction of increasing the purchase price and lowering the selling price, thereby sharply reducing the very high profits of the activity. This, for instance, was the serious motivation behind the decision to merge all the independent companies in the Netherlands into the *Verenigde Oostindische Compagnie* or Dutch *East India Company* (VOC), which was intended to make it more efficient in trading (and in fostering the Dutch presence) on foreign markets, thanks to its size and financial strength. In this, the interests of merchants converged with those of governments, which, in their turn, were interested, as is detailed below, in avoiding too pronounced market fluctuations.

From the point of view of the governments, the creation of such monopolistic positions had many purposes. The concession of a charter was openly considered to be the same as the concession of a patent, which encouraged people to invest both time and money in new inventions. It was also considered to be a sort of reward for risk-taking initiatives. In the case of English merchants, the early versions of the charters used a fairly standard *incipit*, citing the "Company of *Adventurers* of England Trading in …", with a clear reference to the risk-intensive characteristics of the activity being close to that of exploring new and unknown lands – something with which it very often coincided, as, for instance, was the case with the Canadian territories. The support given to the foreign initiatives of merchants had several goals. The first one was the fact that, not only for fiscal reasons, but also for other reasons of a more social nature, the Crown had an interest in establishing a certain level and relatively steady flow of the goods demanded in the internal market (provided there was no competition with the domestic producers). In the end, it was better to create a monopoly in order to keep supply and demand balanced, which allowed somebody (the merchants) to make good, but not excessive, profits, and, at the same time, served to avoid fluctuations in the market, which was what pre-industrial societies hated most. All this was even truer in the case of goods – not just pepper and sugar, for instance, but also the stimulants to which Europeans increasingly became addicted, such as coffee, tea, or tobacco, or intermediate products such as dyes. The second reason can probably be best understood from a "mercantilist" point of view. Chartered companies, such as the *Hudson Bay Company*, or the *East India* companies mentioned above, were in essence making (huge) profits abroad, especially when they engaged in multiple exchanges, which were repatriated and served to increase the total stock of the home nation's domestic wealth. This was especially relevant for governments concerned with trade as the instrument for preserving and increasing the wealth of the state. France was particularly unsuccessful with its chartered companies, but it has to be stressed how both the *Compagnie des Indies Orientales*, and the *Compagnie des Indies Occidentales*, both founded in 1664, were explicit attempts, designed by Jean-Baptiste Colbert, to challenge the British and Dutch monopolies.

This motivation, connected to the domain of political economy, also concerned a third relevant issue that will be analysed in the following discussion. Chartered companies were, in fact, officially private companies, but they were also instruments for a sort of colonial penetration into distant areas – something destined to become a strategic component in the process of European colonisation, particularly in Asia. Charters were often accompanied by an exchange of letters between governments, and they served not only as credentials for the merchants, but also as a sort of political international agreement based upon private trade monopoly.

A fourth point, also crucial, is the legal status of these companies, and the relationship that this had with the issue of raising capital. A fairly consolidated view in the literature sees the diffusion of chartered companies as a sort of necessity in order to pull together sufficient financial resources to organise long-distance trade when its volume – for the reasons suggested above – exceeded a certain threshold. This is, of course, a quite complex issue, particularly from a theoretical point of view. Chartered companies were, from their inception, stable (at least for the period of the charter) associations of merchants. In some cases, they were not really a small group of partners at all: when it was founded, the British *East India Company* counted 219 members, a number which clearly gives the idea of the difference between these bodies and the pre-existing partnerships. The charter was, at the beginning, issued nominally, that is, to the merchants involved in the venture. But very soon things changed. Due to their role as agents for government interests, the financial strength and the stability of companies became increasingly mandatory, and this opened the way to solutions that were new, and quite revolutionary, in international business. The case of the Dutch *East India Company* was quite extreme, but is, nonetheless, significant, and will help to clarify this point. The Dutch *East India Company* was chartered in 1602, and, like its British counterpart, was granted a monopoly on the trade between the Provinces of Holland and Zeeland and the vast area of the Pacific Ocean between the Cape of Good Hope (South Atlantic Ocean) and the Straits of Magellan via the Indian Ocean. The monopoly was to last twenty-one years. As far as the ownership structure was concerned, the VOC was a joint-stock company, in which each stockholder had the right, according to the charter, to withdraw his capital at the end of each decade. Soon, however, this clause was modified, and the stockholder could only sell his shares, but not withdraw his capital, a measure clearly intended to favour the stability of the company in terms of assets. Here, institutional differences mattered. From the beginning, the VOC system was acutely different both from the concept of partnership and from the shareholding types already in place, particularly in the Netherlands, in international trade in the second half of the sixteenth century. From a closed, small circle of stable shareholders, its ownership became much more dispersed. Shares became tradable, even upon a speculative basis. The evolutionary process of the British *East India Company* (EIC) is probably even more instructive of the way in which the issue of raising capital was managed over time. At the beginning, in fact, after its foundation as a chartered company in 1600, the EIC was a company which raised capital from private investors for each individual expedition. Each stockholder was thus gaining profits on each and every expedition (sometimes, waiting for his expected returns for years) in which he invested his money – and profits could also be paid in kind, for instance, in pepper or other spices. From the very beginning, the necessity of retaining the shareholders' capital in the venture was clear to the EIC, and this resulted in serious tension between the management and the shareholders themselves, who, in their turn, were seeking a balance between investment and liquidity. However, it took almost sixty years to come to a fixed value per share (oscillating around one hundred pounds), something which was already firmly in place, and quite effective, in the Netherlands. In the meantime, the constituency of shareholders continued to grow and increasingly included subscribers from outside the mercantile community, such as courtiers, aristocrats and wealthy families.

A fifth peculiarity of chartered companies lay in their commitment to invest in the ownership of stable facilities abroad. This, of course, depended on the size of the company, on the volume and frequency of trade, and on the convenience of storing merchandise, instead of trading it on the spot market. Trading large quantities of goods over long distances created the necessity of being able to count on stable operational facilities and hubs, such as yards, warehouses and factories – as places in which traded goods were collected, stored and prepared for delivery – and sometimes even military installations and buildings, where necessary. An impressive example of this can be found in the network of trading outposts under the control of the *Hudson Bay Company*, which constituted the backbone of the institution's presence in a territory which extended from the northern section of Hudson Bay to today's central section of the borders between the US and Canada.

As already observed, investment in physical facilities also had symbolic significance, as it stressed the presence of an organised institution in places often characterised by high levels of risk and uncertainty. In addition, at least at the beginning, privileged companies tended to own, rather than lease, the ships that they used to trade; in some cases, such as that of the EIC, the company even invested in a shipyard for the production of the necessary vessels.

Besides their investments in physical goods, as we will see in detail in the following section, these companies also had to undertake other kinds of investments, especially in skilled human capital, capable of managing a complex organisation characterised by the relevant agency costs. In principle, this was not concretely visible, as it was in the presence of factories and warehouses, but it did absorb a high and relevant amount of the company's resources. To this, one should add the fact that at least the most important chartered companies soon found themselves having to create a stable military force, not only for reasons connected to the necessity of reducing local risks, but also to confront, in a somewhat aggressive way, competition from rivals. The case of the EIC, which progressively established strong military control over large sections of the Indian peninsula, may be quite exceptional, but is by no means an isolated case. A few years after its foundation, the British *East India Company* found itself increasingly at odds with the Dutch and the Portuguese, both of whom already had an established presence in the Indian Ocean, and, in 1612, this escalated into open war (the Battle of Swally). The power of the company grew progressively throughout the first half of the seventeenth century, when the Crown granted the EIC the right to mint money and use military force for the administration of the areas in which it was present, thereby *de facto* outsourcing the colonial rule of India to the *East India Company* until 1858, when this power was transferred to the British Crown. It was, in fact, a "state within the state", as it has been defined by one of its biographers, Kirti Chaudhuri, and the EIC also found itself having to invest resources in operating a complex system of courts of law and local administration.

Sixth, as a necessary premise for their very existence, chartered companies had the support of their governments (or of the political constituencies which preceded the Peace of Westphalia, the series of treaties which, in 1648, officially gave birth to the concept of the modern state). The companies were strongly incentivised to use private initiative to pursue not only mercantilist goals, but also to strengthen their international political influence. This point, which is particularly delicate, requires further reflection. As stated above, the concession of a charter and the creation of a monopoly (which could, in principle, damage domestic consumption) was something that the political powers of the time could agree upon, either for personal interests (something which often happened), or to promote more "general" issues.

The creation of a stable presence abroad, frequently characterised by the support of organised military force, was part of a strategy of "sovereignty outsourcing" which governments put in place by means of leverage on private interests (and greed). The political economy of the emerging European states was thus, in the mid-seventeenth century, largely based upon chartered companies. In contrast with the past, when military force was used to protect mercantile activities from piracy and other risks, in the phase of chartered companies, trade activities became inseparable from the use of some kind of military force, and political purposes came together with commercial ones. The above-mentioned merger at the origin of the VOC, for instance, was a private initiative put in place following the strong recommendation by the States General. The government of the Dutch Republic progressively established greater control over the company, which *de facto* operated as a quasi-governmental body abroad. The close relationship between international trade, power, and chartered companies was even greater and more evident in the case of Britain, which was probably as interested in the establishment of her political influence in (and outside) Europe as the Dutch were motivated by commercial and trade issues. This led to a *de facto* identification of a private company and its bodies with its country of origin: in India, the presidents of the British *East India Company* were considered as being synonymous with the governors of the British monarch. In the cases of both the Dutch and the British, it was not at all rare for courtiers or members of the royal family or of the government to be shareholders. In the case of France, the relationship was even stricter, because the state control of trading companies was probably higher than in other European countries. The political economy of chartered companies, in sum, involved a great deal of competition among countries, not only for mercantilist strategies, but also for reasons connected to international power and reputation. While bigger states explicitly engaged in direct competition even involving military clashes, smaller states tried to follow their steps by attempting to establish monopolies for trading with East India. This, for instance, was the case both of Denmark, which established her own *East India Company* (*Ostindisk Kompagni*) in 1619, and of Sweden, which adopted the same strategy in 1731 (*Svenska Ostindiska Companiet*).

3. Structural features

Chartered companies varied greatly in terms of size, geographical coverage, and financial structure. But notwithstanding this, what all these impersonal joint-stock companies had in common was the fact that they were created both to handle and to manage a volume of trade which was considerably higher than that which had previously been performed by pedlars and small traders, who had hitherto been the backbone of Asian trade, even over long distances.

Data are available for the largest companies, which also left pertinent archival information. The records of the Dutch VOC provide us with a fairly clear idea of the size of the operations carried out by the Dutch chartered company in Asia.

On average, from 1602 to 1795, the VOC sent twenty-five ships per year to Asia (that is, to Batavia, Coromandel, Bengal, Ceylon and, from the beginning of the seventeenth century, to China). Around the middle of the seventeenth century, the fleet amounted to more than 100 ships. The deployment of personnel was also impressive. Between 1602 and 1795, mostly during the eighteenth century, the VOC sent several hundred thousand people – sailors, seamen, soldiers, administrative personnel, staff, churchmen, servants – to Asia, for a more or less limited stay, on *circa* 1,500 ships of various sizes built in the company's own shipyards. The VOC was not only the largest employer in the Netherlands; it also had to hire outside the United Provinces, mainly in Germany. The personnel located in Asia rose steadily over time. Data for 1625 show around 5,000 people, which had doubled by 1689. One century later, the VOC personnel in Asia amounted to 25,000 people. Of these, 11,000 were related to the military, 6,000 were seamen or in service on board, 2,000 could be classified as "craftsmen", and another 1,700 were employed in the administration. In addition, together with Europeans, there were a not negligible number of local servants, labourers and slaves. According to the available data, the cost of maintaining the personnel constituted a burden that steadily increased over time, actually eroding returns to the point of producing negative results, particularly in the second half of the eighteenth century. Given these numbers, it can without hesitation be suggested that chartered companies constituted a new organisational form of international business. Stemming from the ancient (and flexible) instrument of the *societas*, these companies removed the constraint on the limited amount of capital through the introduction of anonymous stock ownership. At the same time, they also provided an elegant solution to the liquidity problems that could keep potential investors away, given the immediate birth of a secondary market for the shares – which sometimes, as in the case of the *South Sea Company*, led also to serious problems of speculation.

There has been, and still is, a debate – one which mainly involves modern and contemporary business historians and historians of organisations – about the "modernity" of these organisations. According to some scholars, the volume of the operations handled by chartered companies abroad and the complexity of their organisational structures establish them as the antecedents of modern multinationals and other international organisations. For others, they constitute exceptional cases which are to be considered as significant; in addition, the volume of the transactions annually carried out by even the most sophisticated of these organisations is not even comparable to the weekly volume of transactions taking place in a small-size, contemporary multinational company. It is not, however, in the spirit of this chapter to enter into this debate, or to take a position on one side or the other. Even if they were exceptional outliers, chartered companies constitute an important step in the evolution of international business organisations, creating, introducing and refining procedures and management methods which would be widely adopted in the following centuries. The study of the way in which the transformation in the structure and the volume of trade impacted on long-distance mercantile activities deserves a great deal of attention, and is also essential if we are to understand fully the structural characteristics of the forms of international business which followed the "age of chartered companies".

Apart from their dimensions in terms of volume of trade, employment, working and fixed capital, the issue of the *frequency of transacting* in *different and distant markets* is a key topic. Starting with the issue of the frequency of transacting, chartered companies were undoubtedly similar to medieval international merchants in one regard: they were still basically intermediaries between two or more markets. In their simplest form, they transferred merchandise from one market to another (in contrast to merchants, however, chartered companies progressively integrated into shipping, as we will see). Yet their nature deeply transformed the relationship which they had with these markets. First, the end, or final, market was a market in which chartered companies sold the products that they imported from abroad. The fact that they traded large quantities of items (at least, larger than those traded by individual merchants) meant that they were not selling to retailers, but to wholesalers. In the case of both the British and the Dutch *East India Companies*, the sales took place through a system of auctions in which the protagonists were the wholesalers. As far as procurement was concerned, market relations were also affected by the presence of this new kind of company. In contrast to individual merchants, chartered companies were buying large quantities of goods, and this created, in some cases, temporary or even permanent "monopsonistic" positions, in which the bargaining power was basically on their side. In general, chartered companies bought either from local wholesalers or directly from the producers (when it was convenient to skip the intermediaries), upon the basis of evaluations which took the value of the goods purchased and their transport costs into account. The company's factories were the places in which the transactions with the wholesalers and the producers took place, and where the goods were finally stored before their delivery to the home market or to other markets. Local trade was the most delicate part of the business of these companies, and this meant that the local agents and personnel were increasingly acquiring the status of idiosyncratic resources, which embodied the crucial knowledge of the complex local markets in which the companies were investing substantial resources. It is, of course, very difficult to provide generalisations in this regard; the operations of chartered companies in foreign markets were, in fact, characterised by a huge variety of situations, depending on local practices and routines. The trading problems that the VOC, for instance, faced in India were different from those which other chartered companies were facing in China, or Canada, or even on the West African coast.

A second relevant issue concerns the frequency of transacting. Engaging in business in multiple markets, both between Europe and Asia, and inside Europe and Asia – and, in the case of the largest ones, such as the British *East India Company*, on a global scale – required a respectable number of daily operations. If one also includes all those involved in the shipping, transportation, distribution, and administrative activities in normal market transactions, it is probably no exaggeration to talk of hundreds of thousands of transactions being performed every year, in relatively poor conditions in terms of transport, communication and information technologies, which, of course, made the whole process remarkably slow. The volume of transactions suggested above is low if it is compared with those of a contemporary multinational enterprise doing business inside a global value chain, but it is probably not very far from the volume of transactions performed in a nineteenth-century European firm trading and investing abroad with only one or merely a few branches.

There were, however, additional advantages in scale and scope. In the end, this extremely complex situation on the part of the markets generated an invaluable advantage for the largest companies, an advantage which they were able to hold over all other competitors, and also over the smaller, geographically focused companies. Companies such as the Dutch or British *East India Companies*, which were diversified giants that were present in a high number of locations and markets, and which traded simultaneously in a wide variety of goods and items, were able to enjoy to the full the advantages generated by their control of information. To an extent incomparable to that available to individual merchants and smaller competitors, they knew how to collect, process and store information, were able to compare a much greater range of prices, forecast supply, decide to buy where items were cheaper, and were even able, as outlined above, to exert some influence on the way in which these prices were set. In addition, their status as *de facto* interfaces between domestic governments and local powers gave the companies access to particular information which concerned issues that were not immediately related to trade, but which nonetheless strongly affected it, such as political changes and turmoil.

Dealing with a higher volume of transactions and information across distant markets meant that chartered companies faced completely new challenges in terms of internal structure and organisation. The companies were instruments for managing the complexity of long-distance trade and growing geopolitical goals and tensions in the most efficient way possible. The price which the companies paid for all this was, however, problems in at least three broad areas: organisational structure, managerial and administrative procedures, and governance. The companies that successfully dealt with these issues gained a considerable advantage over their competitors in terms of stability and longevity. However, in order to exploit these advantages fully, these companies had to establish mechanisms with which to collect, process and refine this mass of incoming information to be processed, transforming it into a stable competitive advantage, and, at the same time, coordinating the activities of their personnel. To put it another way, chartered companies were organisations which were set up with the precise aim of economising on the transaction costs which resulted from the increase in the volume of international trade over very long distances.

Box 2.2: The divergence and adaptability of European imperialism (seventeenth–eighteenth centuries): the case of the *Levant Company*

The *Levant Company* (1581–1825) was formed by the merger of two companies which had already been active in regions of the Eastern Mediterranean; the *Turkey Company*, which had been active in trade with the major ports of the Ottoman Empire, and the *Venice Company*, which had been formed to do trade between Venice and its colonies and England. Both predecessors of the *Levant Company* had been formed between the 1570s and 1580s, in order to facilitate the trade in commodities arriving in the Mediterranean basin via the land routes and the caravans from the East: spices, cotton, raw silk, Indian dyes, and tapestries, in return for cloth, kerseys (coarse woollen cloth), and conyskins (rabbit skins and fur) from England. The complementarities of the trade of the two companies and the high costs of their operations eventually led to the formation of a single company, namely, the *Levant Company*, by means of a new charter in 1592. The newly established charter of the *Levant Company* covered the coast of Asia Minor and Syria, the Barbary Coast states (the modern-day states of Morocco, Algeria, Tunisia, and Libya) in North Africa, Egypt with Alexandria and Damietta, and Greece with the Aegean islands, the Ionian Islands and the Adriatic coast.

Relations between the English "factors" in the Eastern Mediterranean ports and the main political entities were determined by bilateral treaties, the Capitulations, which granted mutual privileges to both sides in each other's dominions, which were re-negotiated and renewed several times. The concessions agreed in the Capitulations included the protection of English merchants and their products from molestation or confiscation, favourable trading conditions and the right to appoint consuls, who were to settle the disputes among their co-nationals and represent them to the *Sublime Porte* (how the Ottoman rule was commonly named), a practice already applied by the French, earlier in the sixteenth century. Thus, the *Levant Company* emerged as both a commercial corporation and a diplomatic body in the Eastern Mediterranean.

Deeply linked to the particularities of the Levant, where neither new lands nor new products were to be discovered, the British merchants had to infiltrate an already well-established and well-organised state successfully. The Ottoman market was unfamiliar to British traders, and a number of rival traders, both local and foreign, provided strong competition. To facilitate its activities, the *Levant Company* concentrated on a few strategic ports – which were usually *entrepôts*, where the trade routes from the Asian hinterland ended – to set up its "factories" (trading centres), where it amassed goods for re-distribution to both the Mediterranean and Western Europe. For this purpose, it selected a number of major ports which combined the attributes of: a) a local consumer market for British products; b) an *entrepôt* for the intra-Mediterranean trade; and c) an outlet to the sea for the commodities produced in the Mediterranean hinterland that financed imports from Britain.

The most suitable organisational form for the Levant trade proved to be the *regulated company*, a hybrid business organisation. While the *Levant Company* was initially a joint-stock company, it functioned more like a loose co-operation of individual merchants, who were only subject to the regulations and restrictions imposed by their own corporate bodies. Instead of joint stocks, joint capital was formed on the eve of a venture by a partnership of a number of participants who wished to lease a ship and purchase their selected merchandise. Upon the ship's return, the partnership was dissolved and the accounts were settled among the partners in proportion to their original investment. This procedure would be repeated for every venture.

The entry of members into the *Levant Company*, at least until the late eighteenth century, was strictly regulated. The condition of permanent residence within the City of London, in addition to the recommendation and support of its existing members, was preserved to safeguard the exclusive structure of the *Levant Company*. Those eligible for membership were charged a small admission fee. Ethnic and gender discrimination, at least initially, was strong, as membership was denied to both women and Jews.

During the eighteenth century, the *Levant Company* underwent a process of organisational transformation. The increase in competition, a direct result of the changing circumstances of the British–French rivalry that eventually led to the Napoleonic wars, opened the way for an ever-increasing number of players who could – and did – participate. The survival of British trade in the Eastern Mediterranean was tightly linked to the efficiency of its individual members in gaining access both to the already existing trading networks and to local knowledge.

Though the *Levant Company* enjoyed a monopoly on British trade in the region, its members had, from the early eighteenth century, introduced the practice of co-operating with free traders and local intermediaries, especially Greeks, Jews and Armenians, in order to overcome the uncertainty embedded in the profound differences of everyday economic practices and entrepreneurial culture. The suspicious "Levantine ways" of business involved striking a balance between speculation and corruption. The customary bribery of state officials in order to maintain fiscal and mercantile privileges, issues of commercial credit and trust which were built upon networks of kinship and ethnicity, the linguistic difficulties, and the particular market preferences all served to complicate European trade and business in the Levant.

The local intermediaries were granted the same privileges as the British merchants by offering the *Levant Company* a large amount of capital. However, in the late eighteenth century, the monopoly became ineffective: Levant shipping and trade was not only conceded to a wide number of beneficiaries, British and foreign, but co-operation with local carriers and merchants also gained ground, replacing the older, traditional practices of rigid monopoly. In the age of the Napoleonic wars in the Mediterranean, local players managed to penetrate the British monopoly of trade in the Eastern Mediterranean, with the approval of the *Levant Company* itself. Due to the status of neutrality that they enjoyed, local Ottoman traders were allowed to trade without danger and to undertake shipping on their own behalf, thereby accommodating British trade. Progressively, the monopoly of trade was removed and even foreigners could profit from the influx of British commodities in the Ottoman Empire. By 1809, the *Levant Company*'s status was transformed into a fusion of different ethnicities, and was no longer a monolithic, centrally governed body. This decision, taken by the British Government, led to the repeal of the monopoly in 1825, thus opening the way to the democratisation of trade.

This box was written by Alexandra Papadopoulou.

★ ★ ★ ★ ★

4. Organisational structures

A first, relevant point is that, even with some differences, these companies broadly shared the same organisational structure, which was the consequence of the process of their formation. Almost all of them were headed by a *Court*, a sort of board of directors, which represented the central and main directive body of the company, located in the country of incorporation, which was, of course, close to the main sources of finance (either the stock exchange or the Chamber of Commerce). The *Court* or board, which was responsible for most of the strategic decisions, was a delicate mechanism. The Dutch *East India Company*, for instance, was formed by the main shareholders (as well as the stakeholders, to wit, the six Chambers of Commerce of the country, that is, Amsterdam, Zeeland, Delft, Rotterdam, Hoorn, Enkhuizen), was frequently closely connected with the government and the Crown. As stated above, differences had arisen, from the very beginning, between the members of the board, the majority shareholders and the minority shareholders, differences which were progressively solved by increasing the tradability of shares – thereby providing an exit option for unhappy shareholders.

In order to take the main strategic decisions, committees, composed of salaried managers with functional responsibilities, supported the *Court* as staff units. Accounting, shipping and procurement were typical examples of their functions, tasks and responsibilities, but almost all of the typical functional areas present in the modern enterprise were represented, albeit with different names or titles: the treasury (finance), which supervised the financial transfers of the company; private trade (internal audit), which was in charge of the private activities of the directors of the company; and others. These committees, of course, changed over time both in name and in composition, but not in substance, which was that of the staff and support of the main bodies. The central body took the strategic decisions concerning the type and quantity of trade, both between the home country and the foreign location(s), and concerning the countries in which the company was present. The Dutch *East India Company* again provides a good example. The Board (called the "Gentlemen Seventeen") was in charge of deciding about the shipping and the crews going to Asia, the amount of goods and precious metals to be shipped, the auctions of the goods received from Asia, the merchandise to be requested in future shipments (quality and quantity), and the appointments and promotions of personnel in Asia.

The *Court* and its committees were based in the home country of the company, and was a relatively lean structure when compared to the part of the organisation located abroad. In the most sophisticated chartered companies, the area of the charter was divided into foreign trading areas under the responsibility of a local council headed by a president, akin to modern multi-divisional structures divided on a geographic basis. In turn, the local councils were interlinked to the managers of the local factories (trading centres) or trading posts in which most of the basic exchanges took place.

The *East India Company* had several outposts abroad, basically "factories" (trading centres) with storage warehouses and buildings for the personnel and administration, in several locations normally close to the main communication routes, either on land or by sea, with some being more relevant than others in terms of the volume of traffic. In the case of the VOC, the main hub was Batavia, the name the Dutch gave to the Indonesian harbour which they seized in 1619, now called Jakarta. Batavia was the largest factory (trading centre) connected with the mother country, and the most heavily presided over by Dutch civilians and military, and was where the main administrative body of the company in Asia was located, since Batavia organised all the shipping from Asia, including the maintenance of the fleet. Batavia was also the central "records office" for all the Asian trade, and the administration there collected the bulk of the most strategic information available to the company. In addition, other factories were also present, some of which traded directly with the Netherlands, such as Canton, Malacca, Hugli, in West Bengal, and Ceylon, now Sri Lanka. When a region became strategic in terms of the quality and the quantities of trade, as happened to China in the first half of the eighteenth century, a separate committee was formed at home, basically a specialised staff unit, which was then added to the central bodies.

Batavia was the seat of the General Council, the organisation which oversaw all trade in Asia, headed by a Governor – which meant the presence of an intermediate body abroad, between the central top decision-making office, and the operative units. This body acted as a conveyor of information, both top-down (that is, from the central body to the operative units), and bottom-up, since the "factories" made all their requests to the mother country through it.

As suggested above, this was also the first level at which the identification between the company and the government at home took place, since, quite often, it was the Governor, or an analogous body, who acted as the home country's Ambassador abroad or even as the representative of the Crown in the case of imperial rule. The Council took on the functional roles of its staff abroad, overseeing, for instance, the bookkeeping, shipping, and military matters. This structure was replicated on a smaller scale in the local "factories" (trading centres) scattered throughout Asia.

The individual factories also developed over time, according to a model of progressive growth and consolidation. The first settlement was basically set up in order to facilitate trade and to coordinate the shipment of goods. The second phase involved the creation of stable storage units, followed by another phase in which the factory embedded itself in the local production system in greater depth through exclusive contracts and by binding suppliers through finance via a system of cash-in-advance payments. In the last phase, the factory completely internalised the local market transactions, thereby integrating the market into its production system. This phase actually coincided with the transformation of the company's activity from pure trading to a mixture of trading and production. As many scholars have stressed, integration into production – which, it is important to remember, did not always take place – was a response to a series of pressures, ranging from the necessity of sending a steady flow of goods to the mother country, to the temporary or structural shortages of the precious metals necessary to make purchases at local level. One could not, in short, wait for the shipments of silver sailing from Amsterdam actually to arrive before starting the necessary transactions to amass, say, the pepper, cloves, or nutmeg that Europe was so desperate to obtain. In addition, control of production allowed local factories to create a buffer against price fluctuations, and thus to maximise the profits for the company itself. Another incentive for backward integration was, of course, the necessity to control the quality of the goods traded; the VOC had already directly employed cotton spinners from the mid-seventeenth century in order to allow the production of the textiles to be exported to the Netherlands. In the same way, direct control was achieved almost immediately with regard to natural resources such as precious minerals. Lastly, (and logically), companies vertically integrated into production or services when the latter were not immediately available locally. Both the *Muscovy Company*, which had already set up a cordage factory in St. Petersburg for its own needs at the beginning of the seventeenth century, and the shipyards and warehouses established by the Dutch *East India Company* at the Cape of Good Hope, in order to provide maintenance and provisions for the ships sailing to Asia, provide telling examples here.

The organisation, both in the case of the VOC and in others, was thus a sort of pyramid, with lean headquarters in the Netherlands taking strategic decisions upon the basis of the administrative support provided by specialised staff committees, while the day-to-day operations were managed abroad by another section of the hierarchical organisation, the head of which, in the case of the VOC, was in Batavia, controlling a number of operational units and providing administrative and maintenance support.

Intuitively, a relevant issue in this kind of structure, as well as in similar ones, is the issue of information, which allows the headquarters to take decisions and to give orders to the bottom of the pyramid, and simultaneously allows the bottom to provide additional evidence for the use of the administrative central bodies. Clearly, given the status of the existent communication technology, information also circulated very slowly for this kind of bureaucratic structure. It has been calculated that a whole cycle of information exchange between Batavia and Amsterdam took – on average – two years to be completed, either travelling by the sea route (around the Cape) or by land, on the residual caravan routes across India and Asia Minor. What was different from the past was not the *availability* of information in the short run, but the *quality* of information, and its *reliability*, given the crucial capabilities and relations now internalised by the company. A second relevant outcome of this situation was that, from the beginning, the units operating abroad were characterised *de facto* by a high degree of autonomy in their decision-making.

5. Internalising international competitive advantages: opportunities and risks

As suggested in the previous sections, chartered companies soon moved from pure trading (bilateral or multilateral) to a mixture of trading and both backward (in production) and forward (in shipping) integration. Companies integrated in shipping not only by chartering vessels, but also made crucial investments in shipbuilding, something that clarifies the strategic and idiosyncratic nature of the technologically appropriate forms of

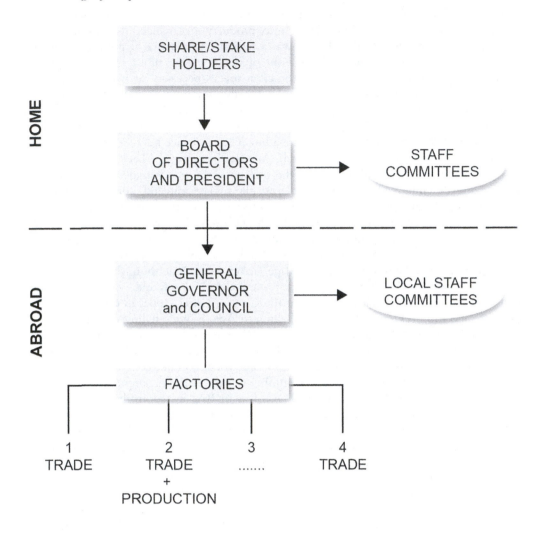

Figure 2.1 Organisation of a chartered company

infrastructure (in this case, ships) to such an extent that companies preferred to internalise their own production, instead of relying on independent shipping services bought on the market. In addition, according to some research, it was clear to the boards of the companies that renting ships was cheaper than building them, given the immobilisation of capital in both ships and shipyards. The alternative was, thus, clearly not rational in economic terms; the fact that the companies' ships also performed military roles, thus, must have also played a relevant part, as this completely shifted the incentive systems in the direction of direct control of their construction.

Independently of the importance of forward and backward integration (which, in any case, both changed over time and varied from case to case), the most relevant innovation (and difference from the previous phase) was that chartered companies internalised – from the very beginning – *the* most relevant assets in global trade, the crucial resources of information and political relations: in a word, agents. The increase in both the volume and the frequency of transactions, and hence of the transaction costs, not only made administrative coordination (that is, the creation of expensive bureaucratic structures) more convenient than coordination carried out through market mechanisms, but also increased the strategic relevance of idiosyncratic resources in trade intermediation. And it was not simply a matter of volume and frequency, but also of specific and refined knowledge. Most of the trade of chartered companies took place in distant and exotic markets, which involved a high degree of skill in transacting, also in the light of the volume and value of each individual transaction. To complete a purchase successfully in, say, Malabar, or in Bengal, very specific knowledge was necessary, ranging from the language, to local customs, to competences relating to the type of goods (for example, the various quantities of spices, and the different varieties of the different spices), their quality and how to handle them, and, last but not least, to a certain degree of embeddedness in local societies and of closeness, or proximity, to the local élites and the concomitant ability to deal with them). Medieval international merchants relied – to a certain extent – on independent agents (and established pure market transactions which were enforced by social control and trust), beyond which they tried to strengthen market relations by means of the family, when the agent was a relative or had familial ties, or upon ethnicity-based ties. Thus, chartered companies moved a step beyond, promoting the internalisation of previously market-based relationships.

The internalisation of agency contracts transformed the agents into the servants of the company. Yet this did not solve the delicate issue of controlling agency costs, which, due to distance and communication problems, tended to rise further. This situation, which, according to many authors, lay at the base of the decline of the model of the chartered company at the end of the eighteenth century, was a task which was as challenging for the top management as that of designing the administrative structures described above.

Yet agency issues fill company archives. Everywhere, from Russia to India and from Canada to China, employees were inclined to misappropriation, cheating under various forms, corruption, and the use of the company's own name and facilities for their own private self-interest. The list is basically identical to that which one can find filed in courts today against managerial malpractices, aggravated by the fact that the degree to which this behaviour could be monitored was extremely low. This was crystal clear to everybody familiar with company affairs. Adam Smith, writing at the end of the eighteenth century, when the burden of corruption was already sinking these organisations, expressed his anger at the insurmountable conflict between managers and shareholders, explicitly referring to the case of chartered companies, and emphasising what is still a common issue to this day, that is, the misalignment between the interests of the principals and those of the agents.

The records filed in the archives (those which have survived) of the companies focus mostly on one particular type of agency problem, namely, the habit that local managers had of engaging in private trade. These skilled professionals who were in full control of the crucial information about both the quality and the availability of goods, and about the local market conditions, frequently engaged in private transactions, creating fictitious companies and building huge fortunes at the expense of both the companies that they represented and their respective shareholders. For instance, something that frequently happened was that agents raided the merchandise in the company's warehouses privately, or even carried out trade upon a dual basis, keeping the most profitable business for themselves, while involving the company in the less convenient business. The long distance from the mother country, along with the scarce monitoring capacity undoubtedly provided an incentive for this kind of behaviour. On the top of this, the fact that contracts normally lasted from three to five years was also an incentive for those who wanted to get rich quickly to exploit their chances as best they could.

Given this situation, the companies naturally put in place the appropriate devices to limit agency issues. These strategies varied from one company to another, depending on the specific situation in the local market. For instance, some companies completely banned private trade, while others kept it under control, allowing their employees to make wealth privately to a certain extent, albeit not excessively. The British *East India Company*, for instance, provided space on the company ships for its employees to store a small number of items for private trade when they travelled back and forth from and to Asia. Another strategy was to keep average salaries high, and also to require bonds and guarantees from the agents. Social control (by other managers and peers) played some role as well, and this was strengthened by selecting employees from the same areas and communities, and binding them to the company through the swearing of oaths.

These attempts to bring agency costs under control allowed the companies to create relatively efficient administrative structures, which differentiated agencies from individual merchants in long-distance trade. However, corruption was endemic in institutions which made huge profits at home thanks to monopolistic rents, and which thus had incentives to lobby the power holders in order to maintain the *status quo*. Corruption was also endemic abroad, where agents and employees were often able to pursue their own interests more than those of the company, and where bribery was often the "normal" way of interacting with local authorities. In sum, chartered companies proved to be efficient mechanisms for coping with the sharp increase in both the volume and the span of long-distance trade, but also proved to be very limited instruments, particularly with regard to the difficult monitoring activities. Chartered joint-stock companies demonstrated, in sum, how much a close control over the organisation's assets had become a strategic issue, particularly in organisations which were expanding both the size and the scope of their activities to an extent never been seen before. Given the status of communications technologies, however, this would remain a problem without a solution for quite some time.

Conclusion

By the mid-nineteenth century, the age of chartered companies was over. Albeit for different reasons, some monopolies lasted until the second half of the century, while some chartered companies were even founded at the end of the century, especially in the light of the intensification of European colonial presence in Africa. More than for pure trading purposes, companies such as the *German West African Company* (*Deutsch-Westafrikanische Gesellschaft*) and the *German East Africa Company* (*Deutsch-Ostafrikanische Gesellschaft*), both founded and chartered at the beginning of the 1880s, were chartered to establish *de facto* national monopolies in the exploitation of a sector which was gaining growing relevance, that of natural resources, particularly in mining. But this was a completely different story. The giants that dominated international business activities during the whole of the eighteenth century had, by that time, either been dissolved or radically transformed into private trading companies. This, for instance, was the case of the *Hudson Bay Company*, which had lost its monopoly rights on the fur trade by the 1830s, more or less the same period during which the British EIC's monopolies on tea and its trade with China came to an end. In other cases, dissolution came because of internal financial distress (the VOC was disbanded for this reason and after several rescue attempts by the Dutch government at the end of the eighteenth century), or of political problems both at home (for instance, the *Royal African Company* lost its political protection, its political connections and consequently its monopoly rights in 1689, after the Glorious Revolution), while abroad, for example, the *Muscovy Company* did not survive the deterioration of diplomatic relations between the British and Russian governments.

The legacy of the age of chartered companies, however, appears to be of paramount importance to the framework of international business. For the purposes of this book, it is worth mentioning at least three:

First, both the management of chartered companies and of local servants/employees developed as skilled human capital. As discussed above, capacity in trading developed as an idiosyncratic skill, to such an extent that it was necessary to put trading initiatives under strict control and to regulate them. The training of high-quality human capital, however, also resulted in the development of entrepreneurial capabilities that were free to emerge once the limitations of the monopolies were removed, and sometimes even before; according to some scholars, the decline of the British *East India Company* coincided with the increasing propensity of its employees to engage in trade for themselves.

The innovation in the administrative structures and the creation of organisations based upon a vertical principle of authority, reinforced by the integration or internalisation of crucial relationships (such as those with agents) and market exchanges into the organisation itself were a second, and, maybe, an even more important, legacy. In a certain sense, chartered companies established a model that was to be replicated in the decades that followed the collapse of chartered companies as a world-scale system of colonisation through trade.

Last, but not least, chartered companies introduced, or, rather, put into practice, a new model of financing international business activities. In particular, they succeeded in collecting huge financial resources by exploiting the instrument of incorporation to the maximum, which allowed a separation between ownership and management, and the deployment of adequate resources for ambitious and expensive long-distance trade. Resources, in the form of tradable shareholdings, were collected in the home country, where financial markets were developed and where the companies' headquarters were located. However, almost the totality of their business activity, both in the form of trade and – albeit to a very minor extent – in production, was performed abroad. In this, chartered companies anticipated other forms of international business firms which, as the following chapters will show, were to become diffused in the course of the nineteenth century.

Bibliography

Chauduri, Kirti N., *The English East India Company: The Study of an Early Joint-stock Company, 1600–1640*, London: Cass, 1965.

Gaastra, Femme S., *The Dutch East India Company: Expansion and Decline*, Zutphen: Walburg Pers, 2003.

Tracy, James D. (ed.), *The Political Economy of Merchant Empires*, New York: Cambridge University Press, 1991.

3 International business in the First Industrial Revolution (1800–1870)

1. Eighteen-thirty-three AD

August 1833 was far from being a quiet summer for the British Members of Parliament. On 1 August 1833, the Slavery Abolition Act was passed, freeing all the slaves in the territories of the British Empire. At the end of the same month, another kind of slavery was abolished, with the introduction of the Factory Acts, which aimed at regulating child labour, at the same time introducing a form of compulsory education. It was, in the end, a very progressive and human-rights-oriented month.

On 28 August of the same year, another Act was passed. Its name was the "St. Helena Act", which transferred "the island of St. Helena, and all forts, factories, public edifices, and hereditaments whatsoever in the said island, and all stores and property thereon fit or used for the service of the government thereof" to the Crown. After decades of more or less violent quarrels among the Spanish, Portuguese, British and Dutch, the tiny island had, after a Charter conceded by Oliver Cromwell in 1657, been the property of the *East India Company* (EIC), which had used it as a sort of "trading station" on the way to and from the East Asia route. Napoleon had died in exile there some years before the St. Helena Act; luckily for the company's shareholders, however, the British Government had met the expenses relating to the hospitality afforded to the former French Emperor.

By 1833, however, the EIC had to give back the 47 square miles of rock, and St. Helena became officially part of the British colonial Empire. The good (or bad) news for the company was that the Act concerned not just St. Helena. With a bit of (perhaps involuntary) British sense of humour, the Act, named after probably one of the smallest British possessions overseas, did, in fact, include two other momentous decisions. The first was the first serious attempt to curb the authority of the *East India Company* in India through the direct appointment of a Governor-General directly responsible to the Crown. The second was even more symbolic: under the form of a renewal of the charter for another twenty years, the Act deprived the *East India Company* of all its residual monopolistic privileges, and, in particular, its trade monopoly with China. With the 1833 Act, in sum, the company became a sort of *primus inter pares*, and the biggest (but by no means the most efficient or profitable) of the British trading companies in Asia found itself no longer protected by a charter, even though British imperial rule over the subcontinent was to become total in 1858.

It was the end of an era which had lasted for at least two centuries. At the beginning of the 1830s, the *East India Company* was, beyond any doubt, far from the splendour that it had enjoyed a hundred years before. Yet the decline of its dictatorial power was, nonetheless, a remarkable event, something that people used to label as "epochal", even though, quite probably, few contemporaries realised the relevance of the event at the time.

It is also probable that the "epochal" relevance of another event taking place at the same time passed equally unobserved: again, on the 28 of August of the same year (1833), at the port of Gravesend, in Kent, a ship had docked: the *SS Royal William* had left Pictou, Nova Scotia, in Canada, a few weeks before. The voyage had been calm and without notable events, except for the fact that the paddled, double steam-engined vessel had crossed the Atlantic, probably for the first time, solely by means of steam power, resorting to her sails only when boiler maintenance was required.

Due to one of the accidents of history (provided, of course, that history *has* accidents), on this relatively obscure day at the end of August 1833, two events had taken place, in a very short space of time. One was the symbolic end of an era in which merchants had dominated international business, and chartered joint-stock companies had enjoyed monopolistic positions in exchange for a primary role in the mercantilist strategies of their respective governments. The other was one of the first, robust, achievements of a new phase in the history of mankind, which had started some decades before: the radical, economic, social and cultural transformation which we have come to know as the "First Industrial Revolution". Although the two events are profoundly different in themselves, they nonetheless symbolise the radical transformation in the complex world of international business brought about by the rise and affirmation of a new technological paradigm of production, transport and communications. Not by chance, both events took place not only at the same moment in both time and history, but also in the same place: Britain. And both of these events mark a momentous watershed in the history of international business activity.

★ ★ ★ ★ ★

This chapter will discuss the impact of the new technologies of the First Industrial Revolution (and of their developments) on the complex world of the international economy and of the entrepreneurs and the organisations acting within its framework. The chapter will first deal with the technological transformation that impacted most on international business (in a broad sense). The First Industrial Revolution transformed the world of the international economy, not simply because it allowed faster and more reliable connections in terms of physical and immaterial communications, thereby eradicating many of the structural constraints to entrepreneurial action that we explored in the previous chapters. More radically, the First Industrial Revolution transformed the very nature of capitalism, or, rather, made it multi-form, adding to the word and concept of the noun "merchant" a new adjective, namely, "industrial". This great transformation had a structural impact on the nature of international trade in that it promoted an increase in the use and circulation of raw materials, semi-finished inputs, and finished goods for final consumption. Besides this, it also introduced some changes in the nature of foreign activity. On the one hand, technological innovations in information and communication techniques (see below) made trading faster, eliminating intermediaries and middlemen; on the other, entrepreneurs started to invest abroad in order to replicate the competences that they had developed at home in other promising markets. If, in sum, international trade was renewed, then cross-border productive activities started to acquire relevance as a consequence.

International production strategies brought new problems into the picture. It was one thing, first of all, to trade, even over long distances and with a relatively limited amount of fixed investments, as was the case of some chartered companies (see Chapter 2); it was quite another to set up production facilities, which required capital and other assets, long-term investments and, above all, the availability of a completely new type of skilled human capital, somewhat different from that involved in trade. In this process, new hierarchies among industries, and even among countries, emerged.

Second, these changes took place within a framework characterised by a process of increasing economic integration among different geographic areas of the world economy. The revolution in transport and communications technologies played a major part in the process, which is now known as the "first globalisation" (something which is, however, much debated with regard to its extent and duration). At the very minimum, two other general premises, which pushed the process of integration to an extent never reached before, were of equal relevance. One was the increasing role of cosmopolitan culture, which was, first of all, a European phenomenon, although not exclusive to Europe. The second, and probably even more relevant and of immediate impact, were institutions, both national and international, which removed the main obstacles to the process of cultural and economic integration across different regions of the world.

A third conceptual framework discussed in this chapter concerns the impact of the First Industrial Revolution not only on the nature of foreign activity, but also on the structures and the strategies of the enterprises operating abroad. The phase extending from the sunset of the age of privileged monopolistic chartered companies (see Chapter 2) to the last three decades of the nineteenth century is frequently considered, in international business literature, as a transitory phase, a sort of prelude to the emergence of the so-called "modern multinational" model (see Chapter 4) which was to dominate both the last part of the nineteenth century and a large part of the twentieth century. Yet, this phase not only saw the emergence and consolidation, as outlined above, of the globalisation process fostered by the First Industrial Revolution, it also witnessed the emergence of various new models of international business activity, each one the result of a process of adaptation of entrepreneurial initiatives to both the opportunities and the constraints provided by the general context.

2. International business in the First Industrial Revolution: migrating entrepreneurship

Discussion of the origin of the First Industrial Revolution is beyond the aim of this book, as is an analysis of the impact of this epochal transformation on the economic structure of the countries that progressively came to be affected by the "contagion" of industrialisation. What is of greater relevance here is to assess the way in which the outcomes and the changes introduced by the technological shift impacted on the forms of international business activity.

The first, very well-known, effect of the revolution was the rise of the factory system, which meant, in short, the partial substitution of labour with machinery (capital), which, in its turn, operated thanks to inanimate sources of energy. As a consequence, the availability of the inputs necessary for the production process started to acquire growing relevance, particularly in the case of those countries in which these inputs were not immediately available. This, incidentally, is one of the reasons that are put forward to explain the primacy of Britain in the process of early industrialisation, that is, the ready availability of the necessary inputs in terms of energy sources and raw materials.

In contrast to what one might expect in theory, this did not translate into an immediate process of cross-border investment strategies that were finalised by vertical integration in order to secure primary sources of raw materials, for at least three reasons. First of all, the "average" firm of the First Industrial Revolution was a relatively advanced production unit, in terms of production technology, in comparison to the artisanal workshops which had dominated the secondary sector (manufacturing) until the end of the eighteenth century. However, it was definitely smaller than the large integrated multi-unit corporations which would appear in the last quarter of the century. It normally relied on multiple energy sources (mainly steam power, but also water, and, occasionally, on human or animal (horse) power, which reduced the incentive to backward integration). In addition, it also ran "discrete" production processes, which were characterised by a limited degree of integration and were basically fragmented into successive phases. Mechanics, textiles, pottery, even metalworking, were all characterised by the presence of small firms, each one specialised in one phase, or a few, of the production process, which was far from being continuous. This made the need for backward (in energy and raw materials) and forward (in distribution) integration far less pressing than it would be in the following phase. Finally, the First Industrial Revolution was based upon inputs, most of which had had efficient markets forged for them in the age of merchant capitalism, such as energy inputs (for instance, coal) or raw materials (for instance, raw cotton). They were characterised by a relative price asymmetry which would, however, progressively be reduced thanks to technological progress in transport and, above all, in communications, thereby reducing, even if not completely eliminating, one of the strongest incentives underlying backward integration strategies. The First Industrial Revolution, in sum, did not immediately create a vibrant international economy based upon cross-border investments and production, although, from the very beginning, it did influence international business in a more indirect way.

First of all, it affected entrepreneurship. If, during the first few decades of the nineteenth century, much of the inputs passed through market exchange (even international market exchange) with limited effect on cross-border investments, things went differently for other elements, mostly of an immaterial nature. For the first time in history, the industrial revolution created a new combination of the factors of production which led to an above-average increase in productivity in some industries, which spread everywhere. This phenomenon has been discussed at length in the literature, as has the contribution of entrepreneurial creativity in aggregating the "productive forces". Moreover, the great transformation created new competences, both entrepreneurial and in the management of the production process. These competences were fundamentally different from those of the merchants, traders and agents who used to act as intermediaries connecting supply and demand over short and long distances, and extracting profits from asymmetric information and from the continuous re-investment of working capital. The consolidation of the factory system thus coincided with the increase in the bulk of technological and administrative capabilities, which could easily move across borders. On the one hand, this was because these capabilities travelled embodied in individuals; on the other, it was because – in contrast to the mercantilist era – not only were there very few obstacles to impede the transfer of this human and financial capital abroad, but also imperial rule was basically facilitating, when it was not actually incentivising, the process of entrepreneurial globalisation. Most of these investments were of a market-seeking nature, sometimes combined with the strategies of resource exploitation, including cheap labour. While, for some of them, it is difficult to talk of multinational activity (but easier to talk of migrating entrepreneurship), for others, the divide is definitely unclear. A good example which allows us to clarify many of the concepts put forward in this section is provided by the investments made by Swiss entrepreneurs in textiles (mainly in silk and cotton) in Italy, before the unification of the country in 1861.

Dozens of cases follow more or less the same pattern. After some initial training as agents, technicians or even future owners by inheritance in Swiss cotton factories mostly located in the Central German-speaking cantons of Switzerland, the decision to emigrate led them to establish factories, mainly in cotton spinning and weaving, in both the northern and southern regions of Italy. Their entrepreneurial, technical, administrative, and managerial competencies, combined with some favourable local conditions, in particular the availability of a cheap and docile workforce, and of favourable fiscal regimes especially in the south of Italy, resulted in the creation of flourishing entrepreneurial initiatives. In the majority of cases, however, this was not a "real", definitive emigration. The linkages both with Switzerland and, for many, with the original family-business activities, persisted, under the form of share ownership, and served to provide financial resources, technical assistance, machinery and personnel. The case of Swiss entrepreneurs was not isolated. Migrant entrepreneurs could be found everywhere in Europe, and, in some cases, the decision to invest abroad took a shape that was close to the replication abroad of the managerial competences that they had developed in their countries of origin, thus anticipating the model of the multinational enterprise which was to become so pervasive a few decades later.

The cross-border migration of entrepreneurs during the first two or three decades of the nineteenth century exemplifies some of the effects of the First Industrial Revolution on international business. Entrepreneurship was thus the factor of production whose degree of internationalisation was immediately influenced by the technological transformation. Soon, however, other effects of the technological change began to affect the realm of the international economy. It was the era that symbolically started at the end of August 1833.

3. The information and communication revolution

The main area in which the First Industrial Revolution would affect the domain of international business was, of course, technology. The last decades of the eighteenth century had witnessed the invention and diffusion of the steam engine, and of radical innovations in metalworking and mechanics. After a few decades, and following the Napoleonic Wars, these seminal innovations had generated a number of radical technological breakthroughs which directly affected one of the most crucial aspects of international business activity, that related to transport and communications technologies. The generation and propagation of inventions and innovations was the result of an increasing European propensity towards what has been defined as the "Industrial Enlightenment", that is, a mentally and philosophically favourable attitude towards the industrial applications of scientific speculative research. To some extent, this process was also endogenous to the rise of the factory system and to the transition from mercantile to industrial capitalism. The many applications of the general-purpose technology of the steam engine included the train and the steamboat. Once the technology for generating energy "on-board" was relatively mature (a state achieved by the 1820s), railways started to be diffused throughout the United Kingdom, and, particularly during the 1840s, quickly spread throughout the continent of Europe, in North and South America (around the 1850s), and, to a minor extent, to Asia by the end of the 1850s, including Japan, where railway-building was a sort of symbol of the Meiji Restoration, with the first steam locomotive entering service in 1868.

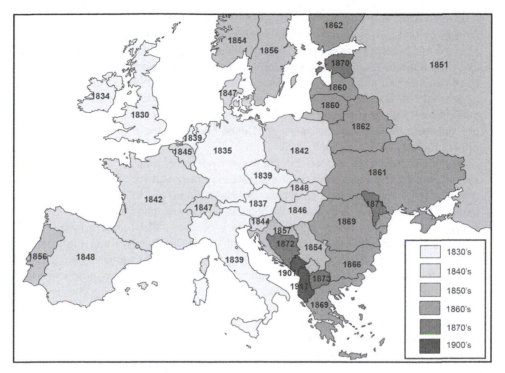

Map 3.1 First railway line by country

Railways became synonymous with modernisation, connecting domestic markets, and linking centres to peripheries. In the first stage, railways were essentially connecting internal markets. Built very often on impulse by the government, through deliberate subsidisation, railways allowed entrepreneurs to reach distant locations more rapidly and at relatively low cost, and, on occasion, to cross borders in search of new markets, particularly when the domestic one was too small for their ambitions (see Box 3.1). Particularly in the case of small European countries, such as Belgium, the Netherlands, and Switzerland, this allowed local entrepreneurs to tap the advantages of a market of continental size.

Box 3.1: "*Ganz Natürlich*" from the Swiss Alps to Europe: the early internationalisation of *Nestlé*

The man giving his name to one of today's biggest food processing firms started like many other nineteenth-century entrepreneurs as a one-man business. Henri Nestlé, born Heinrich Nestle, was born in Frankfurt am Main in Germany on 10 August 1814. He was in his twenties when he left Germany in 1843 and emigrated to Switzerland, where he settled in Vevey on the north shore of Lake Geneva. Nestlé applied for admission as a chemist in the Swiss canton of Vaud where he worked as a druggist's assistant until he started his own business as a merchant. It was at the age of fifty-three that major success came for Henri Nestlé with milk-based infant food.

After only eight years, in 1875, Henri Nestlé sold his successful firm for one million Swiss Francs to three experienced entrepreneurs in the region.

In the 1860s, Henri Nestlé made little money with a special kind of gas that the city of Vevey used to illuminate the streets. When the city decided to build a gas plant, Nestlé was forced to look for another source of income. It is not known exactly when he started his research into milk for infants, but it was probably between 1861 and 1863. It took several years and many futile attempts for Nestlé to come up with a useful product from his experimental research. Nestlé himself dated the final breakthrough of his research back to autumn 1867.

Nestlé's achievement in food for infants was not really original. There were other similar products on the market, as the substitution of breast milk with other types of milk had been practised for a long time. But Nestlé managed to combine all the various ingredients known to be adequate sources of infant nutrition at that time into one easily usable product. Nestlé's invention was a powder that became a kind of milk after being mixed with water. Some trials with babies had shown that the Nestlé's product could also be given to newborn children, not only to babies who were already several months old. The immediate increase in the demand for his product made Nestlé realise from the start that he had to produce large quantities in order to meet this demand. In 1868–1869, he bought several new machines, a necessity for the large-scale production of milk for infants. The set-up of the production process was such that the milk delivered in the morning had become bottled milk for infants by the evening. This was due to hygienic reasons: the primary product, milk, has to be processed immediately. Therefore, the milk required for the production of the daily output of milk for infants had to be delivered every morning to the Nestlé production site. Procurement and production had to be parallel and synchronised. This made the securing of a steady supply of high-quality cow's milk essential.

Nestlé started building up relationships with the neighbouring farmers, and especially with the *laiterie*, the regional association of milk producers. From 1872, Nestlé bought all the milk delivered to the *laiterie* for the production of his milk for infants. However, the supply was not constant, and sometimes he had to produce cheese with surplus milk, while other days saw a shortage of milk. Thus, in order to create a more stable supply of milk, Nestlé decided to establish farms which were to serve his factory directly.

By the end of the 1860s, Nestlé's production facilities allowed for the output of 1,000 boxes of milk daily. He internationalised his business immediately because Switzerland was too small a home market. The first step towards internationalisation was in Germany, the country which he knew best: his home country. This was also why he could rely mostly on friends and relatives to find his first retailers in Germany. From the middle of the nineteenth century, economically motivated emigration overseas from Switzerland, especially to North and South America, had grown constantly: between 1851 and 1860, over 50,000 persons had emigrated; in the 1860s and 1870s, 35,000 had emigrated; and during the 1880s, again over 50,000 persons went overseas.

It was principally the size of the home market that made it not promising enough to concentrate exclusively on Switzerland.

International distribution was facilitated by the extension of the Swiss railways from the 1860s onwards. The first railway company was established in Zurich in 1836, but it failed to obtain all the cantonal concessions that it needed for its plans for a line to Basel, and it had to be wound up in the face of financial difficulties. Despite this slow start, enthusiasm gradually caught on. In the next three decades, 2,500 km of track were laid – and one of the great tunnelling feats of the century was constructed, the 15 km long (9.3 mile) Gotthard railway tunnel, which was opened in 1882. A second alpine line was opened under the Simplon Pass in 1906. Branch lines began to be built in the 1870s, and two-thirds of them were built as narrow gauge lines in order to reduce costs. Fifty branch lines were built in the period from 1874 to 1877, including the Gäu Railway between Solothurn and Olten (completed in 1876) and the Broye valley lines near Freiburg (1877). Thus, the railways connected western and north-eastern Switzerland. Thanks to the efforts of private companies, the main cities were linked together, and, despite initial fears, there were few competing lines. Even the agricultural areas were served by trains, which was vital for their economic development, and it was the railways which allowed the quick distribution of industrial processed food to the surrounding markets at low cost.

What made customers buy milk for infants from Switzerland? After all, in all of the countries supplied by Nestlé there were already similar products on the market. The answer lies in the raw material used in the product: Swiss milk. Even before the invention of Nestlé's milk for infants, Swiss milk had been widely known for its high quality, and the low infant-mortality rate in some Swiss regions was attributed to the superior quality of the milk; and it was a clever move on Nestlé's part to advertise his product by exploiting the purity of Swiss nature (*Ganz Natürlich*: All Natural) and its high-quality milk. Along with Swiss chocolate, Nestlé's milk for infants became one of the first branded products in Switzerland. In the second half of the nineteenth century, the Swiss Alps became fashionable with alpinists and tourists from the United Kingdom. Already in the second half of the eighteenth century, mountains were increasingly losing their image as places inhabited by demons and ghosts, and were perceived as beautiful and health-beneficial regions. In particular, the beginning of the nineteenth century saw the first ascents of various peaks, in what became known as the Golden Age of Alpinism, and, at the fore, it was British alpinists who were enthusiastic about the Swiss Alps. The end of the nineteenth century saw a race to see who would be the first to climb some of the more challenging Swiss mountains, and the last peak to be conquered was the famous Matterhorn, which a group of British alpinists climbed in 1865. Thus, the Swiss Alps were a fashionable tourist resort at the time. In the 1870s, Swiss entrepreneurs embarked on a new kind of railway, thanks to the invention of the rack-and-pinion system, which enabled trains to climb steep slopes. More and more tourists came to enjoy the Swiss mountains, benefiting from the European railway system which enabled them to travel to the top without exerting themselves. And another reason for the positive image of healthy nature attached to Switzerland stemmed from the publication of Johanna Spyri's Heidi books in 1880 and 1881. Nestlé very cleverly attached his product to this positive Swiss image.

Apart from linking his product to the origins of its raw material, Nestlé also stressed the close connection with scientific authorities. His cooperation with medical doctors and scientists was a new phenomenon at the time: he invited doctors to test his milk for infants and encouraged them to write professional opinions afterwards. Some doctors also distributed Nestlé's milk for infants, thus boosting demand. In addition, drugstores were directly supplied with samples so as to attract customers.

His milk reached Germany, France, the United Kingdom and Italy. By the beginning of the 1870s, Nestlé milk was being used in hospitals around the world: Argentina,

Australia, Belgium, Mexico, the Netherlands, the East Indies, Austria, Russia, Serbia, Scandinavia, Spain, and the United States.

After the Franco–Prussian War (1870–1871), Nestlé enlarged the factories, and, in January 1874, almost thirty people were working in Vevey. Output was doubled between July 1871 and July 1873, and Nestlé was confronted with an increasing problem concerning overseas distribution. Still the only manager in his firm, he could cope with the supply for Switzerland, Germany, France, the United Kingdom and Italy. But the growing overseas demand and its implication of long-distance management and distribution was too much for the sixty-one-year-old Henri Nestlé.

In 1875, Nestlé sold the successful business that he had built up in only eight years to three business associates. These men transformed the firm into a joint-stock company and gave the company, now called Farine Lactée Henri Nestlé (Henri Nestlé's milk flour), the necessary management and financial foundation for another 133 years of successful performance.

This box was written by Marina Nicoli.

★ ★ ★ ★ ★

Steamship routes were as relevant as railways in promoting the interconnection of very distant countries and markets, and probably played a more decisive role in international and even intercontinental trade relations. The steamship technology became relatively mature at the same time that the railways began to be diffused throughout Europe. The first Atlantic steamship line dates back to the early 1840s, less than a decade after the above-mentioned *SS Royal William* had made what was probably the first Atlantic crossing by steam power.

Steam locomotives and steamships were momentous technological innovations, directly generated, as suggested above, by the same "general-purpose" technology, the steam engine patented by James Watt, and were closely intertwined with the First Industrial Revolution. The generation and diffusion of steam transport was, of course, endogenous to the factory system, contributing at the same time to the consolidation of cross-border trade activities. What is worth stressing here is the fact that the introduction of the new means of transport carried, in itself, not just the possibility of accelerating the transfer of people and goods at a cost and a speed rarely attained before. More importantly, the new technology made travelling and transport in general progressively less and less dependent on the conditions prevailing in the external environment and more reliable, thereby contributing to a further reduction of the uncertainty which had characterised the global economy during the previous centuries.

The revolution brought about by the application of the steam engine to transport was, however, only one side of the story, albeit an extremely remarkable one. After decades of experimentation, the 1830s witnessed the successful patenting, simultaneously in both the United Kingdom and the United States, of the telegraph. Improvements in telegraph technology, in terms of cost, reliability, and speed of transmission, took place quickly, and led to the rapid replacement of the other means of communications that had been in use up to that point. In some ways, it is symbolic that the *Pony Express*, the horseback postal mailing system in use in the US between Sacramento (California) and St. Joseph (Missouri) closed on 26 October 1861, exactly two days after the inauguration of the overland telegraph connection between the west and the east coasts of the United States. An organisational miracle, it took the *Pony Express* a (record time of) ten days to deliver a letter across the Great Plains and the Rocky Mountains. Overnight, however, it was a matter of just a few minutes, if not seconds (and of a few dollars, compared to an average price of over ten dollars per item (at contemporary prices) with the *Pony Express*), to send a message from Salt Lake City in Utah to San Francisco in California.

Similar networks were, of course, being built across Europe and Asia, in an endless effort of connection. By the 1860s, the main telegraph connections were established across Asia, Europe and North America, and allowed an increasingly intensive flow of communications across the regions of the globe.

Overland, the "telegraph road", characteristically made of wires and poles, followed and, in some cases, accompanied the construction of the railways, both for practical reasons relating to the maintenance of infrastructure and because of the necessity that communications implied. It was no mere coincidence that, from the very beginning, the telegraph was closely connected to communications in transport, and particularly to railway lines.

Given the state of the technology available at the time, it is indisputable that, in this period, a real globalisation in communications could once again take place across the oceans. Telegraph wire communications – which, until the introduction of a new form of technology, the telephone, remained the sole instant cross-distance form of messaging technology in the 1870s – could, in fact, efficiently connect distant markets on the same continent, but not yet the vast continents separated by oceans, which were, however, slowly but surely building up the global economy. Symbolically, the two above-mentioned revolutionary means of transport and communications, the steamship and the

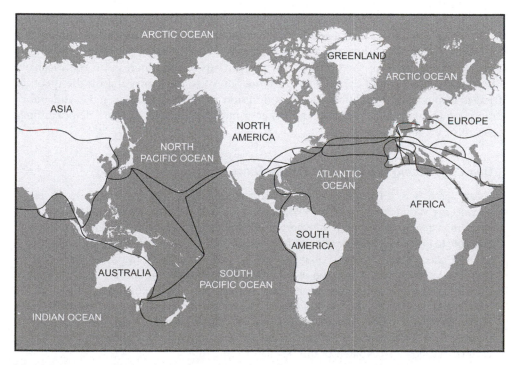

Map 3.2 Main overland and sea telegraph routes and connections, nineteenth century

telegraph, together overcame the limits of technology and allowed a further relevant step to be made in what could rightly be defined as the first information and communications technology revolution of the modern era.

On 16 August 1858, the first telegraphic message was sent across the Atlantic. It was a ninety-word message, and took around 16 hours to be sent (not a short time, but enormously faster than a journey by ship at the time, which would have taken at least three weeks). The sender was Queen Victoria, and the message was addressed to the US President, James Buchanan. The electrical signal went through a cable that had been laid in the Atlantic Ocean from Newfoundland to Ireland. Following subsequent improvements, the transatlantic telegraph cable started to operate regularly in the second half of the 1860s, opening a new era in communications which would last for more than a century, when satellite networks came into use, breaking the technological monopoly of wires. Between the 1870s and the beginning of the twentieth century, almost all the continents were linked by submarine cable networks, most of which were built and operated by British firms.

Very quickly, information became a relatively "staple" commodity. During the second half of the nineteenth century, the cost of a telegraph message was reduced to one-third or even less of the initial cost. The main effect of this drop in price was, however, largely indirect. The telegraph not only allowed information to be sent quickly over very long distances, it also made it available to the general public, by means of other technological innovations, which simultaneously transformed the publishing industry (what we would call the "media", in modern day language). Between the 1840s and 1850s, at the same time that the diffusion of the telegraph was taking place, the first prototypes of rotary printing machines were patented, which dramatically increased the speed of printing. In the 1810s, the technological progress allowed 400 pages to be printed per hour; in the 1840s, the printing capacity was ten times higher, and in the 1850s, the capacity was up to 8,000 pages per hour. In the 1860s, the introduction of a rotary press machine with a continuous paper roll pushed printing capacity up to 12,000 pages per hour. The effects were, of course, both on the printing cost per page (given the increase in the mechanisation of the process, and the consequent reduction of labour costs) and on the quantity of pages printed per time unit. The mass diffusion of news, including news and information concerning costs, prices and market trends, accelerated further, democratising access to news and information.

Box 3.2: *Around the World in Eighty Days*

Jules Verne was a French novelist, poet, and playwright. His most famous novel, *Around the World in Eighty Days*, published in 1873, is about a Victorian Englishman who bets that, with the new transport and communications technologies, it will be possible to travel around the world and return to London in a little less than three months, such a "short" span of time for that period. The novel was taken to be pure fiction at that time (and has since become a must-read for generations), but, in reality, it was not so far from the truth. A few years later, in 1889, the American journalist Nellie Bly took a trip around the world, attempting to turn the fictional *Around the World in Eighty Days* into reality. She arrived back at her starting point 72 days, 6 hours, 11 minutes and 14 seconds after her departure. The following are excerpts from the Collins Classics 2010 edition of the novel.

The matter under discussion [...] had occurred three days before, on the 29th of September. A package of bank-notes, making the enormous sum of fifty-five thousand pounds, had been taken from the counter of the Principal cashier of the Bank of England. [...] "Well", replied Ralph, "there is not a single country where he [the robber] can take refuge". "Phsaw!" "Where do you suppose he might go?" "I don't know about that", replied Andrew Stuart, "but after all, the world is big enough." "It was formerly," said Phileas Fogg in a low tone. [...] "How, formerly? Has the world grown smaller perchance?". "Without doubt," replied Gauthier Ralph. [...] But the incredulous Stuart was not convinced, and when the hand was finished, he replied: "It must be confessed, Mr Ralph, that you have found a funny way of saying that the world has grown smaller! Because the tour of it is now made in three months." "In 80 days only," said Phileas Fogg. [...] "80 days, since the section between Rothal and Allahabad, on the Great Indian Peninsular Railway, has been opened. Here is the calculation made by the Morning Chronicle: from London to Suez via Mont Cenis and Brindisi by rail and steamers: 7 days; from Suez to Bombay, steamer: 13 days; from Bombay to Calcutta, rail: 3 days; from Calcutta to Hong Kong (China), steamer: 13 days; from Hong Kong to Yokohama (Japan), steamer: 6 days; from Yokohama to San Francisco, steamer: 22 days; from San Francisco to New York, rail: 7 days; from New York to London, steamer and rail: 9 days [...]". "Yes, 80 days!" exclaimed Andrew Stuart [...] "but not including bad weather, contrary winds, shipwrecks, running off the track, etc." "Everything included," replied Phileas Fogg. [...] "I would like very much to see you do it." "So be it," said Mr Fogg, and then, turning to his companions, continued: "I have twenty thousand pounds deposited at Baring Brothers. I will willingly risk them."

By eight o'clock, Mr Fogg was ready. He carried under his arm Bradshaw's Continental Railway Steam Transit and General Guide, which was to furnish him all the necessary directions for his journey. [...] Phileas Fogg and his servant got into a cab, which was rapidly driven towards Charing Cross Station, at which one of the branches of the South Eastern Railway touches. [...] There Phileas Fogg gave Passepartout [his servant] the order to get two first-class tickets for Paris. [...]

On Wednesday, the ninth of October, there was expected at Suez, at eleven o'clock a.m., the iron steamer Mongolia, of the Peninsular and Oriental Company, sharp built, with a spear deck, of two thousand eight hundred tons burden, and nominally of five hundred horse-power. The Mongolia made regular trips from Brindisi to Bombay by the Suez Canal. It was one of the fastest steamers of the line, and always exceeded the regular rate of speed, that is, ten knots an hour between Brindisi and Suez, and nine hundred and fifty-three miles between Suez and Bombay. [...] Eleven o'clock was striking when the steamer came to anchor in the roadstead, while the escaping of the steam made a great noise. [...] The Mongolia, whose fires were well kept up, [then] moved along rapidly enough to anticipate her stipulated arrival. Nearly all the passengers who came aboard at Brindisi had India for their destination. [...] The 14th, the Mongolia put in at Steamer Point, to the north-west of Aden harbour. [...] The Mongolia was not due at Bombay until the 22nd of October. She arrived on the 20th. [...] It was at half-past four p.m. that the passengers of the Mongolia had landed in Bombay, and the train for Calcutta would leave at precisely eight o'clock.

At eight o'clock in the morning, and fifteen miles before they reached Rothal, the train stopped in the midst of an immense opening, on the edge of which were some bungalows and workmen's huts. The conductor of the train passed along the cars calling out, "The passengers will get out here!" [...] The newspapers are like certain watches which have a mania of getting ahead of time, and they had announced the finishing of the line prematurely. [...]. Passepartout, [...] hesitating a little said: "Monsieur, I believe I have found a means of conveyance." "What?" "An elephant belonging to an Indian living a hundred steps from here." The elephant [...] moved rapidly through the still dark forest. [...] Towards ten o'clock, the guide announced the station of Allahabad. [...] Phileas Fogg ought then to arrive in time to take a steamer which would not leave until the next day, October 25, at noon, for Hong-Kong. [...]

The Rangoon, one of the vessels employed by the Peninsular and Oriental Company in the Chinese and Japanese seas, was an iron screw steamer, of seventeen hundred and seventy tons, and nominally of four hundred horse-power. She was equally swift, but not so comfortable as the Mongolia. The weather, which had been quite fine until this time, changed with the last quarter of the moon. [...] But the passengers would have to blame the Rangoon rather than the ocean for their sickness and fatigue. In fact, the ships of the Peninsular Company, in the China service, are seriously defective in their construction. The proportion of their draught, when loaded, to their depth of hold, has been badly calculated, and consequently they stand the sea but poorly. Their bulk, closed, impenetrable to the water, is insufficient. They are "drowned", to use a maritime expression, and, in consequence, it does not take many waves thrown upon the deck to slacken their speed. These ships are then very inferior – if not in motive power and steam escapes – to the models of the French mail steamers, such as the Imperatrice and Cambodge. Whilst, according to the calculations of the engineers, the latter can take on a weight of water equal to their own before sinking, the vessels of the Peninsular Company, the Golconda, the Corea, and finally the Rangoon, could not take on the sixth of their weight without going to the bottom. [...] The diary of Phileas Fogg put down the arrival of the steamer on the 5th, and she did not arrive until the 6th. [...]

The Carnatic having left Hong-Kong on the 6th of November, at half-past six, turned under full head of steam towards the Japanese shores. [...] At high tide on the morning of the 13th, the Carnatic entered the port of Yokohama. [...] The steamer making the voyage from Yokohama to San Francisco belonged to the Pacific Mail Steamship Company, and was named the General Grant. She was a large side-wheel steamer of two thousand five hundred tons, well equipped, and of great speed. [...] By making twelve knots the steamer would only need twenty-one days to cross the Pacific. [...] It was seven o'clock in the morning, when Phileas Fogg [...] and Passepartout set foot on the American continent. [...] Clippers of all sizes were moored there, steamers of all nationalities, and those steamboats with several decks, which ply on the Sacramento and its tributaries. There were accumulated also products of a commerce which extends to Mexico, Peru, Chili, Brazil, Europe, Asia, and all the Islands of the Pacific Ocean. [...]

"From Ocean to Ocean" – so say the Americans, and these four words ought to be the general name of the "Grand Trunk", which traverses the United States in their greatest breadth. [...] New York and San Francisco are therefore now united by an uninterrupted metal ribbon, measuring not less than three thousand seven hundred and eighty six miles. [...] Formerly, under the most favorable circumstances, it took six months to go from New York to San Francisco. Now it is done in seven days. [...] On the prairies the road progressed at the rate of a mile and half per day. A locomotive, moving over the rails laid yesterday, carried the rails for the next day, and ran upon them in proportion as they were laid. [...] At eight o'clock a steward entered the car, and announced to the passengers that the hour for retiring had come. This was a sleeping car, which in a few minutes was transformed into a dormitory. The backs of the seats unfolded, beds carefully packed away were unrolled by an ingenious system, berths were improvised in a few moments, and each passenger had soon at his disposal a comfortable bed, which thick curtains protected from all indiscreet looks. [...] Cries of fright made themselves heard from the inside of the cars. [...] The train had been attacked by the Sioux. [...].

At thirty-five minutes after nine at night, the train stopped in the depot, near the very pier of the Cunard line of steamers, otherwise called the British and North American Royal Mail Steam Packet Company. The China, bound for Liverpool, left thirty-five minutes before! [...] None of the other steamers, nor the ships of the White Star line, nor those of the Inman Company, nor those of the Hamburg line, nor any others, could serve this gentleman's project. The Pereire, of the French Atlantic Company, would not start until the 14th of December. And besides, like those of the Hamburg Company, she would not go directly to Liverpool or London. [...] This gentleman was seeming to fail in his last attempt, when he perceived, moored in front of the Battery, at a cable's length at most, a merchantman, with screw, of fine outlines, whose smokestack emitting clouds of smoke, indicated that she was preparing to sail. [...]

At twenty minutes before noon, the 21st of December, Phileas Fogg finally landed on the quay at Liverpool. He was now only six hours from London. [...] This evening, the five colleagues of the gentleman were assembled in the grand saloon of the Reform Club. [...] At the moment that the clock in the grand saloon indicated twenty-five minutes past eight, Andrew Stuart, rising, said: "Gentlemen, in twenty minutes the time agreed upon Mr Phileas Fogg and ourselves will have expired."[...] "Forty-four minutes after eight," said John Sullivan [...] At the fortieth second, nothing. At the fiftieth still nothing! [...] At the fifty-seventh second, the door of the saloon opened, and the pendulum had not beat the sixtieth second, when Phileas Fogg appeared, followed by an excited crowd, who had forced an entrance into the Club, and in his calm voice he said: "Gentlemen, here I am!" [...] Thus Phileas Fogg won his bet. In 80 days he had accomplished the tour around the world! To do this he had employed every means of conveyance, steamers, railways, carriages, yachts, merchant vessels, sledges, elephants.

Jules Verne, *Around the World in Eighty Days*, first published in French, Strasbourg: Pierre-Jules Hetzel, 1873.

4. Global migration in a global world

The combined effect of better communications and transport technologies served to promote a radical revolution not only in business and trade, but also, more in general, in terms of social and cultural dimensions. The impact was enormous in terms of the individual's perception of the "global dimension" of a world which was very rapidly starting to "shrink" to a measure which was attainable even by the most ordinary individuals, even if it were normally not for leisure, but rather for reasons of necessity. Probably the most tangible proof of the rise of a truly global world can be understood through the lens of the macro phenomenon of mass emigration, which, during the second half of the nineteenth century, reached levels never experienced before. And, to a large extent, emigration was, incidentally, another effect of the revolution in both land and sea transport technologies. Particularly from the 1870s onwards, a growing stream of migrants left continental Europe. The main reason, particularly among workers in the primary sector, was poverty. And poverty was a direct consequence of the importation of grain to Europe, from both the Russian and the American mass-producing regions, which travelled fast and safely by steamship or by train, at a transport cost that was low enough to allow it to be competitive with local crops.

Independently of the geographic areas involved, the nineteenth century, and particularly from 1850, was a period of mass migration. The commercial trade routes discovered and put into operation during the previous two centuries were now travelled by a steadily growing mass of human beings who took advantage of the decreasing transport costs, increased speed of travel and the low barriers to mobility. According to the data available, immigration from Europe accounted for almost half of the population growth in the US in the second half of the nineteenth century up to the First World War. Some 30 million people migrated from Europe to the US alone, not to mention South America, between 1840 and 1914. If one adds the migration flows from North and South East Asia to this, the total number easily doubles. Mass transatlantic migration is, of course, a multi-faceted phenomenon, involving the demographic, social, cultural, and even emotional spheres. For the purposes of this book, it is crucial to remember that mass migration coincided with at least three important phenomena, a fact which is not always sufficiently stressed in the research into the effect of migration flows on host economies. The first is the availability of abundant, and frequently skilled, human capital; the second, a process of urbanisation in the "peripheries" of the world; and the third, the creation of consumer communities abroad, which, once beyond the poverty threshold, would foster opportunities not only for local, but also for foreign, entrepreneurship.

Mass migration of individuals was an epochal phenomenon not only due to technological factors which enabled people to settle in very distant places where they could (expect to) maximise their economic utility function but also benefit from another kind of mobility, social mobility, probably the most important achievement of nineteenth-century Western societies. Physical and social mobility was, in itself, the consequence of institutional elements which, directly or indirectly, lowered the legal barriers to mobility, wherever they were present.

The nineteenth century was, in fact, a phase in which institutions further enhanced the technological effects on the mobility of people, goods, and capital. This, in its turn, was the effect of many determinants, of a political and even a cultural nature, which contributed to the creation of generally favourable conditions to what can rightly be defined as precocious globalisation, and these conditions, in their turn, were mirrored in institutions which increased the overall degree of "openness" in many aspects. And this phenomenon, which was largely, but exclusively, European, can probably be understood by looking more at the cultural and social sphere, than merely at the economic one. The "climate" which prevailed in the nineteenth century can probably be appreciated even more when it is looked at from the point of view of those who actually experienced its disintegration at the outbreak of the First World War (see Chapter 5).

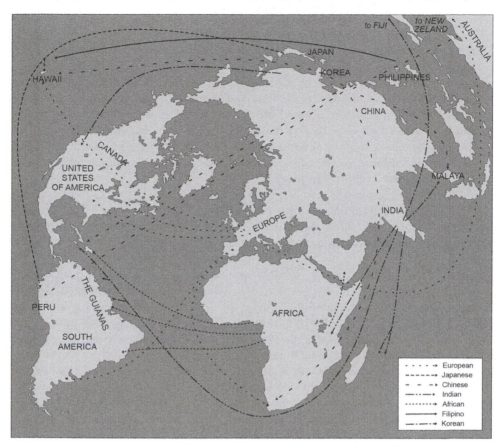

Map 3.3 Migrations in the nineteenth century, 1800–1914

What an extraordinary episode in the economic progress of man that age was which came to an end in August, 1914! The greater part of the population, it is true, worked hard and lived at a low standard of comfort, yet were, to all appearances, reasonably contented with this lot. But escape was possible, for any man of capacity or character at all exceeding the average, into the middle and upper classes, for whom life offered, at a low cost and with the least trouble, conveniences, comforts, and amenities beyond the compass of the richest and most powerful monarchs of other ages. The inhabitant of London could order by telephone, sipping his morning tea in bed, the various products of the whole earth, in such quantity as he might see fit, and reasonably expect their early delivery upon his doorstep; he could at the same moment and by the same means adventure his wealth in the natural resources and new enterprises of any quarter of the world, and share, without exertion, or even trouble, in their prospective fruits and advantages; or he could decide to couple the security of his fortunes with the good faith of the townspeople of any substantial municipality in any continent that fancy or information might recommend. He could secure forthwith, if he wished it, cheap and comfortable means of transit to any country or climate without passport or other formality, could dispatch his servant to the neighbouring office of a bank for such supply of the precious metals as might seem convenient, and could then proceed abroad to foreign quarters, without knowledge of their religion, language, or customs, bearing coined wealth upon his person, and would consider himself greatly aggrieved and much surprised at the least interference. But, most important of all, he regarded this state of affairs as normal, certain, and permanent, except in the direction of further improvement, and any deviation from it as aberrant, scandalous, and avoidable. The projects and politics of militarism and imperialism, of racial and cultural rivalries, of monopolies, restrictions, and exclusion which were to play the serpent to this paradise, were little more than the amusements of his daily newspapers, and appeared to exercise almost no influence at all on the ordinary course of social and economic life, the internationalization of which was nearly complete in practice.

In this way, at the beginning of his *The Economic Consequences of the Peace*, first published in London in 1919, John Maynard Keynes describes what another great novelist and historian, the Austrian-born Jewish Stefan Zweig, defined as "the world of yesterday".

The world thus shrank, and not just for technological reasons. In the last quarter of the nineteenth century, without exaggeration, around one half of the populated land (by geographical extent) was under some form of imperial rule. Empires and colonial possessions – not only, but mainly, of European origin – of different sizes covered the world. The British Empire, by far the largest, included Canada, a vast part of Africa including the regions along the Nile down to the Cape, Persia, the Horn of Africa, India, an innumerable number of islands in South East Asia, Australia and New Zealand, plus the strategic port colonies in China. France's empire had more fluctuating borders, but, in the second half of the nineteenth century, reached West Africa and the area known as *Indochine* (Indochina), which included the Cambodia, Laos and Vietnam of today. The Russian Empire was dominant (in terms of size) in Asia and, in the middle of the century, had tried to push forward its southern borders, openly challenging British rule in the north of the Indian sub-continent. Empires were large in the Old World too, such as the Austro-Hungarian Empire and the Ottoman Empire, which included large areas of the Balkans, Greece, Turkey, the Middle East, and vast regions on the north-east African coast. As a latecomer to the "New Imperialism" and the "Scramble for Africa", Germany, after its political unification at the beginning of the 1870s, extended her colonial rule in Africa and New Guinea. In addition to formal colonies, there were spheres of influence mainly for European countries – which was the case of China, for example, which was formally independent but, from the second half of the nineteenth century, under the strong influence of Britain. Empires were, of course, diverse in terms of internal political structures and institutional organisation, but they nonetheless provided a framework in which the mobility of (select groups of) individuals, goods and finance was relatively free. In theory, in the late nineteenth century, a British citizen like Phileas Fogg could travel over two-thirds of the world *without ever leaving* the borders of the Crown's possessions

In addition to this, in countries that were not (or, rather, were no longer) under some form of imperial rule, immigration was relatively free. In the Americas, both in the North and the South, laws restricting immigration came into use only around the end of the nineteenth century, and initially regulated the immigration of socially dangerous persons. The purpose of attracting immigrants was even part of the constitutional laws in countries which desperately needed to increase their population quickly, such as

Argentina. The impact of institutions favourable to mobility was not exclusively on the mobility of individuals. The nineteenth century, particularly its second half, was, both in Europe and in the territories under European rule, be it direct or indirect, characterised by a widespread favourable ideological attitude towards free trade and free market exchange, sometimes bluntly imposed against national sovereignty, as occurred in the case of China, which was violently forced by the West, notably the British, to "relax" its hostile attitude towards the opium trade, to the anger of Emperor Ch'ien-Lung. All the available historical evidence points in the direction of an average level of import duties declining sharply in the decades around the middle of the century, when almost all the main European countries, their colonies and Japan started to relax barriers to the importation of goods, both from the primary (agriculture) and secondary (manufacturing) sector. The trend towards liberalisation lasted at least until the 1870s, when protectionist policies were re-started as a reaction to the importation of cereals from the US and Russia. The sole places that resisted this trend were located in the New World, in both the Northern and in the Southern hemispheres. The US maintained high import duties, which exacerbated the tensions between the manufacturers of the Northern US states and the export-oriented landowners of the Southern US states up to the start of the Civil War. Southern US states maintained a high level of protection in general, also for reasons linked to the necessity of raising government revenues. But, above all, there were the effects of technology: duties and tariffs could hardly combat the decline in the transport cost per unit. Notwithstanding these restrictions on trade, the progress towards an increasing globalisation of markets went on relatively undisturbed.

5. Input mobility

A relevant consequence of the nineteenth-century information and communications revolution combined with favourable institutions was, thus, a growing integration of commodity markets. Economic historians interested in trade dynamics have clearly stressed how, after the Napoleonic wars, intercontinental trade grew at a per-annum rate that was more than three times higher than in the three centuries before.

And yet, commodity-market integration on a worldwide scale was a major achievement of the nineteenth century, and is witnessed by another phenomenon which took place for the first time in history: the convergence of the prices of similar goods in different markets. The cornerstone of arbitrage techniques, which allowed merchants and

Table 3.1 European and world intercontinental trade growth rates, 1500–1992

Period	Per annum % growth
1500–1599	1.26
1600–1699	0.66
1700–1799	1.26
1500–1799	1.06
1800–1899	3.85
1900–1992	3.65
1800–1992	3.70

Source: Revision and simplification of O'Rourke and Williamson (2002, Table 1, p. 419).

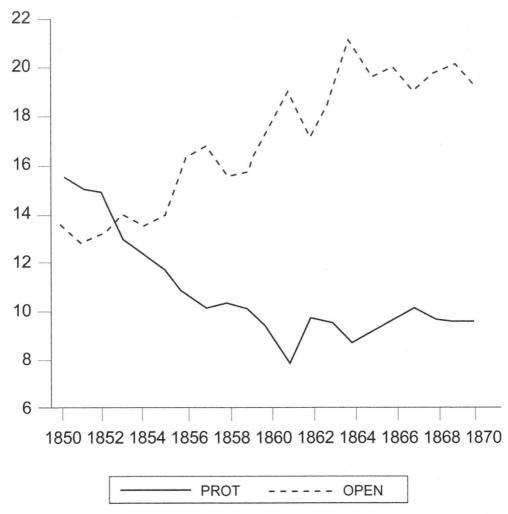

Figure 3.1 Average openness (ratio of imports to GDP), protection (ratio of customs revenue to total imports), 1850–1970

chartered companies to amass enormous fortunes by leveraging on information asymmetry, vanished in a few decades thanks to the mixture of new communications and transport techniques. The gap in the prices of different merchandise, from silk to bar iron, from tea to raw cotton, or wheat, fell radically between the 1850s and the 1870s. The price convergence also benefited from another institutional achievement, that is, the monetary stability introduced by the gold standard, a system of relatively stable exchange rates among currencies whose value (and thus the exchange rate) was based upon a fixed quantity of gold. Historians have stressed the positive relationship between the establishment of the gold-standard system and the volume of trade among countries; the rate of adherence to the system was about 30 per cent of the countries of the world in the 1860s, climbing to 60 per cent at the end of the century.

Commodity-market integration, price convergence and exchange-rate stability, whatever their causal relationship, had one structural effect which would permanently influence the way in which economic actors – entrepreneurs and companies – made their way through the global economic scenario. For the first time in history, and on an unprecedented scale, production inputs became easily transferable at relatively low cost. This transferability concerned labour (through migration – see above), different kinds of resources, and capital, in various forms.

Capital, basically financial capital, was migrating very intensively, as financial centres in Europe, the Americas, Asia, and even Oceania simultaneously became more and more efficient, better (self-) regulated and closely intertwined through consistent and steady flows of investments. According to the data available, capital mobility at a global level rose steadily until the First World War, to a level that has only recently been re-attained, followed by a sudden closure that lasted for almost the whole of the interwar period. A subscriber of the (mass-printed) British journal the *Economist* at the beginning of the 1870s could easily choose where to invest his money from among several hundreds of joint-stock companies, mainly in railways and mines, both in the UK and abroad, in British possessions as well as in distant locations from Mexico to Australia, even to a small village somewhere in the Piedmontese Alps where *Pestarena Gold Mines Co. Ltd.* operated, employing locals in order to exploit some veins in the mountains, which they considered to be very promising.

The hierarchy of capital exporters mirrored, as can be expected, the hierarchy in terms of the economic leadership that had emerged during the first half of the nineteenth century. Britain was by far the principal investor abroad with (mostly portfolio) holdings of around one billion pounds, twice that of its main competitor, France.

Foreign investments and loans – a category in which we will, for the moment, include a wide array of investments, from the ownership of foreign bonds to international loans, to the purchase of sovereign debt, to more direct forms of investment aiming at the control of the resources of production activities, in sum, all that was not "domestic" *strictu senso* – rose steadily during the second half of the nineteenth century. Again, according to the available information, at least until the First World War an overwhelming part of foreign capital flows privileged the private sector over governments as borrowers under various forms. Most of these private investments were, as we will see, "portfolio" investments, the purpose of which was simply to obtain a reasonable return on the sum invested. It is quite difficult to provide a quantitative estimate of the total amount of capital committed. Some calculations suggest a total foreign investment amount of slightly less than fifteen billion dollars in 1913, an amount which was, according to Geoffrey Jones (2004), close to 10 per cent of world GDP (more or less the same percentage as today). Given the relative absence of restrictions, however, the incentive to record capital flows by governments was low (with the consequent inability of historians to provide more than rough estimates).

The same ideology which backed the free trade philosophy lay in what has been acutely defined as the "first global bazaar",[1] behind the globalisation of capital, which took the status of a vital input which fuelled the international economy, exactly as labour supply and basic natural resources did in mining and agriculture respectively. Restrictions on the exportation of capital were virtually absent as long as a country adhered to the gold standard system, and investors were thus free to allocate their capital around the world as they saw fit, and to profit from the market opportunities which continuously arose, and to benefit from the declining cost of information which impacted on international financial markets as well. From another perspective, the mobility of capital provided an indispensable fuel for entrepreneurial initiatives that extended throughout

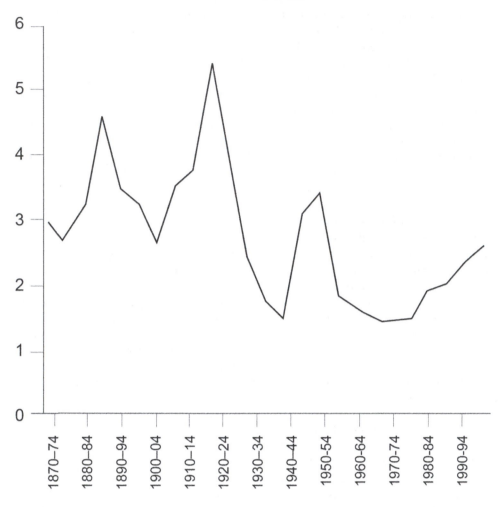

Figure 3.2 Capital mobility index (in % of GDP), 1870–1996

the world, coinciding both with the industrialisation of the peripheries, with the creation of global infrastructures, and with the steady growth of the market for commodities and natural resources, which had begun as a consequence of the First Industrial Revolution, but became definitively consolidated when new capital- and energy-intensive industries, heavily based upon non-renewable natural resources, became the core of the Second Industrial Revolution (see Chapter 4).

6. Forms of enterprise in the first global economy: merchants and traders

The emerging first global economy had, as shown above, enormous impact on both the volume and the extent of international trade. As demonstrated in the previous sections, the origins of the globalisation process were basically of a technological and institutional nature; yet the effects were also momentous at the micro level of the form which entrepreneurial initiatives took in reaction to the new opportunities that the new global context made available. The information and communications revolution, on the one hand, and the increasing degree of openness in trade and finance, on the other, created favourable conditions for international entrepreneurship. In some cases, the existing practices were adapted to the new context. In others, new organisational forms emerged. The second part of this chapter will thus be dedicated to the investigation of both the new and the established forms of international business in the context of the first global economy. The trends described below will concern: a) the organisational evolution of merchant trading activities during the central decades of the nineteenth century in the light of the institutional and technological transformations of the time until their progressive transformation into proto-multinational structures; and b) the diffusion of a particular type of foreign direct investment, that is, the so-called "free-standing company". In this case, the chapter will show how a particular form of foreign investment could be the consequence not only of technological and institutional changes, but also the result of particular conditions in international capital markets – a relationship which has still not been explored in sufficient depth in the existing literature.

The reader should also be aware of the fact that the trends described in this chapter, and particularly in the following pages, took place in a relatively discontinuous way. The organisational evolution of merchant trading firms into more complex structures which eventually resulted in multinational companies is quite easy to trace, although it is not linked to a specific place or period of time. In addition, the story of merchants evolving into multinationals and of free-standing companies overlaps with the diffusion of the (much more well-known) model of the "modern multinational" in the final quarter of the nineteenth century – which will be explored in the following chapters. All this tends to highlight that the nineteenth century is not only relevant – and moreover fascinating – because of the impact of technology and institutions on international business, but also for the huge variety of the forms of enterprise which populated the complex framework of the global economy. For rhetorical reasons, this chapter will deal with two of these forms, leaving the analysis of the modern multinational to the following chapters; these forms, to some degree, have to be considered as offshoots of the same epochal phenomenon that, again, goes back to the First Industrial Revolution, the "great divergence" between the West and the East, and the first globalisation of the world. Last, the chapter overlaps with another "macro phenomenon" that took place throughout the century, namely, the relative decline of Britain as the dominant manufacturing and trading nation in the world, and the emergence of the United States and of other continental European nations, primarily, Germany. This process is, of course, reflected in the volume of foreign investment activity, but also, as we will see, in its forms and structures. Again, for the sake of clarity, this chapter will deal with a phase which is basically dominated by British investments, which constitute the most significant part of the story told here, albeit not the whole story.

The previous chapter emphasised the role of chartered companies in international trade – and, to some extent, international production – between the seventeenth and eighteenth centuries. The emergence of these chartered companies, which have been defined as the "giants of an earlier capitalism",[2] did not eliminate the activity of international merchants. As noted above, some of them remained independently active, even if sometimes in a subordinate position with regard to the more complex and articulated joint-stock organisations. Others disguised themselves as the companies' servants or employees, running their own business sometimes in an open (and tolerated) agency conflict. For others – as shown in the case of the *Levant Company* – things did not change too much, since the charter was simply a device that made individual trading over long distances easier. In other cases, the international activity took place over routes or through businesses that were not under chartered control. An interesting example of this is provided by the trade activities of British merchants in the Mediterranean. Sicily, for instance, between the end of the eighteenth and the beginning of the nineteenth century, was targeted by independent trading houses that not only exported mining products and other raw materials to Britain, the demand for which rose steadily during the industrial revolution, but also local Marsala wines, which were appreciated on the British market just like other fortified wines, such as Madeira and port, were, and were traded by British merchants who managed complex networks of local producers and domestic retailers.

Some of these companies collapsed, for many reasons, before the industrial revolution, while others continued their activity, even though, as we have seen, they progressively lost their privileges, such as the *Hudson Bay Company* or the British *East India Company*. In addition, their overall efficiency is sometimes challenged by the most recent research. However, the decline of chartered companies left an ocean of opportunities open for individual merchants, who operated under very different conditions than those in which their "ancestors" had carried out their business during the previous centuries. British merchants and traders dominated the first three-quarters of the nineteenth century. As suggested above, one effect of the First Industrial Revolution was to transform the British Isles relatively quickly into a hub to which the raw materials necessary for industrial production were imported, and from which manufactured goods reached almost every corner of the globe.

The evolutionary steps of the British merchant houses are, in some way, paradigmatic, even though Britain soon became home to other foreign merchants who established themselves in the most dynamic market of the world. Germans, Greeks and Jews of various nationalities, were, in fact, operating side by side with British merchants (see Box 3.3).

Box 3.3: The Greek business community in London: the case of the Ralli Brothers

When Pantoleon (Pandias) Ralli, the head of the Ralli Brothers firm, died at his home, at 5 Connaught Place West, London, on 9 July 1865, the estimated capital of the family house was well over half a million pounds sterling. The only firm that was substantially richer was that of the five Rothchilds brothers, but they were financiers, not merchants. Pandias sat on his throne, like the "Zeus" that he was nicknamed, of the vibrant Greek community of London, the business centre of an extended network of interconnected branches and offices in Europe, Asia and the United States. His activities were diversified in trade, shipping and finance.

However, in 1810, only half a century before, the Rallis had been just another typical Greek merchant family from the Eastern Mediterranean, who had originated from the island of Chios, under Ottoman rule. The patriarch of the family, Stephanos Ralli (1755–1827) was a successful local merchant, engaged in intra-Ottoman trade in silk, wool and linen between Chios, Smyrna and Constantinople. His five sons, Zannis (a.k.a. John) (1785–1859), Augustus (1792–1878), Pandias (a.k.a. Zeus) (1793–1865), Toumazis (1799–1858) and Eustratios (1800–1884), had all been brought up on Chios, and had also served as apprentices in his business.

From the eighteenth century onwards, the Ralli family, like most Greeks, were caught between empires, assuming a number of different identities as they were divided among competing empires: the Ottoman, the Habsburg, the Venetian, the Russian and the British. Finding themselves in a field in which different political and economic actors and institutions intermingled, and in which overlapping authorities collided, the Greeks moved through the cracks of the system, obtaining a status of protection from both sides, taking advantage of Western Europeans seeking allies and agents in the Levant, in order to overcome their "liability of foreignness".

This "liability of being foreign" describes the cost of conducting business in an alien environment, in which the newcomer, in this case the European merchants, were often at a competitive disadvantage due to distance, asymmetric information and limited know-how of the local market. This common organisational problem was largely alleviated by recruiting agents on the spot selected from a local pool of middlemen, a solution which proved to be more profitable, efficient and flexible. Local agents proved to have better information about the economy, the law, the ethics, the language and the politics of the host country.

The Greeks had for a long time been favoured by the European powers which had settled in the Levant (the French, British, Dutch and Swedes), and long-lasting alliances and partnerships had been established. By assuming their role as intermediaries for the Westerners, they were the dragomen (i.e. translators in countries speaking Arabic, Turkish or Persian), warehousemen, scribes, brokers and money-changers, who were protected by a system of patents and protection. The licences to trade and the protection system (the Turkish capitulations, or *ahdnames* (also *achtiname* and *ahid-nâme*), were bilateral acts entered into by the contracting parties which facilitated trade between the Ottoman Empire and the European nations/powers) were, in fact, the springboard for the Ottoman subjects to become integrated into the networks of the European merchants. The legal framework which regulated western commercial activity in the Eastern Mediterranean was strictly defined by the "capitulatory regime" that had been introduced in the early sixteenth century. Furthermore, the capitulation regime regulated the relations between the Westerners and their local partners. The European communities had the right to bestow *beraths* on the subjects, i.e. patents of protection, which entitled the possessor to all the economic and political benefits of the foreign merchants with whom he entered into contract.

During the hazardous period of the French and Napoleonic Wars, from 1799 to 1813, international trade in the Mediterranean underwent a progressive transformation. While some players were expelled from the Mediterranean, others profited from the uncertainty and expanded their share of the market. Beyond the armed conflicts, the French and Napoleonic Wars introduced economic warfare which was implemented in the form of embargoes on the exports of the enemy to the European markets through the imposition of Napoleon's Continental Blockade in 1806 and the British counter-measures of 1807.

Local players took advantage and emerged to fill the gap caused by the embargoes imposed by the belligerent powers. In the age of consecutive wars in the Mediterranean, the status of neutrality adopted by the Greeks protected their vessels from hostilities, especially from capture and ransom, which were frequent among the privateers of the European states. While, up until 1810, the vast majority of ships reaching Eastern Mediterranean ports were British with British captains having London as their port of departure, after 1810, the British trade changed completely, increasingly reflecting a melting pot in which a number of different ethnicities were featured. The vast majority of ships were by now no longer British.

As a consequence, the nature of shipping changed, moving into more flexible forms undertaken by other, local seafaring populations. Among them, the Greeks held a prominent position which centred on the maritime base of Malta. The repeal of the monopoly of the *Levant Company* had led to the democratisation of trade and to the participation of small-scale merchants, who exploited the British networks to carry out their business. The Greeks gained even more privileges, including the right to establish commercial houses in London. The Ralli family, along with other Greek merchants such as the Petro-cochino, the Maurocordati, the Macri, the Negreponte, the Scaramangas, and the Schi-nas, all Greek-Ottoman families originating from the island of Chios, all featured among the consignees of the *Levant Company* cargoes in the early nineteenth century.

After 1810, the Ralli merchant house followed the British routes into inter-nationalisation. By 1814, Pandias and Zannis Rallis formed the firm called *Pandia and Zannis Ralli & Co.*, in Malta and Smyrna, and, a year later, in Constantinople. At that time, both Smyrna and Constantinople were commercial hubs of the intra-Ottoman and Eastern Mediterranean trade routes for Indian and Asian silk, spices and grain. In 1816, Pandias and Zannis Ralli arrived in London and a year later established a firm in cooperation with another Chian family, the Petrocochino family. Until 1825, the business continued to expand through either branches or agencies in Messina, Venice, Vienna, Marseilles and Trieste.

From 1825 until 1850, the Ralli Brothers' trade continued to grow and the firm spawned new partnerships and trading bases round the Mediterranean, in Russia and in the Middle East, notably in Marseilles, Odessa, Constantinople, St. Petersburg, Taganrog, Rostov-on-Don, and Tabruz and Rescht (Persia), while it also gained a firm grasp in markets in Manchester and Liverpool in Britain. From these bases, the firm's agents reached far into the interior, even as far as Turkestan, conducting a cash and barter trade, typically exchanging grain, wool or raw silk for Manchester cottons and textiles. At that time, the Ralli brothers and their close relatives were dispersed to manage the company's branches and agencies, each with an area under his super-vision: Zannis Ralli was in Odessa, Toumazis Ralli in Constantinople and Trebizond, members of the Ralli and Scaramanga families managed their firm in Taganrog (the Ralli family had married into the Greek Scaramanga trading family), Stefanos Scar-amanga in Rostov-on-Don, Peter Ralli in Rescht, Palli and Agelasto in Tabruz, Stephen Skilizzi in Liverpool, Augustus in Marseilles, Eustratios first in Syros and then in Manchester, and Pandias Ralli was the head of the firm in London.

The exchange of the Black Sea grain trade from the port of Odessa and the Sea of Azof for British textiles lay at the heart of their activities. Until the repeal of the Corn Laws (1846) and the repeal of the Navigation Acts (1849), Russian wheat could be directed to Western European markets by the organisation of a very complex, and very efficient, system of overlapping transport networks that linked the markets of the Eastern Mediterranean and the Black Sea with Britain. This system was feasible through the establishment of a chain of *porto franco*, or (duty-) free ports, which usually operated as entrepôts for British trade, such as Leghorn (Livorno) and Malta. Malta and Syros developed as entrepôts for transit trade and became nodal points for maritime exchanges and information. A vast amount of grain reached them from the Black Sea on Mediterranean (mainly Greek) vessels to be trans-shipped on British vessels to British ports in order to satisfy local demand.

From 1830 until 1860, the Ralli family, along with the other members of the Chian business group, dominated Russian exports to Britain and Marseilles. From 1841 until 1845, the Ralli branch in Odessa was the first most important exporter of animal fat and wool and the second most important exporter of wheat, after Michel-Emmanuel Rodocanachi, the influential Greek trader and banker of London, to the British ports. At the beginning of the 1850s, it was the firm Ralli and Scaramanga in Taganrog which controlled almost half of the total exportation of these products to Britain.

The establishment of the Ralli Bros firm in London from 1825 onwards provided Chian merchant houses with access to the top British institutions, such as the Bank of London and the Virginia and Baltick Coffee House, the precursor of the Baltic Exchange. In 1854, Pandias Ralli, the head of Ralli Bros, and Michel-Emmanuel (a.k.a. Michael) Rodocanachi was one of the twenty-four members of the Baltic Exchange Committee who emphasised "the beneficial relationship between the Baltic and Greek members". When, after the Crimean War, the Virginia and Baltick Coffee House was re-organised into the Baltic Exchange, two of the twelve members of the directorate of the new company were Pandias Ralli and Michel-Emmanuel Rodocanachi. Access to the Baltic Exchange, the largest independent freight shipping market in the world, provided power and esteem in the British markets, which competed with the most powerful British firms. London became a hub of the Chian Diaspora network, following the Chios massacre (the mass killing of Chiot Greeks perpetrated by the Ottoman troops in 1822, during the Greek War of Independence), and the foundation of the Ralli Bros offices in Finsbury Circus led to the formation of a Chian business "cluster". Pandias Ralli also became the Greek Consul in London, and John Ralli was appointed to the office of the American Consulate in Odessa.

However, it was the coordination of trade and shipping between Russia and Britain that ensured the Chian merchant house's long-term competitiveness. Ralli Bros was embedded in a business group of sixty families, more than half of whom originated from the island of Chios, and who were bound together through a dense network of kinship ties, had a similar communal background and had a history of longstanding successful business relations. They represented a strong geographical concentration by entering new markets as a business group, or, in a sense, showed that the establishment of one family in a market was followed by the establishment of others. This created a chain of Chian Diaspora merchant communities in numerous commercial centres of the Mediterranean, the Black Sea and Britain: Odessa, London, Marseilles, Leghorn (Livorno), Trieste, Alexandria, Syros, Constantinople and Smyrna, and Taganrog, in which agencies operated to coordinate the grain trade.

This pattern of business organisation reduced the costs of moral hazard, opportunistic behaviour and intermediation. Mutual trust between members made them part of a "moral economy", in the sense that trustworthy behaviour could be expected, normative standards understood, and opportunism foregone. This allowed the unhindered circulation of products, resources, information and human capital. And it was based upon this type of mechanism of direct representation in the export and import markets that Ralli Bros introduced complex trading practices such as tramp shipping, of having no fixed schedule or ports of call, and tramp trading. The cargoes loaded in Black Sea ports were sold by Ralli Bros in the Baltic while the ship was still making its journey.

The sufficient capital resources and credit embedded in their networks of business connections allowed the Ralli Bros to employ a conservative policy of never issuing "paper" (bills of exchange), but to conduct business in cash to the maximum extent possible, which enabled it to protect the firm from the vulnerability to which so many small trading houses were exposed in the recurrent trade crises. They shared a sectarian outlook that interlocked families in chains of partnerships, marriages and loyalties that overcame the distance between the various business partnerships.

Inevitably, some families were more successful than others, but the very process of the separation of the strong from the weak seemed to make the outstanding firms even more powerful. As in biological evolution, the strong chose the strong as partners, so that, out of a crowd of small and middling firms, a core of dynastic houses persisted, with partnership changes, for much of the nineteenth century. The Ralli Bros, as part of the Chian business inner core, was linked to the largest number of the most powerful and oldest families, which is also indicated in its networks of business partnerships and agents throughout the period 1830–1865.

After 1860, a year which signalled the organisation of an integrated grain trade on a global scale, Ralli Bros completely re-structured their business strategies by geographical differentiation. First of all, the blockade of grain exports from the Black Sea ports during the Crimean War (1854–56) had brought their trade in cereals to a halt and left room for the rise of their US, Canadian, Argentinean and Indian competitors. In 1851, foresight had led Pandia Ralli to change his strategy and enter the Anglo-Indian and North American markets dynamically. Ralli Bros opened offices in Calcutta in 1851 and Bombay in 1861, and also had an office in Karachi which was operated by another Chian merchant, John Negroponte. From these branches, as it had done in Russia, the company reached out into the vast undeveloped interior of India. Ralli Bros also expanded to the US, with offices in New York, New Orleans, Savannah (Georgia) and Charleston (South Carolina).

The death of Pandia Ralli in 1865 signalled the end of the Ralli house as it had been known up to that point. The firm was handed over to Stephen Augustus Ralli (1829–1902), Pandia's nephew, who managed to maintain Pandia Ralli's authority in the firm and his leadership of the Greek community until the end of the century. Stephen Augustus Ralli, who had been trained in the London house (both of Pandia's sons having died in early life), constituted a new "Ralli Brothers", based upon the Indian and Anglo-American trade, leaving the Russian business to the Scaramangas, while the Constantinople and Persian branches were discontinued. It was based upon its British branches in London, Manchester and Liverpool, along with the two new branches in Dundee (1903) and Hull (1903), and its Indian branches in Calcutta, Bombay and Karachi, and the newly established branch in Pondicherry (1903). The main commodities traded were jute, rice, wheat, cotton, linseed, various oilseeds, rapeseeds, gunny, saltpetre and lac dye. Except for the British branches, in Europe the branch in Marseilles was to be maintained under the name of Ralli Frères (1892), while a new branch in Antwerp was founded in 1904 in an effort to enter the new maritime hub of Central Europe.

This box was written by Alexandra Papadopoulou.

★ ★ ★ ★ ★

These merchant houses operated in a more or less standard way. They were originally individual entrepreneurial ventures, seldom transformed into family firms and/or partnerships. They were located in both the main industrial areas and in promising markets where these traders initially imported their goods (mainly cotton textiles) from British

Table 3.2 The Ralli house, 1825–1850

Markets	Number of Companies	Name of Companies	Year of Establishment
Great Britain			
London	1	Ralli Bros.	1825
Manchester	1	Eustratio Ralli & Co.	1826
Liverpool	1	Stephen P. Schillizzi	Between 1837–1865
France			
Marseilles	2	Argenti & Ralli	1816–1834
		Ralli, Schilizzi & Argenti	1834
Russia			
Odessa	2	John S. Ralli & Co.	1826–1859
		John Eustratio Ralli & Co.	1859–1865
Taganrog	1	Ralli & Scaramanga	–1865
Saint Petersburg	1	Ralli & Scaramanga	–1865
Rostov	1		
Ottoman Empire			
Constantinople	2	Stephen P. Schillizzi & Co.	1853–1871
Trebizond	1	Stephen P. Schillizzi	–1871
Persia			
Tabruz & Rescht	1	Ralli & Agelastro	1837–1858

manufacturing districts, exporting local merchandise – acting as intermediaries – while accumulating precious know-how and building up contacts. A second step was the diversification of activity through a process of vertical integration (into shipping, for instance, but sometimes also into production) or quasi-related horizontal expansion, mainly into banking services, in a broad sense, from the discounting of bills to the sale of foreign securities on the London market. According to Geoffrey Jones – the scholar who has analysed this process of evolution in greater depth than anyone else – by the 1870s, some stable and established firms had emerged from the crowd of merchant houses, bankers and traders disseminated almost everywhere.[3]

While British mercantile expansion in Canada, South America, and, in particular, India, South East Asia and China provides a telling example of the positive relationship between trading activities, imperial rule over markets of huge geographical extension, and easy money, the favourable institutional and technological conditions created by the rise of the first global economy also provided invaluable opportunities for entrepreneurs from peripheral economies (see Box 3.4). Often, networks based upon common ethnic origins were still at work as they had been centuries before, and the diffusion of the limited liability and of the joint-stock form provided further incentives for the consolidation of these collaborative networks.

During the first three-quarters of the nineteenth century, in sum, some general trends can be identified in the kaleidoscopic universe of international business activities. After the age of chartered companies, mercantile and trading activities continued to account for a vast proportion of international business. The favourable climate of the first global economy resulted in flourishing entrepreneurial activities, both in the core economies already characterised by the outcomes of the First Industrial Revolution and in the more peripheral ones which benefited also from huge emigration flows which literally created markets that had not existed before. The intermediation activity was no different, in theory, from that undertaken centuries before by the international merchants described in Chapter 1, and was also based upon the services of specialised agency houses. What was different, first of all, was the size and the geographical span of trade, and the exploitation of the trade opportunities in markets which were different from those of origin. For instance, British private trading companies such as *Jardine, Matheson and Co.*, emerging from the consolidation of existing partnerships, were heavily involved in the lucrative business of the opium trade with China, which brought the two countries to war in 1839. In the mercantile tradition, these traders generally remained almost allergic to investments in fixed assets, limiting their diversification strategies to shipping and banking. However, it was not rare, particularly in Asia and South America, to find merchants investing first and foremost in plantations and mining. By the last quarter of the nineteenth century, in sum, there were already some former merchant houses which had diversified into banking or into shipping, as well as into a wide array of trades, ready to take the form of multinational, diversified business groups.

Box 3.4: Enrico dell'Acqua: A "prince-merchant" from the periphery

Enrico dell'Acqua was born in 1851 in Abbiategrasso, a small town near Milan, and, after brief commercial studies, he took over his grandfather's trade in cotton textiles produced by small, local firms. Within a few decades, he was able to strengthen and enlarge this activity, creating an empire that extended to international markets, and which featured an integration of trading and manufacturing both at home and abroad.

The Altomilanese area, North-West of Milan, at that time was a specialised area, a local system of production which had taken shape from the eighteenth century onward. The system was based upon the extensive use of the local labour force (peasants) who, in their free time or during the winter, occupied themselves by weaving. Their activity was coordinated by a merchant-entrepreneur, i.e. a person who bought raw cotton and distributed it directly to the peasants' homes, paying them for their work at the loom. The successive phases, such as dyeing, were performed in centralised plants (sometimes, but not necessarily) owned by the merchant entrepreneur himself. At the end of the whole process, the goods were sold, quite often anonymously or, from the early decades of the nineteenth century, branded with the name of the merchant entrepreneur (the *ditta* or firm). Although cotton manufacturing was important for the region's economy, it was nonetheless rather backward, characterised by a low degree of mechanisation and heavily dependent on foreign nations for raw materials as well as machinery. The products were of very low quality and were sold mainly in local markets. Even after the political unification of Italy (1861), the markets continued to remain basically regional. Transport costs, low consumption and purchasing power, as well as a scarce knowledge of the market itself, deterred northern merchants and entrepreneurs from selling their products in the southern part of Italy. When Enrico became fully in charge of the business in 1871, he started to introduce some changes to the structure, both in the organisation of the production process and in the distribution. At the beginning of the 1870s, a mechanised weaving plant was established in Castrezzato, near Brescia. Raw textiles were then dyed and finished in another factory in Busto Arsizio, about 30 km north of Milan. *Enrico Dell'Acqua & F.llo*, as the firm was now called, started to sell in southern Italy and mainly in Apulia (Puglia). To implement this strategy, dell'Acqua decided to sell directly to the retailers, cutting out the intermediate wholesalers. In order to contact the retailers directly, salesmen were despatched to every part of the regions of southern Italy. At the same time, dell'Acqua started to collect the most detailed information possible about the potential markets for his products.

In the mid-1880s, dell'Acqua started to plan the replication of this strategy on an international scale. In order to pursue this policy of internationalisation, the following alternatives were considered: Africa, Asia and Latin America. What all these territories had in common was the presence of Italian emigrants. Dell'Acqua was convinced that a truly big opportunity existed if trade followed emigration. Dell'Acqua's intuition was to generate close connections with the colonies of emigrants and exploit the strength of their social and cultural ties, i.e. the strong feeling of being Italian and buying "made in Italy" products. Latin America, in particular, was characterised by a large and growing concentration of Italians scattered throughout Argentina and Brazil. According to dell'Acqua, whose opinion was supported by official statistics and other information, the South American market was very appealing, not for luxury products, but for mass-consumption goods: standardised items, such as textiles and other household and personal goods. Dell'Acqua decided to send questionnaires to the postal offices in Brazil and Argentina in order to obtain detailed information about the structure of the potential market. This was a true market investigation of the local social and economic situation concerning population, the number of Italians, local production, transport networks, financial institutions and the presence of manufacturers, dealers and retailers.

In 1810, Argentina became an independent country. Independence was followed by liberal reforms which fostered a general development surge in both trading and banking. After 1850, the integration of Argentina into the international market sped up the process of economic growth. Thanks to innovations in transport and preservation techniques, it also became possible for Argentina to export perishables and foodstuffs (mainly meat and cereals). As a result, average GDP growth was 4.5 per cent per year. Beginning in the 1860s, this allowed Argentina to import increasing quantities of European-produced goods. This situation also made Argentina attractive for foreign capital, especially for investments in railways. Due to the overall relevance of the primary sector (agriculture) and the availability of an immense quantity of land, the state promoted a wide-ranging colonisation policy through the encouragement of mass immigration. Immigration flows from the Old Continent grew steadily from the 1850s onwards, reaching impressive levels: from 65,000 in 1886 to nearly 100,000 the following year, and nearly 220,000 at the beginning of the 1890s, with the majority coming from Italy. Consequently, Italians made up around 13 per cent of the country's total population according to the 1895 census. The Italians were mainly peasants. However, they also included craftsmen from a wide range of industries and activities such as light mechanics, distilleries, groceries and the building industry. Imports of Italian goods (mainly foodstuffs but also tobacco) thus accompanied this mass migration, while more sophisticated products (including machinery) came from England, France, Belgium and Germany. Imports from Italy grew steadily, quickly surpassing those of the other European countries. From 1887 to 1896, imports of Italian goods as a whole increased by 25 per cent in volume, compared to a 13 per cent increase for

Britain and a 40 per cent decrease for France. The trade in handmade goods was organised as follows: through importing "houses" (*importadores*), wholesalers (*registreros*), and retailers (*tiendas*). The import houses bought the goods in Europe and sold them to the wholesalers, who, in turn, sold them to the retailers scattered all over the country.

After completing the market analysis, dell'Acqua sent a set of samples selected according to the climate and habits of the different regions to all the Argentine wholesalers. At the beginning, his finances came from both his family's personal wealth and a credit of 600,000 lire extended by the entrepreneur and banker, Federico Mylius. In 1887, dell'Acqua left Italy for Buenos Aires. At that time, *Enrico Dell'Acqua & F.llo* was organised as follows: production took place in the Castrezzato factory in Italy; two "houses" that carried out the purchasing activities were located in Italy (one in Milan, and one in Busto Arsizio), and two foreign branches (one in Buenos Aires, one in São Paulo) acted as wholesalers for the Latin American market. Almost immediately, dell'Acqua decided to change track and to target the retailers (the *tiendas*). From the Buenos Aires and São Paulo offices, commercial travellers were sent almost everywhere. The outcome of this strategy was encouraging. At the end of the year, the total sales in Argentina, Uruguay and Paraguay had reached nearly 825,000 lire, with three-quarters from the cotton trade. In the following years, sales shot up to unexpected levels. Immediately after the first settlement, dell'Acqua started to open commercial houses (trading companies) in the largest towns of the commercially most attractive countries. These would be the pillars of a distribution network based upon a large number of salesmen. The enlargement of the distribution network was to be coupled with the introduction of new brands aimed at strengthening the company's market power over the other importers. The organisational structure of the company was based upon a head office in Milan that oversaw a number of branches in South America, linked to the head office by profit-sharing agreements. The local branches were independent in terms of commercial practices and strategies in their own local market. The expansion project, however, was undermined by the deep economic crisis in Argentina that resulted from both financial factors and natural factors, such as bad harvests. Given the positive trend of business by 1889, when the crisis broke out, dell'Acqua had enlarged both the commercial operations and the credit to the retailers. In order to solve the problem, dell'Acqua had to return once more to using Italian capital. Thus, he was back in Italy again in the middle of 1889 with the purpose of creating a new trading company to export Italian merchandise to South America and to import South American goods to Italy at a later date. The new firm was to take over all the activities, credits and debts of *Enrico Dell'Acqua & F.llo*. The start-up phase was turbulent; creditors were unhappy, and banks were progressively suspending their support. However, their involvement was considerable, with the result that they finally decided to support his project. On 25 February 1890, a new limited partnership company, *E. Dell'Acqua & C.*, was founded. The capital amounted to 1.5 million lire. The structure was based upon a wide network of suppliers, a head office in Milan, and branches in Buenos Aires and São Paulo.

After the crisis of 1889 in Argentina and the similar crisis that hit Brazil the following year, protectionism spread in South America. In 1890, the Brazilian government introduced customs duties of 100 per cent "ad valorem" on all kinds of goods. The situation warranted a change in dell'Acqua's strategy. The first factory was established in São Roque, a small town in the Brazilian province of São Paulo. Dell'Acqua also involved local partners in the new start-up, which began in 1892; it was essentially the first modern plant in the country.

In the meantime, dell'Acqua was convinced that the economic crisis was going to end and kept exploring the countryside through his extensive network of commercial travellers. In 1894, dell'Acqua set up another factory in Buenos Aires dedicated to hosiery and mechanical weaving, bleaching and dyeing. In the second half of the 1890s, the whole organisation took a definitive shape. The headquarters were located in Italy (in Busto Arsizio). This office was in charge of both the general management of the company and the purchasing of the merchandise. It was divided into two branches: the commercial branch, receiving orders from South America and buying goods on the Italian market; and the accounting section, responsible for the company accounts and for the branch-office operations. Four sales agencies were located in Argentina, three in Brazil and one in Peru, each one established as an independent firm with only administrative reporting to headquarters. An agency employed twenty commercial travellers, each in charge of several retailers. The agencies were connected to the factories in Buenos Aires and São Roque. The main agency was that of Buenos Aires, and here the merchandise was sold both through the network of travellers and through a truly Argentinean method: the *remate*. This was a kind of auction system that allowed the sale of large quantities of goods through the sale of small batches of goods and the ability to obtain information about the trends in local market consumption immediately. In Brazil, the relevant agencies were in São Paulo and in the State of Bahia. The latter, in particular, was actually a kind of spin-off of the former. It was created when Enrico dell'Acqua found it impossible to convince a wholesaler to introduce new brands and decided to detach some of the São Paulo employees in order to start his own commercial business. In a similar way, the Lima agency was set up with the aim of overseeing the development of the business in Venezuela, Colombia, Peru, Bolivia and Chile.

As a whole, the company employed over 2,000 people at the end of the nineteenth century. Relying upon the *tiendas* scattered throughout South America required prompt management of operations and stocks aimed at granting the availability of goods. The strategy and the structure of the company proved to be a successful mixture. In nearly a decade, the brand 'Vedetta', introduced by *Enrico dell'Acqua & C.*, conquered more than 700 marketplaces in Argentina, Brazil, Uruguay, Paraguay, Venezuela, Chile and other countries.

Based on Luigi Einaudi, *Un Principe Mercante. Studio sull'espansione coloniale italiana*, Turin: Bocca, 1900.

7. Forms of enterprise in the first global economy: free-standing companies

On 20 November 1869 (just a few months after the opening of the Pacific-Atlantic Continental Railroad), the *Economist* published (pages 1366–67) an article entitled "The Suez Canal". It was a relatively dry – in the journal's style – celebration of the opening of the water connection between the Mediterranean and the Indian Ocean, which would revolutionise the world of shipping and, in part, all trade between Europe and

Asia, cutting the duration of the journey between India and Britain from three to slightly less than two months. The article sincerely praised the stubbornness of Ferdinand de Lesseps, the person who had played a prominent role in the realisation of the project, arranging everything from the collection of capital to the necessary political support, to the organisation of the work in person. In a snobbish British style, however, the anonymous writer explained to the reader that the canal, built by French technicians with a lot of French and Egyptian capital (plus a considerable amount of forced labour) was not, in fact, going to change the direction or even the intensity of trade between the West and the Indies significantly, and that, if any change *was* going to take place, it would go in the direction of strengthening the already dominant position of Britain in world trade. Somewhat sardonically, the *Economist* reported the droll opinion of the French engineers working *in situ*, who had been heard to say "that the Canal has been cut by French energy and Egyptian money for British advantage".

The *Economist*'s comments proved, however, to be slightly excessive, with regard to at least two aspects. The first concerned the impact of the Suez Canal on the general conditions of Euro-Asian trade, even though it must be admitted that its administration faced financial difficulties due to the low volume of traffic that continued to persist for nearly twenty years after its completion. By the beginning of the twentieth century, however, the Suez Canal had progressively become one of the foremost trade routes between Europe and Asia, the tonnage transiting through the artificial isthmus growing almost steadily until the First World War, and after the war, up to nearly 10 per cent of total world trade. From the very beginning, the percentage of British tonnage exceeded two-thirds (and sometimes even three-quarters) of the total transit. On this issue, the *Economist*'s reporter was right. Britain took a significant part of the advantages offered by the Suez Canal, to such an extent that, in the mid-1870s, the British government decided to acquire all the shares sold by the Egyptian government, which had found itself in serious financial straits.

Secondly, it was not exactly true to say that the canal had been built by French energy with Egyptian money. The situation was, in fact, a bit more complicated. The *Suez Canal Company* (or, officially, the *Compagnie Universelle du Canal Maritime de Suez*) started to build the Canal in 1859 after de Lesseps obtained concessions and support from the Egyptian Viceroy. The *Suez Canal Company*'s administrative headquarters were in Paris, while its operative seat was in Alexandria. The capital amounted to two hundred million French Francs, and the shares could be bought – according to the statutes of the company – from the representatives of the company, located in the main financial centres of the world, including Constantinople, London, New York, Paris, Vienna, St. Petersburg and Geneva. The Egyptian government stepped in as a major shareholder, buying more than 40 per cent of the shares, after some initial difficulty in raising the capital, which was, however, subscribed mainly by French investors. However, the canal was, effectively, built by "French energy"; apart from the international committee entrusted to produce the definitive project of the work, the engineers and technicians were all French – and, of course, building on the great French tradition in civil engineering.

To sum up, the *Suez Canal Company* was an international joint-stock company, with its headquarters in Paris, which raised capital on the main European financial markets, in order to finance the construction of a major engineering project in a peripheral area (in this case, Egypt). All the operative activity was, of course, taking place *in situ*; the company relied on French technicians, but employed local workers, while the financial, technical and administrative core was located in Europe, where the majority (and, after the British take-over, almost the totality) of the investors were resident. Thus, the company was not really a trading company, because it was actually investing in real fixed assets – in this case, the canal, some facilities, and the areas close to the canal which were subject to the company's exploitation by concession – and also because the headquarters were not located in Egypt, but in Paris. Nor was the company a prototype of a multi-national company starting from some domestic activity in the home country and then investing abroad, since it was specifically formed to finance the construction of the canal at Suez. It was a company incorporated in one country – in this case, France – in order to do business in another, Egypt. Nor can it be described as an investment trust, that is, a vehicle for investing abroad for purely financial purposes (portfolio investments), since it *de facto* exerted direct strategic control over the operations abroad. For the individual, private investor who bought shares in the company, this was, of course, intended to be a (hopefully profitable) investment in order to obtain financial returns; the *Suez Canal Company* was, however, far from being a simple investment trust; it was a company which both invested and controlled real income-generating assets.

This form of corporate structure might seem relatively atypical today, but it was far from being infrequent when the *Suez Canal Company* was started. The *Economist* reader mentioned above could decide about his investments upon the basis of the lists of shares published in the journal, which included dozens of companies which were similar (if not more promising in terms of returns) to the *Suez Canal Company*. They included ventures which had their headquarters in Europe, with no operations at home except for the administrative activity taking place in a small office in Paris, Brussels, Liège or London, investing the capital which they raised in the construction of infrastructure and utilities, and in the ownership of mines and plantations around the world, under the supervision and management of technicians mainly of European origin.

International business historians have been familiar with these kinds of companies since some decades ago, coining the definition of "free-standing enterprises" or "free-standing companies" in order to define them, and stressing the fact that they were not generated out of an already existing activity in the home market, as is the rule among the "modern" multinationals which had started to spread by the last decades of the nineteenth century (see the following chapters). According to the data available, free-standing companies constituted a relevant portion of the total of the direct investments of the main industrialised countries during the second half of the nineteenth century. By 1914, they accounted for a (very rough) 40 per cent of the total stocks of foreign investments from the European countries, plus Japan, the US, Canada, Australia, New Zealand and South Africa, even if the incidence is even higher for some countries – where more reliable data are available – as in the British case (around 80 per cent). Less than half a century before, in 1870, their incidence had been lower, since more or less two-thirds of British direct investments abroad (for which, it is worth repeating, we possess far better data) fell under the category of "free-standing companies". The data available also allow us to form some hypotheses regarding the sectorial distribution of these companies' investments, which mainly tended to privilege three broad areas. The first was that of mining and primary resources, including agricultural products. The second concerned railways, and the third utilities and services. Both banking and manufacturing were, of course, represented, although in a far smaller proportion. Albeit only to a minor extent, free-standing companies also had their headquarters in other European countries – mainly in Belgium, the Netherlands and France – with little or no substantial difference in terms of the industries targeted, or, as we will see in the following, in terms of their organisational structure.

Created mostly in wealthy and developed European countries, free-standing companies invested mainly in developing peripheries. The term "periphery" here is a deliberately chosen, relatively blurry concept, which includes areas that were urbanising and industrialising at an above-average rate during the last decades of the nineteenth century until the outbreak of the First World War. In continental Europe, as well as Asia and South America, municipalities in fast-developing countries needed infrastructure in transport (for instance, urban tramway lines) and utilities (water and electricity production and their respective concomitant distribution networks), the construction of which required advanced technical skills, and some kind of "patient capital". In Southern Europe, Asia and China, and in both South and Central America, European companies (mainly British, French and Belgian) participated in what was a major "push" towards modernisation. Headquartered in Brussels, London, Paris, Liège, Antwerp and Manchester, and in the other leading technical, financial and industrial centres, these companies oversaw the construction and management of networks of facilities and infrastructure that were essential for the transformation of these peripheries into modern conurbations.

Peripheries were not only promising for the development of infrastructure, they also attracted capital (and would attract more in the future) due to their endowment with natural resources; both the first and the second industrial revolutions were voracious consumers of natural resources. The cables laid under the oceans were coated by *gutta percha*, the natural material imported from Malaya, used in the West for a myriad of different purposes, from dentistry to fabrics even to golf balls. Tea had become indispensable in the diet of Anglo-Saxons (and Europeans), just as coffee had, and, to some extent, poppies, which provided basic active principles for dozens of the pharmaceutical formulae or compositions that were increasingly in demand in Europe. Plantations were thus an attractive destination for European investments, and the common practice was to undertake these capital-intensive initiatives under the form of companies incorporated in the relatively efficient, safe and well-informed European stock markets. The case of mining presents a similar story, in which ventures were formed for the exploitation of rare earth minerals in every corner of the world. *Rio Tinto*, one of today's largest global oligopolists in natural resources, started at the beginning of the 1870s as a free-standing company incorporated in Britain and was initially set up for the exploitation of a mine in Andalusia, Spain. A few years later, a similar story unfolded with *Penarroya*, another company incorporated in Paris, which had been created for the exploitation of lead mines and coal mines in the Sierra Morena (again in Andalusia), and was destined to become a dominant player in the modern global mining industry.

Their particular "shape" had implications on the prevailing organisational structure of free-standing enterprises. At first sight, they may seem relatively unimportant in terms of authority relations and bureaucratic architecture. At the beginning, free-standing enterprises were considered to be quite simple organisational devices. In their simplest form, the very fact of having their headquarters located in an office in one of the Western finance capitals constituted a concrete guarantee for investors. The Board of Directors thus superintended the operations of what was, very frequently, a single-business initiative, located abroad. A director who supervised a local operative structure, appointed by the board at home, ran a mine or a plantation, or oversaw the creation and management of a utility company. The bureaucratic relations between the home headquarters or seat and the operative units were thus considered weak. The Board of Directors was thus conceived basically as a "guarantee" for the shareholders, who had their stocks listed and traded on the domestic markets and known individuals sitting on the boards. Then, the capital collected under the name of the company was put at the disposal of the managers and technicians who, for instance, built a tramway or lighting network in the French Concession in Shanghai, or ran the operations in a silver mine in the Chilean Andes.

Further research has, however, demonstrated that things may have been more complex. The degree of autonomy of the foreign operations of the free-standing company was, of course, considerably high, and probably closer to that enjoyed by the director of an *East India Company*'s factory in Java than to the autonomy level of the top manager of a branch of an American multinational operating in Italy in the twentieth century. The home office, however, had a more complicated role than the (albeit relevant) role of collecting financial resources. Let us review a real situation, well explored in the literature. In 1871, some Scottish investors decided to set up a company in Glasgow, the *Rangoon Oil Company*, in order to invest in the search for oil fields and their subsequent exploitation in India. The company, soon re-named the *Burmah Oil Company* (a predecessor of *British Petroleum*), was collecting money on the basis not only of the prestige of its promoters, but also of the feasibility of their business plans. Senior executives had to display a high degree of personal skills, in order to show that they were able to hire the right people or to rely on skilled professionals. Managers *in situ* had complicated operative roles that included the none-too-easy task of doing business in a complex environment, while the head office performed other strategic functions, such as marketing. The link between the head office – which was clearly much more than a brass plate on a door – was ensured by the secretary of the company, who acted as a sort of liaison officer. As already stated, free-standing companies transferred capital abroad not to strangers, but to skilled professionals who had (sometimes risky) ideas.[4] It was, in sum, a sort of venture-capital transfer to entrepreneurial ventures on a global scale. They were "born global" by definition, being formed with the purpose of operating abroad right from the very beginning.

The British biologist Herbert Spencer is credited with having coined the phrase "the survival of the fittest", in his *Principles of Biology* (1864), after reading Charles Darwin's *On the Origin of Species*, published in 1859. And by the 1860s, the free-standing enterprise was really establishing itself well, with dozens of examples being born every year, proving how this organisational form of international business was particularly well adapted to the environment of the first global economy, and was, additionally, very efficient in managing operations abroad in many different industries, from plantations, to mining, to oil, even to manufacturing and banking.

Behind this overall efficiency, there were some contextual and specific motives, some of which have been mentioned, but not been discussed in any detail, in the previous sections.

A first, general condition was provided by imperial rule. It has been observed that there is a sort of correlation between the number of free-standing enterprises in a domestic economy and the existence of a more or less extended empire or imperial influence exerted by the country that was home to the companies. This did not exclude countries without empires, or with small empires, which hosted free-standing companies, as mentioned above in the case of late nineteenth-century Italy, for example. Nor were free-standing companies operating exclusively within imperial borders. Belgium, which in the second half of the nineteenth century had a relatively small empire when compared to Britain, was home to a relatively high number of free-standing companies which were committed to investments in Southern European countries. It is clear, however, that imperial influence allowed free-standing companies to operate in a relatively safer environment than those operating *outside* the confines of an empire with its imperial rules, law system and enforcement and administration.

There are, however, abundant examples – as shown above, in the cases of *Penarroya* and *Rio Tinto* – of free-standing companies operating outside empires, but nonetheless enjoying a relatively neutral, when not friendly, attitude on the part of the host governments. From the point of view of governments of the host countries, the free-standing companies were, above all, the primary vehicles through which foreign capital, entrepreneurship and technical skill were flowing locally, accelerating the process of modernisation of the periphery within their country. Moreover, there was no serious risk of loss of sovereignty, since local capitalists could always be associated with ownership, as the shares were tradable and negotiable on the main stock exchanges, and even governments (as happened in the case of the *Suez Canal Company*) could become shareholders. In contrast to chartered companies, which sometimes responded to the political and economic goals that were set by their own home government and which were often superimposed domestically, free-standing enterprises started to be perceived, and to act, as "foreign companies operating locally" not only for their own benefit (which was natural), but also for the benefit of the host country.

In the framework of the first global economy, in sum, free-standing companies developed as efficient vehicles for the transfer of financial capital to support global entrepreneurship, benefiting from the favourable conditions of the international capital market in the period of the gold standard. Through a free-standing enterprise, a capitalist could invest his money, with an acceptable degree of risk, in a venture for the exploitation of a business opportunity anywhere in the world, under the leadership of skilled entrepreneurs and technicians, and could benefit from the relative safety of his state's imperial dominions or of the prevailing friendly attitude of a government willing to import foreign, up-to-date technology in infrastructure. As a sort of win–win arrangement, this organisational type would last for decades, until the favourable conditions of the global economy and of international financial and monetary stability collapsed at the outbreak of the First World War.

The increasing, widespread diffusion of free-standing companies from the second quarter of the nineteenth century has, of course, prompted a number of theoretical explanations which endeavour to discuss the rationales behind their existence.

As suggested above, a possible first acceptable explanation can be found in the reasons connected to the nature of international capital markets during the first period of globalisation. Free to move without constraints and stimulated by the favourable climate of the gold standard, foreign direct investments took the form of free-standing companies since they were free to explore different areas in order to support sometimes risky – but generally profitable – new ventures. This, essentially, connects the existence of free-standing companies to the decision(s) taken by investors to allocate their resources in activities characterised by different levels of returns (and risks) in a logic of portfolio diversification. To push this argument further – maybe too far – the logic behind this process of allocation follows the selfsame logic as discriminating between investments upon the basis of interest-rate differentials, a logic which has been a cornerstone of the theory of international investments for a very long time.

More recently, other theorists have tried to reinterpret the existence of free-standing enterprises in the light of the theoretical frameworks in use in the more recent international business literature. One particularly intriguing explanation is provided by transaction cost theory, which stresses how free-standing firms acted as efficient "internalisers" of a particular market, namely, the international market for financial capital, irrespective of whether they possessed any form of firm-specific advantage – for instance, in terms of mastering a superior form of technology. This perspective is, in some way, connected to what has been suggested above, in that free-standing enterprises collected capital in the dominant and most efficient equity markets of the time, and put it at the disposal of international entrepreneurship.

The interpretation suggested by internalisation/transaction cost theory is fascinating and, to some extent, adequate, but it is still not fully convincing. Free-standing enterprises were, in fact, investing both in countries which were characterised by non-efficient equity markets, involving a high level of risk and delayed returns on the investment, as well as in areas in which capital markets were developing and in which both local and foreign entrepreneurs were already operating quite effectively. The aforementioned case of Italy during the last quarter of the nineteenth century is particularly telling, but the same can be applied to other peripheral European countries, such as Spain or Russia. Moreover, free-standing enterprises were also investing in markets which were themselves home to local free-standing companies because of investors who were active outside their national borders. All this points in the direction of adding another explanation to the previous one, in order to explain the existence of free-standing companies as a particular and, to some extent, unique, type of international business activity which matured in the unique general framework of the second half of the nineteenth century.

In order to introduce this explanation it is worth considering the fact that free-standing companies were, to some extent, a consequence of the first industrial revolution, which was, all things considered, eminently a technological breakthrough. As noted above, a great number of free-standing enterprises could be found in the primary sector (agriculture) and in obtaining the natural resources necessary to the manufacturing activity of the first industrial revolution. In this case, one might content oneself with the explanation of their existence being based upon the internalisation of capital markets as suggested above. In order to run a natural rubber or a palm oil plantation in Malaya or Burma, it was necessary to have a trustable director who was content to spend a substantial part of his twenties and early thirties in a relatively none-too-healthy tropical climate, to employ some local personnel, obtain some (patient) capital which was to be collected where it was abundant, some leading investors, and a relatively skilled headquarters on home territory which had the necessary skill to market the harvest efficiently. Another large number of free-standing companies, however, dealt with activities which were as (patient) capital-intensive as plantations, but which required an even higher degree of technical skill. To run a mine or to coordinate the digging and manage the navigation of a canal such as that of Suez, or to set up a regional, or even local, tramway network, or a waterworks or the supply of electricity to an expanding city, was definitely a different kind of business. The headquarters of a hypothetical Belgian free-standing company created to build and manage a railway network in the northern Italian regions in the 1880s had different tasks from a Dutch counterpart running a palm oil plantation somewhere in Burma. It had to deal with local administration and municipalities in order to obtain mileage subsidisation and payment for various services, to invest in infrastructure and building materials, and to employ suitable skilled human capital to coordinate the building of the network and its daily operations, something which involved both personnel on the spot, and able technicians of Belgian origin. In sum, this Belgian company was not only collecting investments and delivering returns, it was also connecting the supply of skilled labour (both in technical and managerial terms) with the growing demand for technical advancement coming from the peripheries in the developing world. As noted by the most important expert in this subject, the US scholar Mira

Wilkins, free-standing companies acted as powerful connectors in the realm of the global economy. And, in some cases, this coincided with some kind of "specialisation", which, at the time, was more visible at country level than at the level of the individual companies. Belgium was thus home to free-standing companies in railways, tramways and gas distribution. France was a leader in public works and other utilities, such as waterworks. Britain and the Netherlands were more "specialised" in mining, primary resources and real estate.

Conclusion

Multinational trading companies and free-standing companies, the two main protagonists of this chapter, can, to some extent, be considered to be the microeconomic outcome of the epochal transformations introduced by the First Industrial Revolution in the complex framework of the first global economy. It would have been difficult, almost impossible, for either of these organisational forms to have developed without the revolution in transport and communications which took place in the central decades of the century, and, at least in the case of the free-standing companies, these organisations were also among the main promoters of the revolution itself. Both mobilised huge quantities of resources, both in financial terms and in terms of human capital and technical skills, to an extent never experienced in the previous centuries. Both rose as particularly efficient devices in the global economy, and contributed in a clear way to the consolidation of the Western leadership in the first decades of the process known today as the "great divergence". Both, however, had either almost disappeared or been radically transformed by the first decades of the twentieth century, especially after the outbreak of the First World War. This metamorphosis is particularly striking because of its rapidity: once dominant, the free-standing company had become a relatively rare species by the 1930s, while the majority of the trading companies described above had undergone the inexorable process of transformation into multinational business groups.

Clearly, such a rapid change – which sharply reduced the variety in the forms of international business which were considered to be proper throughout the whole of the modern and early contemporary period – was determined by the decline of some of the conditions in which the previous forms had prospered, to wit, the unique framework of the first global economy described above. It was, however, also determined by the emergence of new forms of enterprise, in their turn generated by new technological breakthroughs, which profoundly altered the existing conditions of international business.

Notes

1   Maurice Obstfeld and Alan M. Taylor, *Global Capital Markets: Integration, Crisis and Growth*, Cambridge: Cambridge University Press, 2004, p. 129.
2   Ann Carlos and Stephen Nicholas, "Giants of an Earlier Capitalism: The Chartered Trading Companies as Modern Multinationals", *Business History Review*, Vol. 62, No. 3 (Autumn, 1988), pp. 398–419.
3   Geoffrey Jones, *Merchants to Multinationals: British Trading Companies in the Nineteenth and Twentieth Centuries*, Oxford: Oxford University Press, 2002.
4   Mira Wilkins, "Long-Term Investments in the Gold Standard Era", in: Marc Flandreau, Carl-Ludwig Holtfrerich and Harold James (eds), *International Financial History in the Twentieth Century: System and Anarchy*, Cambridge: Cambridge University Press, 2003, pp. 51–76.

Bibliography

Jones, Geoffrey, *Merchants to Multinationals: British Trading Companies in the Nineteenth and Twentieth Centuries*, Oxford: Oxford University Press, 2002.

Jones, Geoffrey, *Multinationals and Global Capitalism: From the Nineteenth to the Twenty-first Century*, Oxford: Oxford University Press, 2004.

Hertner, Peter and Jones, Geoffrey (eds), *Multinationals: Theory and History*, Aldershot: Ashgate Publishing, 1986.

Wilkins, Mira, "The Free-Standing Company 1870–1914: An Important Type of Foreign Direct Investment", *Economic History Review*, 2nd series, 41(1988), pp. 259–282.

Wilkins, Mira and Schroeter, Harm (eds), *The Free-Standing Company in the World Economy (1830–1996)*, Oxford: Oxford University Press, 1996.

4   Enterprises and entrepreneurs in an age of globalisation (1870–1914)

1. A nineteenth-century born-global

When, in 1872, he founded the company that to this very day still bears his family name on its corporate website, Giovanni Battista Pirelli was twenty-four years old. He had graduated just two years before from the *Politecnico di Milano* (the Polytechnic University of Milan), just before spending some months abroad, travelling throughout Europe in order to decide upon a promising new business to start up on his return *in patria*. It was not an easy task. Within two decades, Italy would have been rightly considered one of the most effective examples of a latecomer country, one which had successfully proven itself able to undergo a process of industrial and social modernisation. But, at the beginning of the 1870s, it was a country that had only just completed the process of its political unification (Rome, the capital, had been militarily annexed to the newborn Italian state in September 1870, when Pirelli had just set off on his modern version of the *Grand Tour* or "training tour" across the Continent). It was a country in which agriculture was the dominant sector, and manufacturing activity was either of an artisanal nature, or based upon networks of peasants employed mainly in the textile industry. According to some calculations, on the eve of the Unification of Italy with the annexation of Rome in 1870, in both Piedmont and Lombardy – the two most economically developed regions of the country – more than half of the total value of exports came from staple products such as raw silk, which – produced in the countryside by peasants as raw material for textile manufacture – worked as a *trait d'union* between the primary and secondary sectors.

Notwithstanding the overall status of the country, Pirelli developed a fairly ambitious start-up project, based upon the industrial production of vulcanised natural rubber for various civil and military purposes. Pirelli was, without doubt, a visionary entrepreneur, but he was also perfectly aware that the production of vulcanised natural rubber (a technical innovation made by the American-born Charles Goodyear in 1844), which he had seen at work during his European travels, had a huge variety of applications in many fields of manufacturing, including the production of seals and other components for machine tools, mainly for the textile industry. Vulcanised rubber complemented the production of *gutta percha*, the natural resin in use in the fabrication of telegraphic submarine cables and for coated cables in general. In a phase in which the Italian government – and not just the Italian government – was making huge efforts to build an efficient network of communications infrastructure, there were good opportunities for the domestic producers of such a strategic item in a market that was largely dominated by British firms. Between the end of the 1870s and the beginning of the following decade, thanks also to the technical competence of Pirelli's partner Francesco Casassa, the company successfully obtained a monopolistic position in the Italian domestic market in just a few years. Following its consolidation on the domestic market, the company opened a new production facility in La Spezia (Italy), a strategically positioned port in the Mediterranean, and integrated vertically by investing in a ship that was equipped for cable laying.

Business historians generally agree that while *Pirelli* was able to consolidate its position thanks to the ambitious entrepreneurial vision of its founder, the company also greatly benefited from the combined effect of an increasingly protective commercial policy adopted by the Italian government and its propensity to privilege a domestic producer of strategic components, instead of relying on foreign suppliers. Whatever the reasons, *Pirelli* very quickly obtained a dominant position in the Italian market, thereby increasing its production and marketing capabilities and skills. This was, however, a sort of first step. In terms of dimensions and opportunities, the market for cables, both submarine and others, was a peculiar one. First, governmental bodies and agencies, both at local and national level, dominated on the demand side. Second, the market was, by definition, international, especially for a company such as *Pirelli*, which was resident in a country that was developing quickly, but was still characterised by a restricted absorption potential. In view of this, by the end of the 1880s and the beginning of the 1890s, *Pirelli* had started a policy of international commercial expansion, starting with the Mediterranean (Spain, Greece and Egypt). The opening of commercial branches abroad was, in some cases, followed by the establishment of production facilities, particularly when the local market was particularly promising, or when producing was more convenient than exporting, especially in the case of adverse commercial policies adopted by local governments. In 1902, thirty years after its foundation, *Pirelli* opened its first "greenfield" (realised from scratch) production plant abroad, in Spain, near Barcelona (mainly for the production of cables). This was followed by another plant in Argentina (1917) for a more general range of products, after which the company spent some years consolidating in the local market through the activity of commercial branches and partnerships with both local and foreign companies in the electric industry. In the meantime, another plant for the production of electric cables was inaugurated in 1912 in the country which led the industry, the United Kingdom. It was a 50 per cent joint venture between the Italian company and one of the industry's main players, a British company called the *General Electric Co. Ltd.*, not related to the more famous American company of the same name. The Southampton factory of the *Pirelli Cable Works Ltd.* was a relevant step in *Pirelli*'s corporate history: the Italian partner provided the technological capabilities, while the British partner basically took care of the commercial aspects of the joint venture. After the First World War, *Pirelli* continued its expansion abroad, in a sort of endless expansion that culminated in the creation of an international holding company (the *Compagnie Internationale Pirelli*), based in Brussels for fiscal reasons, which was in charge of the Italian company's foreign subsidiaries. The disruption that the First World War brought to the international trade-flow had, in the meantime, pushed *Pirelli* into securing the supply of the raw materials vital to its operations through the acquisition of rubber-tree plantations in the Far East. This was a strategy common to all the big players in the industry.

In the fifty years following its foundation, in sum, the Italian company had quickly consolidated its international presence, both in commercial terms and in terms of vertical integration, and even with production abroad. After the First World War, *Pirelli* continued to follow its strategy of foreign expansion in Europe and South America. In 1928, another British plant was opened, in Burton-on-Trent, in order both to circumvent a sharp increase (+33 per cent) in custom duties on tyres, and as a reaction to the penetration of the British market by *Pirelli*'s main competitors, *Goodyear* and *Firestone*, that was in progress at the time. In 1929, another plant producing cables and tyres was opened in Brazil. Together with the opening of new branches, the Italian company started, at the beginning of the 1930s, a policy of agreements with its main competitors, in order to regulate the international market of rubber products. Among various kinds of agreements, a relevant role was played by *Pirelli* through its participation in a patenting pool, together with the American firm *US Rubber* and the British firm *Dunlop*, in the latex industry, with the formation of a company (the *International Latex Processes Ltd.*), which was *de facto* an international cartel which regulated the whole industry upon a geographical basis.

The story of *Pirelli* was something unusual in Italy, characterised as it was by a relatively inward-looking and domestically-oriented capitalism. But it was, nonetheless, a fairly standard process in various countries and in several industries at the time. In a few decades, something had happened which had had a radical impact on the behaviour of entrepreneurs and enterprises active in the global economy, introducing significant changes in the way in which companies took their strategic decisions and made their competitive choices. These changes, in their turn, also had an impact on the way in which these companies were organised and in the manner in which their internal authority relations were shaped.

Once again, it was technology that played a prominent role in this process. New technologies of production completely transformed the internal structure of some industries, and revolutionised the strategic priorities of the companies under their control, including those linked to the dynamics of internationalisation. This process also revolutionised the relationships between the companies emerging from this process and the general environment surrounding them, including their respective domestic governments and those of the countries involved in their process of internationalisation.

According to many scholars, this process resulted in the creation of a form of enterprise that was active in the global economy but which had never existed before. They were multi-unit, often multi-product, enterprises, and they were simultaneously present in different countries. It was specifically for this new form of enterprise that the term "multi-national" was coined, and the new multinationals were destined to dominate the realm of international business from this moment onward. However, in order to distinguish them from the companies which were active in different markets around the world, we will use the term "modern" multinational.

This chapter will analyse the technological transformations which gave birth to the modern multinational enterprise, and the impact that this had on the structure of firms which were active internationally. In particular, it will deal with the motivations underlying the decision to establish operations abroad taken by domestic companies in the light of the effects of technological change. The impact of the new technologies on internationalisation strategies was, in the first phase, far from being determinant. To some extent, multinational companies developed along similar lines, and the effects of the new technological paradigm diffused themselves progressively. In general terms, *Pirelli* developed along the same lines as its main competitors, *Michelin* in France, *Dunlop* in the UK and *Goodyear* in the United States. Geographic differences, however, also played a role in shaping the internationalisation process of companies, and many US and European firms, as a consequence, experienced a process of international expansion following different patterns. This, in its turn, resulted in divergent models of the multinational enterprise which characterised two different capitalistic environments.

2. The Second Industrial Revolution and the rise of big business

As shown above, both the diffusion of new technological paradigms and the transformations in production processes had a radical impact on the nature, structure and strategies of the business enterprise, and on the attitudes of the entrepreneurs, that were active both at domestic and international level. By the last quarter of the nineteenth century, the spread of a new technological wave, which profoundly altered the behaviour of enterprises and entrepreneurs in a number of industries, was no exception to this rule. What business historians and historians of technology and innovation are used to defining as the "Second Industrial Revolution" was basically a cluster of new products and, above all, of process technologies inherent largely to a) the chemical transformation of raw materials, and b) the assembling of complex products sub-divided into standardised components. Examples of the first category can be found in industries involved in the transformation of the internal structure of materials, such as the forging of metals, (for instance, steel, copper, aluminium), the refining of oil and sugar, the processing of various agricultural products, and almost all the branches of the chemical industry from dyes to pharmaceuticals, fertilisers and fibres. Examples of the second category can be found in light and heavy mechanics, from sewing machines to machine tools, to means of transport, the automotive industry and other machinery. These industries very quickly became the most dynamic branches in manufacturing almost everywhere, characterised by above-average rates of expansion. By the end of the nineteenth century, they were synonymous with modernisation, and were diffused in all the new industrialising countries of the time by means of indigenous entrepreneurial efforts, foreign initiative(s) and even the commitment of nation states desperately struggling to establish a domestic presence in these industries.

Box 4.1 A century of innovations: a chronology

1800	Screw-cutting lathe, standardisation of screw thread sizes (Henry Maudslay) (UK)
1803	First production of sailing blocks using interchangeable parts (Marc Brunel, Henry Maudslay and Simon Goodrich) (UK)
1810	Food preservation technique using tin cans (Peter Durand) (UK)
1816	Milling machine (Simeon North) (US)
1821	Electric motor (Michael Faraday) (UK)
1830	Mass-manufactured steel pen nibs (William J. Gillott, William Mitchell and James Perry) (UK)
1831	Dynamo (Michael Faraday) (UK)
1833	Whitworth's method of producing accurate flat surfaces (Joseph Whitworth) (UK)
1835	Telegraph (Samuel F.B. Morse) (US)
1835	Screw propeller (Francis Pettit Smith) (UK)
1838	Morse Code (Samuel F.B. Morse) (US)
1839	Vulcanisation process of rubber (Charles Goodyear) (US)
1841	British Standard Whitworth system (screw heads) (Joseph Whitworth) (UK)
1842	Steam-powered grain elevator (Joseph Dart and Robert Dunbar) (US)
1844	Wood pulp process for paper-making (Charles Fenerty) (Canada)
1850	First commercial oil-works and oil refinery (James Young) (UK)
1853	Manned glider (George Cayley) (UK)

1853	Mechanised passenger elevator (Elisha Otis) (USA)
1853	Milk powder (Gail Borden) (US)
1856	Bessemer Process for the mass production of steel (UK)
1856	Siemens Martin Process for steel (Charles William Siemens and Pierre-Émile Martin (Germany – France)
1856	Mass production of sewing machines (Isaac M. Singer) (US)
1856	Synthetic dye (William Henry Perkin) (UK)
1858	Rotary washing machine (Hamilton Smith) (US)
1859	First modern oil well (Edwin Drake) (US)
1861	First durable colour photograph (James Clerk Maxwell) (UK)
1861	McKay shoe sewing machine (Gordon McKay) (US)
1862	First automated machine gun (Richard Gatling) (US)
1864	Solvay process or ammonia-soda process (Ernest Solvay) (Belgium)
1866	First self-propelled underwater missile (Robert Whitehead) (UK)
1866	Transatlantic cable (Cyrus Field) (US)
1867	Dynamite (Alfred Nobel) (Sweden)
1867	Typewriter (Christopher Sholes) (US)
1869	Compressed-air brake (George Westinghouse) (US)
1869	First synthetic plastic – celluloid (John Wesley Hyatt) (US)
1873	Barbed wire (Joseph Glidden) (US)
1876	First refrigerated ship (Charles Tellier) (France)
1876	Modern bicycle (Harry John Lawson) (UK)
1876	Otto type of internal combustion engine (Nikolaus Otto) (Germany)
1876	Telephone (Alexander Graham Bell) (UK)
1877	Phonograph (Thomas Alva Edison) (US)
1879	Incandescent light bulb (Thomas Alva Edison) (US)
1878	Gilchrist Thomas process (Sidney Gilchrist Thomas and Percy Gilchrist) (UK)
1878	Telephone switchboard (Almon Strowger) (US)
1881	Roll film for cameras (David Houston) (US)
1884	Paper-strip photographic film (George Eastman) (US)
1884	Steam turbine (Sir Charles Parsons) (UK)
1884	Skyscraper (William Le Baron Jenney) (US)
1885	First automobile, powered by internal combustion engine (Karl Benz) (Germany)
1886	High-voltage alternating electric current (George Westinghouse and Nikola Tesla) (USA)
1887	First practical pneumatic tyre (John Boyd Dunlop) (UK)
1888	Induction electric motor (Nikola Tesla) (US)
1891	Escalator (Jesse W. Reno) (US)
1892	Diesel-fuelled internal combustion engine (Rudolf Diesel) (Germany)
1893	First practical motor car in the United States (Charles and Frank Duryea) (US)
1893	Ferris Wheel (George Ferris) (US)
1895	Cinematographe (Lumière Brothers (France)
1897	Aspirin (Felix Hoffman) (Germany)
1898	Roller coaster (Edwin Prescott) (US)
1899	Loading coil (George Campbell) (US)

1899	Motor-driven vacuum cleaner (John Thurman) (US)
1900	Zeppelin airship (Count Ferdinand von Zeppelin) (Germany)
1901	First transatlantic signal using Morse code and wireless telegraphy (Guglielmo Marconi) (Italy)
1901	Modern tarmac (Edgar Purnell Hooley) (UK)
1903	First powered piloted plane flight (Orville and Wilbur Wright) (USA)
1907	Bakelite (Leo Baekeland) (US)
1908	Ford Model T (Henry Ford) (US)
1910	Haber process to produce ammonia (Carl Bosch and Fritz Haber) (Germany)
1913	Assembly line (Henry Ford) (US)

★ ★ ★ ★ ★

There were three crucial components of this process. The first was the new role that scientific research played in the manufacturing process, progressively displacing the practical knowledge which had largely been based upon trial-and-error practices which had characterised the First Industrial Revolution. Almost all the innovations that transformed the industries listed above, from the Bessemer steel converter to the refining of oil into kerosene, were the consequence of applied research by scientists, who patented innovations which later found practical application in the manufacturing industry. The second was the availability of energy in huge quantity, both from fossil fuels and electricity, for traction, lighting and industrial production. The third was the presence of related innovations in communications and transport, which made the delivery of goods and the transfer of information easier, faster and safer (see the previous chapter).

The impact of the new technologies on the production unit was enormous. According to Alfred Chandler, the business historian who has analysed this phenomenon in greater depth than anyone else, "the firms that transformed old or built new industries constituted a new type of industrial enterprise".[1] In contrast to the enterprises which had populated other industries in which the effects of the new production technologies were felt not at all or barely, these business enterprises were presented with new kinds of opportunities, but also had to face new constraints. They were able to enjoy a substantial reduction in per-unit production costs due to economies of scale, something which could be translated into a brutal weapon in price competition. They had, however, at the same time to commit themselves to the relevant investments in the production facilities, capital goods, and also distribution networks, as well as in the human capital employed at various levels in the coordination of the whole process. This was true both in the case of the giant *Standard Oil* refineries and plants, which progressively concentrated a major part of the US (and the world's) production of kerosene in the course of the 1870s, and in the case of the *Ford* assembly chain in the automotive industry or the disassembly chain put in place in his slaughterhouses by Gustavus Swift in the meatpacking industry. Both combined huge investments in physical infrastructure, in skilled human capital and in managerial hierarchies.

Capital intensity, scaled to a level never attained before, led to many consequences (not least to the ownership structure of the companies, which sharply increased its degree of dispersion), among which one momentous consequence was the mandatory necessity of operating at the appropriate scale, in order to avoid the risk of a dramatic increase in cost-per-unit due to overwhelming production costs. This, in turn, led to an obsessive push to acquire market shares in order to sell the high volumes produced, as well as a strategy of rationalisation of the production capacity. Thus, between the second half of the 1880s and the First World War, an intensive process of concentration, by means of consolidation strategies through mergers, acquisitions and often through the creation of trusts and cartels, took place. Just to mention the most standard case, that of the US, between 1885 and 1920, nearly 5,000 "consolidations" took place, one-fifth of which occurred in 1901 alone. This wave of consolidations led to the birth of industrial giants such as *US Steel, American Tobacco, Dupont* and *International Harvester*. This phenomenon involved almost every branch of manufacturing, but was particularly pronounced in some branches, such as food and beverages, primary metals, chemicals, bituminous products, and also transport equipment, machinery and metal products.

The new industrial corporations grew bigger and bigger through processes of internal and external growth. New plants were built, and new units of production were gathered under the same corporate umbrella. The process resulted in the spread of oligopolistic positions in the new capital-intensive industries. In many industries, companies started a process of diversification from their original field into related fields of production, in order to exploit economies of scale and scope better, particularly in distribution and administration. The phenomenon was extremely complex, and has been effectively summarised by the core research in business history in the course of the last few decades.

It may be tempting (and this has, in fact, been done by several scholars) to identify the diffusion of the large, multi-unit enterprise with the birth of the "modern" multinational corporation. However, this is not completely true. In principle, the rise of the large multi-unit enterprise did not immediately, in many cases, coincide with the inter-nationalisation of corporate activity and its location outside domestic borders. While, in some cases, and, in particular, when small national markets were involved, the inter-nationalisation of the activity first through exports, and then through direct production, took place immediately, in others internationalisation was definitely a further stage fol-lowing the domestic affirmation of the company on the domestic market. In the case of even giant corporations such as *Swift & Co.*, a pioneer in vertical integration in the meatpacking industry, the internationalisation of production came a long time after the acquisition of a semi-monopolistic position in the giant US domestic market.

The rise of big business, however, was undoubtedly linked to a process of internationalisation of production in many cases. The Second Industrial Revolution created a number of premises which led companies to initiate a process of integration of production across borders. These determinants, which will be investigated in depth in the following section, resulted in powerful incentives for entrepreneurs to extend themselves beyond the limits of their domestic borders with modalities and strategies never adopted before. They created new kinds of organisations, which further increased the level of "biodiversity" within the international economy.

3. Big Business and the "Modern Multinationals"

There are several aspects within the rise of large corporations which contribute to explaining why a number of the new firms grew not only larger and became leaders in their respective national markets, but also inclined more and more acutely towards a strategy of internationalisation, both in commercial terms and in terms of direct pro-duction abroad. From the perspective of the firm, or, more precisely, of the corporation, there were some elements which pushed in the direction of greater involvement abroad.

The first powerful driver in the process of internationalisation came from one of the main characteristics of the production processes of the Second Industrial Revolution. Besides the appropriate scale, almost all the innovations that transformed some of the existing industries and created new ones required a structural change in the organisation of production. The previous industrial revolution had, in fact, determined a transition from a workshop-based process to one based upon the factory, upon inanimate energy sources and upon the mechanisation of the production process, which, however, continued to be fragmented and discrete. The cotton factory, the symbol of this phase, was either a spinning or a weaving unit. Both could, albeit not necessarily, be under the same roof or not, and both normally involved a variable number of cottage-workers, spinners and weavers, who added their work hours at home to those performed by the factory workers. Even in the presence of high volumes of production, the process was, nonetheless, far from being a continuous one. The Second Industrial Revolution was instead based upon continuous production processes. A substantial portion of the cost savings in scale-intensive processes derived from the continuous flow of the production process. In other words, in order to be effective, the technical innovations introduced by the Second Industrial Revolution required the production flow to run smoothly and without interruption. This was true both in processes of a chemical nature (for instance, modern steel-making), and for complex assembly lines. In both cases, the production flow could not be interrupted without substantial loss or damage to the final product.

As a consequence, these intrinsic characteristics incentivised entrepreneurs to undertake strategies which were finalised to bring under control the risk of interruptions, shortages and bottlenecks, which could eventually slow down, or even interrupt, the "throughput" of raw materials, semi-finished and finished goods. Vertical integration strategies both backward in procurement and forward in distribution were directed to the internalisation of both the market for inputs and the activity of intermediaries, that is, the merchants who had, in the past, as discussed in the previous chapters, constituted the link between supply and demand.

4. Integrating backward

Backward integration into the sources of inputs became increasingly frequent, even if the internalisation of these markets within a single organisation was anything but obvious; in the end, there were national and international markets for raw materials, both of which had functioned and were functioning reasonably well. According to some calculations, between 1870 and 1913, the world trade in primary products and manufactured goods grew by a factor of between three and four, with a sharp increase in intercontinental flows – still of a relatively asymmetric nature, with the industrialised Western nations exporting manufactures to colonised or quasi-colonised Asian and African countries, which, in their turn, delivered agricultural products and other natural resources. The previously mentioned journal the *Economist* was regularly publishing the prices of raw materials and other inputs, "carefully revised every Friday afternoon by an eminent house in each Department". Here, one can at least see quotations for almost everything, from Java cocoa to French eggs, from Canadian ashes to Messina lemons, Chinese silk and tea, and Scandinavian timber. The prices of various kinds of metals, oils, saltpetre and various provisions were carefully reported. For cotton, one could not only have access to the prices, but also the quantities traded during the previous years in order to obtain information about both relative scarcities and expected price trends. In sum, transparency was very high, and, due to improvements in transport and communication techniques, one could be relatively sure about on-time delivery and about price convergence across different markets. Notwithstanding this, all the items listed by the *Economist* were being employed in discrete processes of production, for which the sudden scarcity of the inputs could pose a serious threat to the ability of the firm to fulfil the orders that it had received, but not damage the whole batch of production, as could happen, for example, with refining or smelting. In the event of a supplier failing to meet an order, a cocoa-butter producer could easily buy what he needed on the Liverpool market, or wait for a week for the next shipment from the Ivory Coast, or even afford to waste a batch of production that was still relatively small in size. In contrast, for a steel company using the Bessemer converter, the interruption of the process due to input scarcity meant not only a huge production batch had to be scrapped, but also that the company would incur other costs inherent to the interruption of production which led to a subsequent pressure to increase the fixed costs on future production prices, and therefore on returns.

A quite obvious policy might be (and, in fact, was) the creation of inventories or stocks which buffered the risk of shortages, but this was, in many cases, not only difficult, but also expensive. And, as the *Pirelli* case described above shows, there were external events – for instance, wars or other forms of turmoil – which had profound long-lasting negative effects on the international markets for inputs. In addition, even in presence of efficient global markets, some inputs were different from others, since some were rare, not renewable, or were simply subject to great, unforeseeable fluctuations in price (as occurs today for the rare minerals which have recently become indispensable for the production of laptop computers, smartphones and tablets).

A second, non-trivial, reason, and one which greatly incentivised strategies of direct control of the inputs for production, lay in two issues introduced by the requirements of the new technological paradigm, which transformed the nature of the inputs as well. First of all, in some cases, even the mere production of these inputs was a process which involved a certain degree of technological knowledge and the skill necessary to ensure a minimum level of quality of the inputs themselves, as, for instance, occurred in the case of oil drilling. Second, the production of primary products became increasingly characterised by a growing capital intensity, due both to the specificities and to the scale of the production process (the example of petroleum is again significant here). Thus, where the availability of a high volume and steady flow of good (and constant) quality inputs became a key component for the competitive standing of the firm, strategies of integration became increasingly very convenient. Production technology, in sum, was the force that made vertical integration a recurrent form of behaviour, something which had seldom been put in place by chartered companies or individual merchants (see the previous chapters).

Backward vertical integration could thus be a viable, if not definitive, solution. Clearly, when possible, the strategies of vertical integration tended to privilege the internal market for a number of intuitive reasons. Many of the "new" firms generated by the Second Industrial Revolution accompanied the expansion of their operations with the acquisition of domestic input sources. For instance, a case in point is that of US oil producers expanding in Texas – which, by the way, had become part of the domestic market only in 1845 – from the beginning of the twentieth century. In other cases – as in the case of *Pirelli* – backward vertical integration could be possible only by crossing domestic borders, and directly acquiring the control of resources abroad. The agribusiness provides a standard reference case here. In order to secure their control of perishable crops, in terms of quality and delivery timing, both European and American companies invested considerable amounts of resources in acquiring the direct ownership of plantations and processing plants. In her fundamental research into American business abroad prior to 1914, Mira Wilkins focuses on US "spillovers" (with explicit reference to geographic proximity, which made the process of expansion much easier) in Mexico, Canada, the Caribbean and South America. In 1914, out of a total of about 2.6 billion US dollars of direct investments abroad (at book value), those related to mining (excluding petroleum) and agriculture amounted to more than one-third of the total, the bulk of which were located in the areas just mentioned. In all these regions, American capital "spilled over" in various directions: in Mexico, investments included copper, lead and coal mines, rubber plant plantations set up to provide an alternative to the British control of the market in the Far East, and, of course, oil. Canada was fundamental, as one can easily imagine, in mining, while the Caribbean attracted backward investments in fruit plantations (in Jamaica, Colombia and Santo Domingo, for instance), sugar and tobacco. The standard case in this regard is that of the *United Fruit Company* (UFC), formed in 1899 through a multi-merger of minor companies, which controlled planta- tions in Jamaica, Santo Domingo, Costa Rica and other countries in the area, where bananas and, to a minor extent, other tropical fruit were cultivated for the US domestic market. Initially, the company integrated its production through the purchase of fruit from independent farmers, but, in the years preceding the First World War, it increased its ownership stake in plantations through a policy involving direct control of the land.

Cases of backward integration which aimed at directly controlling the production and early transformation of inputs multiplied very quickly almost everywhere in industrialised countries. Soon, producers learned that, when large quantities and constant flows of essential goods were at stake, direct control could help them to manage situations in which the "smoothness" of the markets was threatened. For instance, in the case of a renewable natural resource, but one which was limited in terms of quantity, such as natural rubber, already mentioned above, vertical integration (plus appropriate transfer prices) became necessary in order to face the threat of sharp cost increases due, for instance, to changes in custom duty tariffs. Integration policies also began to be undertaken as a strategic move in reaction to similar actions undertaken by the main competitors. This was a very different framework from the one which had prevailed in the preceding centuries.

The Second Industrial Revolution, in sum, created necessities in production that had never been experienced before, which impacted heavily on entrepreneurial strategies, leading to the creation of new investment strategies abroad. The varieties of backward-integration strate- gies are almost endless, and, to different extents, were pursued on both sides of the Atlantic, mainly where the incentives coming from the new production paradigm became sufficiently significant. International business scholars have labelled the investment strategies undertaken in order to secure direct control of raw or intermediate materials – the materials necessary to perform the process of production efficiently in industries characterised by a mandatory continuity in their production flow – as *resource-seeking*.

5. Integrating forward

More or less simultaneously with backward integration, scale-intensive and capital- intensive processes implied another strategy which profoundly affected the shape that internationally active companies assumed.

First of all, particularly, but not only, when the domestic market was small, companies producing on a high scale found a clear incentive to export, thereby seeking new mar- kets for their products. As shown above, the decades preceding the First World War were characterised by a sharp increase in the volume of world trade, not only due to export flows of natural resources and other inputs from the less-developed countries to the industrialised countries, but also due to the flow of manufactured goods between the developed nations and the other countries which were endeavouring to catch up in the process of industrialisation at the time. The Second Industrial Revolution meant, in fact, a growing transfer of the "new" products to markets that were becoming increasingly attractive. Exports were initially a fairly viable solution, also due to the increasing trade openness which characterised the global economy until the First World War (see the previous chapter). To return to the case of *Pirelli*, it is thus not surprising that the Milan-based company was searching for, and finding, its natural market outlet only partially inside its country of origin. From its very inception, it was tapping other different markets, both in the most advanced economies (for instance, the United Kingdom) and in those which were actively involved in the process of catching up, mainly through a process of infrastructure building (this was, for instance, the case of southern Europe and the Balkans, and, in the case of *Pirelli*, of South America). In addition, the Second Industrial Revolution paved the way for the large-scale production of mass-consumption goods characterised by a progressively decreasing price per unit, something which, added to the falling transport prices and low tariffs, enormously incentivised export activity.

All the quantitative evidence available shows, however, that the huge increase in trade volume was accompanied by a parallel increase in the volume of investments which aimed to control productive assets located outside domestic borders. The data are, as one can imagine, highly unreliable. According to John Dunning, on the eve of the First World War "at least $14 billion had been invested in enterprises or branch plants in which either a single or a group of non-resident investors owned a majority of substantial minority equity interest...". The pioneering British scholar in international business also stressed how "This amount represented about 35 per cent of the total long-term international debt at that time; a ratio (...) more significant than at any time before or since".[2]

In sum, entrepreneurs had, for the first time, started to invest unprecedented amounts of capital abroad in a strategic move undertaken in order to control indispensable components of the production process, more than their investment in resources, in order to obtain high, or at least acceptable, returns on the capital invested. These investments were, in part, oriented towards the acquisition, as stated above, of durable and exclusive control of inputs, but not exclusively so. Increasingly, internationally active companies undertook policies of export substitution through direct production abroad. Notwithstanding some relevant differences in the industries involved and the countries targeted, both US and European multinationals precociously expanded abroad, opening plants for assembling, and, more often, producing goods to be sold locally, and even re-exported. Just to mention a few examples, immediately before the First World War some of the leading companies in their respective fields had invested in several locations in both developed and developing countries: *Bayer* had seven plants in the US, the UK and continental Europe; *Nestlé* produced in fourteen countries, including America and Australia. *Saint-Gobain*, the French glassmaker, had started a capillary strategy of expansion in Western Europe (see Box 4.2). *Singer*, which, by the year 1914, was one of the largest companies in the world (ranked seventh, in terms of sales) with an astonishing 90 per cent of the global market in sewing machines ("the nineteenth century antecedent of the motor car, radio, and television"[3]) had expanded from its base in the US to Europe, opening factories in the UK, Germany, Russia and Austria-Hungary, plus a sales network of global reach from the Middle East to southern Africa and the Far East. *Siemens* was producing electrical appliances and machinery in developed and developing European countries. Even more from peripheral countries such as Italy, as the *Pirelli* case shows, and Sweden, companies invested abroad: *Ericsson* opened factories for the production of telephone equipment in Europe and America, while *SKF*, the producer of rolling bearings, was present in Russia, France, Germany, the US and the UK. The Belgian chemical company *Solvay* had opened production plants in all the main European countries and in the US prior to the First World War. A similar geographic diffusion had reached the Dutch company *Naamloze Vennootschap Margarine Unie*, which later merged with the British company *Lever Brothers* to become *Unilever*.

The Second Industrial Revolution was, in sum, introducing something new into international business, something hitherto unknown in international entrepreneurship. In sharp contrast to their predecessors (international merchants and chartered companies), not only were entrepreneurs committing huge amounts of resources to the acquisition of stable and direct control of inputs, and buying ownership stakes in distant countries endowed with natural resources, instead of relying on market mechanisms; they were also starting to produce abroad what, in the past, had been sold through the intermediation of merchants or local agents. This process of forward integration, (or, as some scholars prefer to label it, the further "internalisation" of transactions), has been called a *market-seeking* strategy.

6. Why produce abroad?

However, if resource-seeking practices are intuitive only relatively, for the purposes of this volume it is worth analysing in greater depth the motivations behind the decision to locate production activity abroad, a decision that was probably even more momentous and risky, in some cases, than that of investing in securing the procurement of the necessary inputs. The available evidence allows some generalisations to be made. Entrepreneurs and companies that located production, or even the assembling of complex products, abroad, were driven by a wide set of motivations which can be grouped into the following broad categories, which have, however, to be considered as simultaneous, rather than mutually exclusive, drivers of the process.

Reacting

The first group of motives essentially refers to a sort of reaction to some external shock, which, in some way or other, alters or modifies the existing scenario, diminishing the incentives to export and increasing those attached to on-site production. A first, quite intuitive case much celebrated in the existing literature refers to the companies which took the decision to invest directly in production facilities abroad as a consequence of a rise in customs duty tariffs and other import barriers. This motivation, which is one of the standard theoretical explanations for the decision to produce abroad, found its concrete application from the very inception of the modern multinational corporation. Notwithstanding the general climate favourable to international flows of free trade and the overall growing integration of the world economy, and partly as a reaction to the rising inequality brought about by globalisation in some peripheral countries, the last couple of decades of the nineteenth century and the beginning of the twentieth century right up until 1914 saw a proliferation of protectionist stances, in both the primary and secondary sectors. This was not particularly evident in under-developed areas, such as Africa or Asia in general, which, moreover, were still under colonial rule, but it was abundantly clear in developed countries, such as the United States, Canada, France and, to some degree, in Germany, as well as in developing peripheries, such as Italy, Spain and the Russian Empire. It was also true in South America, as in the case of Argentina, but, above all, for Mexico, Brazil and Colombia. From another point of view, given the effect which they had on the production strategies of international firms, tariffs could more or less consciously be introduced in order to attract foreign direct investments and gain direct access to foreign, modern technologies in industries in which domestic entrepreneurship was lacking or unwilling to commit the required financial resources. Foreign investments, due, to a large extent, to the necessity to circumvent trade barriers, were a substantial component of the Russian catching-up process before the Communist Revolution in 1917. The attractiveness of foreign investments as a conscious instrument of economic and industrial policy, clearly started in a phase (the Second Industrial Revolution) in which the products – otherwise exported – embodied a bulk of specific knowledge that governments wanted to spread domestically. This was clearly a strong incentive for those who had access to these technologies to replicate them abroad, especially when other competitors were threatening to do the same.

Tariffs and incentives are a typical example of external shocks which favoured the risky decision to invest abroad. Another external shock might be an aggressive move by a competitor in these oligopolistic markets. There are several cases of direct investments being undertaken as a strategic move to contrast the foreign expansion of a competitor transferring its production abroad and selling at a cheaper price. According to some research, imitation and pre-emption strategies had already been a common trait of the expansion of US companies before the First World War, as in the case of *General Electric* and *Westinghouse*, which were competing for leadership in both the United Kingdom and Russia at the end of the nineteenth century. This was, it seems, common practice. In the above-mentioned case of *Pirelli*, the decision to open the plant in Burton-on-Trent, UK, in 1928, was clearly due both to the increase in tariffs and to the fact that the main competitors of the Milanese company, including *Firestone* and *Goodyear*, were planning a similar move. Imitation strategies could also be a sort of indirect reaction to competitive threats. One good example is provided by the policies adopted by German electro-mechanics producers in southern Europe, based upon the direct control of local provi-ders of electricity and/or railway and tramway companies. These companies were, in their turn, both generating returns and, at the same time, importing the necessary capital goods from Germany. This strategy was common to the main players in the industry, and resulted in a wave of direct investments from Germany to the rapidly developing peripheries in southern Europe. The creation of companies abroad, which were supposed to act as "bridges" towards other markets which were considered attractive, was a typical move in the case of international oligopolies, a move which was likely to stimulate a reaction on the part of their competitors, including any present at local level.

Being pro-active

It is important to note that the perspective described above considers exports, in some way, as an "optimal" status, and the location of operations abroad as a sort of second best, or "first best under constraints". As we will see in the following chapters, however, there are cases in which the location of operations abroad is far from being a second best, and takes place not as an alternative to exports, but as a strategic move in itself. In some cases, direct production was the sole possibility in order to gain access to additional markets. To put it another way, in some cases, the decision to produce abroad was not primarily the consequence of a change in the framework which made exports less profitable (or not profitable at all). Taking this argument to the extreme, there are cases in which producing abroad is justified also in presence of very low tariffs and other barriers, or even in their absence. A good example in this regard is provided by the history of the internationalisation of *Singer*, which, by the beginning of the First World War, was probably the most effective example of the new "modern" multinational. After strengthening its position on the domestic market, the sewing-machine manufacturer had already begun, as a quite standard move, to expand abroad through exports during the American Civil War (1861–1865), which had depressed the internal market, a strategy reinforced by the negative cycle started by the agricultural depression in the mid-1870s. By the mid-1860s, *Singer* was exporting its products to Europe, starting from markets, such as the British one, which were characterised by a relatively high *per capita* income and a very low level of protection. *Singer*, however, was not making money out of this export activity at the very beginning. There were a number of reasons for this, including the fact that transport costs were simply excessive. *Singer*'s sewing machines were made of cast iron, which made freight costs grow ahead of the average low prices on the British market. The transport revolution, in sum, was determinant in the increase of world trade, but, in some cases, it was still not enough to remove all the barriers to competition. And the same was true for other goods, characterised by heavy weight, low added value, or which were simply highly perishable. A good example can be found the production of chocolate, which, during the second half of the nineteenth century, had evolved from an "élitist" nature to that of a mass-consumption product. This was thanks to the innovations that characterised its production process and the growing availability of raw materials at low prices, again thanks to the transport revolution. The Low Countries, France and the UK were leaders in the mechanisation of chocolate production in Europe. Even if not completely perishable like other foodstuffs, the industrialisation of its production prompted a wave of investments in production plants across Europe, due, in part, to the intrinsic characteristics of the product itself in terms of its acceptable level of quality regarding preservation.

Another case in which exports were a possible, but less viable or less efficient, solution than producing locally, was linked (and still is very much today) to the peculiarities of markets in developing countries from a "political economy" perspective. The case of southern European countries again provides some compelling evidence. As the history of *Pirelli* shows, markets were sometimes heavily conditioned by public demand, particularly in developing countries. To sell cables for communications, electric machinery or similar goods both to central and local administrations, or to obtain orders which often tended to privilege domestic firms, led to the necessity of setting up local facilities, in some cases joint-venturing with local producers in order to leverage their institutional connections. The proliferation of subsidiaries of not only European, but also American, companies in manufacturing industries relating to utilities, for instance, in countries such as Spain, Portugal, Italy and the Balkans, can be seen as the response to specific conditions in the local markets and in some particular industries. For instance, the decision, in 1906, by the German steel producer *Mannesmann* to open a plant for the production of steel pipes in Italy was driven by the promising conditions in the internal market due to the urbanisation process and the expansion of utilities. The Germans, who could rely on a patent for the fabrication of seamless steel pipes which granted them a stable advantage, were, however, well aware of the fact that success in the Italian market, in the presence of protection barriers, was only possible under two conditions. The first was a local factory, which could allow them to maintain control of the production process while, at the same time, grasping the opportunities of the local market; the second was the involvement of a domestic, well-established company which could grant it the necessary political connections. The *Società Italiana Tubi Mannesmann* opened its facility in Dalmine, between Bergamo and Milan, and was an almost equal joint venture between the German company and the Italian *Società Metallurgica Italiana*, of the Orlando family, which had an established presence in the domestic steel industry.

The *Mannesmann* case highlights two additional elements which contribute to explaining why the corporations generated by the Second Industrial Revolution started to produce simultaneously in various locations across the globe. The first had to do with the necessity of adapting to local conditions. The technological change, in fact, had created not only huge market opportunities, but also complex products. Other things being equal, the sale of cotton textiles in a foreign market involved much less complexity in terms of relations with the local consumers than, say, the sale of electro-mechanic machinery, machine tools, telephones or office machinery. In principle, this closeness or proximity to the market was solved first through the establishment of selling agencies and, later, by subsidiaries in charge of the commercialisation of the exported items, and this was what actually happened in many cases as a standard practice. In others, however, agencies and commercial subsidiaries proved to be insufficiently effective in providing useful information about the local market; nor did they prove to be effective in managing the relationships with the relevant local customers, and greater involvement by the mother company was required.

The second element has, again, to do with the technological characteristics of the Second Industrial Revolution. The stories of both *Mannesmann* and *Pirelli* show how the Second Industrial Revolution, much more than the First, created (in some industries more than in others) technological expertise and sophisticated knowledge embodied both in products and in production processes. As noted by the early literature on the rise and growth of the modern corporation, the industry leaders were characterised by a high intensity of knowledge, learning, capabilities and competencies, in production, processing, marketing and organisation. To a certain extent, this could be embodied in the products to be exported, as the local agents could effectively mediate the transfer of (sometimes very) sophisticated knowledge to local markets. In some cases, however, they were not effective (or not committed) enough. The early history of modern multinationals abounds with situations in which the first step in establishing a permanent foreign presence was the decision to establish a local commercial subsidiary in charge of selling complex products on the local market in the most appropriate way. To return to *Pirelli* again, its expansion in South America and Central Europe could, in theory, be managed through independent agents; in reality, the type of products and their technological characteristics pushed strongly towards the establishment of local commercial, and production-oriented, subsidiaries.

Box 4.2: *Saint-Gobain*: foreign expansion, technological change and market-seeking multinationalisation

In the field of plate glass, *Saint-Gobain* has a particular place in history both as a pioneer and as a contemporary leading actor. Created in 1665 by Jean-Baptiste Colbert as a *Manufacture Royale*, in order to substitute for the importation of glass goods into France, *Saint-Gobain* is to this day still a global leader in the glass industry. Its global extension and its diversified and integrated structure, according to many observers, represents the French way of multinationalising enterprises. This company began its activity as a national monopoly, granted under the licence of the French king in the seventeenth century, a licence or concession which it held until the eve of the nineteenth century. In 1830, *Saint-Gobain* became a limited company and started to focus on the international market, expanding its sales abroad through the establishment of an international network of sales agencies (for instance, the first warehouse in New York was created in 1830, followed by London in 1845, and then during the following decade, warehouses were established in many European cities, including Cologne in 1854). Afterwards, *Saint-Gobain* directly invested abroad, creating units in the main European countries, in Germany (1853), Italy (1889), Belgium (1896), Poland (1899), the Netherlands (1904) and Spain (1905). At the same time, *Saint-Gobain* expanded into chemical production in a major way, both as a consequence of a vertical integration strategy to obtain raw materials and of a policy of market-ward diversification. While *Saint-Gobain* maintained a national profile in the chemical field, by the end of the nineteenth century, it had become a leading multinational company in the plate glass industry, which was the result of a deliberate strategy of foreign growth that sought the conquest of new markets. This foreign expansion was accompanied by a reorganisation of its structures that centralised the international management of the whole group. In many respects, *Saint-Gobain* is a paradigmatic example of an enterprise that became a modern multinational through a phase of internationalisation of sales that was followed by export substitution, according to the general theoretical framework of the product cycle theory.

The history of *Saint-Gobain*, however, reveals more interesting insights about the nexus between the development of a multinational managerial structure and technological progress. Having developed its own technology in the manufacturing of high-quality plate glass and mirrors, this company diverged from the business model of small glaziers. While, in this field, cheaper plate glass was traditionally blown and cut, *Saint-Gobain* developed, in an early stage of its history, a two-step technology based upon the flowing of the hot liquid glass material and the further polishing of the plate glass once it had cooled. Blown plate glass, which was essentially used for house windows, was smaller and had many imperfections which made it unsuitable for the manufacturing of goods that demanded perfect transparency, such as mirrors and shop windows. *Saint-Gobain* focused on the "luxury" market of mirrors and big shop windows, which shaped its managerial structure and its commercial strategies. As soon as new applications for this kind of glass emerged, such as in the automotive industry, *Saint-Gobain* was ready to occupy the field and to start new commercial and technological developments. For instance, *Saint-Gobain* introduced the use of this type of glass in the car industry and was able to pioneer the technical research into safety glass, which was achieved during the interwar period. While small "blowing" glaziers had proto-industrial units with local markets and remained without vertical integration or R&D strategies, *Saint-Gobain* had been born a vast and technologically advanced business which already had a national market during the eighteenth century, which it increasingly expanded abroad throughout the nineteenth century, leading the international market at the beginning of the twentieth century.

Before cars had come to represent a further market diversification for *Saint-Gobain*, urban transformations and commercial developments during the second half of the nineteenth century had created new markets for plate glass both in the principal

French cities and abroad. In some cases, these new commercial opportunities were fulfilled by the development of national enterprises that replaced imports, such as *Pilkington* in the UK, *Union des Glacieries* in Belgium, and *Pittsburgh Plate Glass* in the US, while, in other cases, they led *Saint-Gobain* to became an international actor, driving the strategy of the French firm to the creation of foreign direct investments (FDIs). New markets for quality mirror plate glass and rising international competition pushed *Saint-Gobain*, on the one hand, to develop new economies of scale and to integrate its production upward in order to reduce the unitary costs of the "hot phase" of glass production, and, on the other, to develop new and more efficient technologies for the "cold phase." In particular, *Saint-Gobain* succeeded in reducing the price of the top-quality plate glass, while further technological improvements led the company to enter the upper part of the market for window glass. While the classical dichotomy that existed in the glass market between blown window glass and plate glass was not totally erased, technical improvements had merged some of the specific uses of glass at the end of the nineteenth century. Different qualities of plate glass were sold by *Saint-Gobain* with different overall qualities and thickness which, at the lower quality level, competed with the blown window glass while, at the top level, it represented the required choice for big commercial storefronts and mirrors.

The first expansion of the company in Germany during the mid-nineteenth century anticipated this trend of urban transformation, characterised by the commercial expansion of cities and by the blossoming of commercial streets and department stores, and of technical improvements that *Saint-Gobain* carried out in the "cold phase". According to the most authoritative historian of *Saint-Gobain*, Jean-Pierre Daviet, the first units that *Saint-Gobain* owned in Germany did not lead the French firm to become a true multinational. *Saint-Gobain* took over these businesses in the German glass business by exploiting the personal and financial networks of its administrators, and this did not lead to the creation of real global management. Daviet suggests that in the mid-nineteenth century, in spite of the FDIs of *Saint-Gobain* in Germany, the firm was a "multi-nations" enterprise, rather than a multinational. Actually, during the 1850s, the international activity of the group was still marginal and 80 per cent of *Saint-Gobain*'s sales were still concentrated in or around Paris. Things changed at the end of the nineteenth century, when the further expansion of the group was decided in a more competitive commercial environment and in a more advanced technological context. The decision to create a unit in Italy, which pioneered the big wave of foreign expansion in the following decade, corresponded to a deliberate two-fold strategy, made by the head of *Saint-Gobain*, to maintain a quota of the international market in order to face the rising competition of the Belgian and UK producers, and to cultivate new markets outside France thanks to the installation of FDI. The expansion abroad was concomitant with the installation of new mechanised processes for the "cold phase" of plate glass manufacturing both in the older units of the group and in the new ones. The creation of new units outside France and technological progress in the manufacturing of plate glass re-shaped the organisation of the glass branch of the group, whose direction was unified in Paris into a general division that managed the *glaceries*, and their output, as a whole.

This intimate link between the transformation of the organisational methods of *Saint-Gobain* during its phase of internationalisation and the technological progress in glass production was epitomised by Lucien Delloye, who became a leading figure on the managerial board of *Saint-Gobain* from the 1880s to the Great War. Entering

Saint-Gobain in 1881, the French engineer was the designer of the new mechanised glass-polishing technology and he was the architect of the go-global strategy of *Saint-Gobain*. Whereas the "cold phase" had, to a certain extent, been performed by hand, he invented a mechanised plate upon which glass could be polished by powerful rotating motors. He directly helped the installation of this new technology in the French units during the 1880s; he supervised its installation in Germany in the first FDI of the group, and was behind the expansion of the group in both Italy and Belgium. He also became the first director of the Italian unit in Pisa, where he supervised the production start-up and the adaptation of the new technology to the Italian plant. After this task, he was recalled to Paris in 1896, where he took the position of General Vice-Director of the Glass Division at *Saint-Gobain* headquarters, helping to design the strategy to invest in Belgium, after which he became the General Director of the Belgian division in 1903. New output and new economies of scale meant, on the one hand, lower costs of production, but, on the other, it also meant technical rigidities in adapting the output to the conditions of the given market. Whereas the glass division had previously only supervised the actual work of each of the units, which were somewhat autonomous in how they carried out their production, Delloye centralised the production programme of each unit through the harmonisation of the supply–demand balance on a global scale. One of the main outcomes of this new managerial organisation was the decision to reduce the output of the Italian unit between the 1890s and the Great War, whose production costs were higher than the other units of *Saint-Gobain*, and to import to Italy from the Belgian and German plants, which were suffering from the harsh competition of *Saint-Gobain*'s competitors in their respective national markets.

This box was written by Marco Bertilorenzi.

★ ★ ★ ★ ★

7. Where to invest, and how?

Producing abroad implied at least two other important decisions: where, and how, two issues which, as one could expect, were radically new for many entrepreneurs attempting strategies of international growth.

In the case of resource-seeking investments, entrepreneurs were free to decide about the location of their investments only to a very limited extent. In the case of renewable natural resources, for instance, cocoa or palm oil, it was possible up to a certain point even to start cultivations in locations that were more convenient than others (for instance, starting a plantation of rubber trees in Brazil in order to diversify purchases geographically and to reduce the dependence on East Asian crops). In the case of other natural resources, the location of the activity depended on the abundance of nature or on pure chance. However, as far as manufacturing was concerned, things were different, and the degree of freedom in decisions about the location of investments was much higher. In general, as in the past, market perspectives and potentials were the key drivers in the process. Once the decision to substitute exports with direct production had been taken, the location of the activity was the result of a mixture of variables of different and

changing nature across space and time. Some years ago, Mira Wilkins proposed a taxonomy based upon concrete historical experiences, which closely reflected the decisional
process and the behaviour of early multinationals.[4] What Wilkins defines as "parameters"
can be translated into variables in an ideal regression explaining the choice among several
potential locations for an investment abroad. Among these variables, one must consider
the number of *opportunities* provided by a given market in comparison to others (e.g. in
terms of market potential, or the absence of local competitors), as well as the set of *political
conditions* in a given country when compared to others (not only in terms of stability and
of openness towards foreign capital, but also in terms of the general climate in which
business activity took place, including the relationship between capital and labour). In
addition, investors tended (as they do today) to discriminate among countries upon the
basis of their physical but, above all, cultural proximity: the selection took place on the
basis of language, for instance, but also on the basis of other elements which increased
the degree of *familiarity* of one location instead of another, such as the presence of emi-
grant communities, or the presence of a common culture, shared beliefs, even considerations about religion. Often, location choices were made upon the basis of *indirect*
considerations. Some locations enjoyed a strategic position. They allowed markets or
areas where a direct investment was hardly feasible to be reached. To return to the *Pirelli*
case, it is clear, for instance, that the decision to open a production plant in Argentina
simultaneously responded to a wide range of factors which discriminated in favour of this
country instead of another. These factors ranged from the high opportunities implicit in a
fast-developing economy to issues of familiarity with the local business community in
which the Italians were already well represented, to the opportunity of leveraging this
location in order to reach other markets in the sub-continent. Bearing in mind the four
parameters listed above, together with the comparatively high degree of protectionism
which characterised their economy, one can easily explain why, by 1914, the United
States was probably ranked first in terms of attractiveness for the location of foreign direct
investments, immediately followed by Czarist Russia (which, in just a few years time,
would lose all its attractiveness), Canada, Brazil and Argentina.

A general consideration, at this point, concerns the "aggregate attractiveness" of some
macro areas in contrast with others. The dawn of the "modern multinational" consolidated – in terms of the distribution of investment activity – the hierarchy of the
countries which had emerged from the First Industrial Revolution and from the process
of the "great divergence" (see Chapter 1) between the West and the (South) East regions
of the world. The aggregate data available on foreign direct investments mask a very
variegated situation. By 1914, foreign investments were, in fact, coming exclusively from
developed countries, with the UK, the US and Germany – the leading countries in the
Second Industrial Revolution – accounting for 75 per cent of the total. Their composition was, however, profoundly diverse in its nature, and this heavily influenced their
location. Clearly, the bulk of direct investments went to areas endowed with the natural
resources necessary to boost the transforming activities of the Second Industrial Revolution. The resource-seeking vertical integration took place first. This had put the primary
sector, and the countries richly endowed with natural resources, at the top of the ranking
as the recipients of direct investments. By 1914, developing economies (Latin America,
Africa, Asia and the Middle East) accounted for two-thirds of the total stock of the
investments. However, the data may be misleading: in Latin America, the *Pirelli* direct
investment in a rubber vulcanisation plant for the local consumer market is considered to
be the same as the backward acquisition of a Brazilian plantation by a US company

involved in tropical fruit processing for the American market. What it is possible to say is that, as the available literature clearly stresses, the majority of the direct investments in advanced economies and a significant stake of those in countries characterised by intense catching-up processes, was in manufacturing, banking and services, and was basically of a market-seeking nature. Peripheral locations in the process of development were normally the destination of resource-seeking investments. This was, however, what allowed the now marginal areas in Africa, Asia and South America to remain in some way (and, as we shall see, in a tributary way) involved in the general framework of the global economy.

A second issue – which is, however, relatively less explored in the literature, partially due to a lack of acceptable quantitative evidence – is "how" the investments took place or, to use the current international business jargon, the prevailing "entry mode" or "entry strategy" used by companies investing abroad. Once the option for direct investment to substitute for market mechanisms had been selected or decided upon, and once the region to be targeted had been selected, it then became necessary to work out the most appropriate form for the investment. This was another new and momentous challenge for entrepreneurs active in the international economy. Again, in the case of *Pirelli*, the company's early internationalisation patterns are quite instructive. The Spanish investment was, to use the standard terminology, greenfield. The same happened in Buenos Aires in 1917. Spain was, of course, an easier and closer location for a company that was still comparatively young, but it shared with Argentina the prospects of fast development, plus a number of other favourable location conditions, which included the absence of serious local competitive threats. The pattern of investment in the UK, which was set up in more or less the same period, was different: the Southampton plant was a greenfield investment (as in Spain and South America), but the *Pirelli Cable Works Ltd*, which was running the investment, was a 50–50 per cent joint venture between the Italian company and its British partner, which was in charge of the commercial and marketing aspects.

It is, of course, not easy to generalise. However, the available evidence points in the direction that, in the phase preceding the First World War, greenfield investments exceeded acquisitions by far, not only in developing countries, but also in the more developed ones. The reasons for this are quite intuitive. Apart from investments in the primary sector, which were characterised by the acquisition of a source of input and/or the creation of exploitation infrastructures, investments in the secondary sector could rarely take place through the acquisition of an activity already in place. The examples mentioned above, including those realised through a partnership or a joint venture, almost all took place through the creation of new plants built from scratch. Reliable aggregate data are quite difficult to find; however, the available research tends to confirm the prevalence of greenfield investments over the acquisition of existing facilities. For instance, out of a sample of 495 foreign investments registered in Britain between 1850 and 1939, 180 took place before 1919, mostly in chemicals and in mechanical and electrical engineering, with a foreseeable prevalence of American and German companies: *Siemens, General Electric, Ciba, Westinghouse, Hoechst,* and *Singer* were recurrent names. Of these 180, around 130 were greenfield investments, and the rest involved the acquisition of an enterprise already in place. The creation of something from scratch was, in sum, the prevalent way in which foreign firms made investments in Britain. In terms of its stage of industrialisation, Italy was at the other end of the spectrum: by the end of the nineteenth century, it was still backward in comparison with UK, but, it was still by far the most promising southern European country in terms of development prospects.

Notwithstanding some structural problems due to the late political unification and the disparities in the level of development across regions, its economy was growing, and industrialisation was progressing quickly. Urbanisation was progressing rapidly, too. All this made Italy quite an attractive location for foreign investments, which, at the beginning, were mainly directed at utilities, transport and other services, and then rapidly converged towards manufacturing. Out of a sample of 422 foreign investments in Italy between 1885 and 2000, 139 of these took place before 1915. Of these, 102 were greenfield, 27 were based upon the acquisition of a local firm, and 10 were joint ventures. The comparison between the British and the Italian cases is instructive: it clearly emerges that, at the beginning, the structural conditions of the economy "hosting" the investment in production coming from abroad were relatively irrelevant in determining the entry mode. Greenfield investments prevailed both in the most developed European country, the UK, and in a promising, but still under-developed, one, such as Italy. In both cases, there were few or no alternatives to greenfield investments, given the absence of local competitors in industries characterised by new products, and/or by new production technologies. To return to an example already introduced above, when *Singer* invested in Britain, the practical absence of local competitors, excluding some small trading houses, made it necessary to build the new factory from scratch; and this was precisely what happened some years later in Russia. This is a fairly "standard" story: the American company decided to open a factory in the Russian Empire after a long period of consolidation of its commercial network, given the constant expansion of local demand, which made it less convenient to ship sewing machines from distant locations, from the UK or from the US. The new factory, built in Podolsk – close to Moscow – was created in 1900 quite literally from scratch by an English-born engineer experienced in working in Russia, and was a replica of the *Singer* factory in Elizabethport, New Jersey. Initially, it manufactured the less technologically intensive parts of the machines, importing the rest, but, within just a few years, it was capable of producing even the most complicated parts.

Box 4.3: Investing in developing countries: *Singer* and *International Harvester* in Russia

The *Singer Company* took its name from a flamboyant entrepreneur, Isaac Merrit Singer. A creative individual, endowed with manual capabilities, he had patented a sewing machine which was more efficient than the others present on the market in Boston in 1851. There were two main problems in this nascent industry: the presence of a high number of patents – which essentially blocked the development of the industry, since nobody could actually produce machines without incurring some form of patent infringement, and the actual market potential of innovation. The first problem was solved through a patent agreement among the most important producers in 1854. The second was a matter of entrepreneurial creativity, and *Singer and Co.* was, in this respect, amazingly successful. Sewing machines were, in fact, a sophisticated product, something that allowed productivity to increase considerably, in households as well as in the textile industry. For this reason, they required appropriate marketing strategies, with which the eclectic but unsophisticated merchants were very unfamiliar. Edward Clark, who was an attorney hired by Singer to solve legal problems concerning patent infringements and who soon became a partner in the company, found himself to be a marketing genius and innovator. Customers were, first of all, attracted by hire purchase plans, which brought the sewing machine into even the most modest household. Second, the direct-sales door-to-door canvassers were carefully trained, something which immediately created a cohort of faithful clients. The returns from this simple idea were astonishing. *Singer* sold fewer than 1,000 machines in 1855, but more than 10,000 four years later. The success meant a natural expansion of sales abroad. Also because of the market disruption brought by the Civil War, Singer's foreign sales had grown to 40 per cent of the total by the mid-1860s. Machines went to South America and, of course, to Europe, coordinated by representatives resident in the UK (George Woodruff in London) and in Germany (George Neidlinger in Hamburg) supervising sales throughout the Continent, including Scandinavia and, of course, the gigantic and attractive Russian Empire. By the end of the American Civil War, *Singer* was the largest producer of sewing machines – an item which was becoming indispensable, practically a must-have for every household – in the world. With a move which was, in some ways, prophetic, the company had opened a factory in Clydeside, Glasgow, UK in 1867, to supply not only the British but also the continental market. Its position was strengthened by its key competitive strength: strict control of a sales network of representatives and canvassers, which was unique in the world. The network was so effective and so efficient that it required a constant flow of products, if *Singer* wanted to maintain its dominant position in markets – such as the European one – in which aggressive competitors were challenging its dominance. The British plant and the main plant in the US, in Elizabethport, NJ, did not have sufficient capacity to fulfil the demand of the market. A new plant was again opened in Glasgow. Another foundry was started in Vienna at the beginning of the 1880s, and another in Canada, also because of an increase in custom duty tariffs. By the last decade of the nineteenth century, *Singer*, under the dual pressure of market requirements and the need to maintain its dominant position in the global market of sewing machines, had became a modern multinational, producing in several countries and replicating its effective marketing strategy and sales network. Up to then, however, it had mainly targeted developed countries, on both the sides of the Atlantic. A new challenge was coming from underdeveloped, or, rather, developing markets. It was the time of Imperial Russia.

Cyrus Hall McCormick was a creative inventor, like Singer. He had devoted his efforts not to small machines, but to large ones, patenting and selling through instalment programmes a machine for mechanically harvesting grain. In the labour-saving American economy of the nineteenth century (and in particular of the first half of the nineteenth century, when McCormick started his career), machines such as McCormick's reapers were destined to have great success. And the success was, in fact, very great, particularly among prairie farmers. Other markets than American grain fields, however, were attractive to the company. Continental Europe, in which some areas were characterised by an intensive grain-based economy, was very attractive. Exports were also a possibility for *McCormick*; however, a mix of deterrents (high freight rates, the relative high cost of the American labour force overpricing the machines, the difficulties inherent in monitoring agents and licensees effectively, the aggressiveness of other American competitors and European ones, as well as a sort of European tendency to prefer European mechanics) hindered the company's success until the 1880s, when the second generation also became in charge of managing the concern and devoted intensive effort to the building of an effective sales organisation. Marketing the reapers in distant markets proved to be a formidable challenge.

To be effective, and to beat the competition, it was necessary to keep inventories and spare parts at the disposal of the clients (as malfunctioning was, in the case of these machines, a serious issue for farmers). On the top of this, as was the case with *Singer*'s sewing machines, the training of the end users of the harvesters increasingly acquired a strategic function. All these tasks were not easy to perform in distant and different business environments, with the result that, for years, the company was reluctant to undertake ambitious moves which went beyond the exportation of its products. A particularly sensitive case in this respect was that of the Russian market, which was not only very attractive with regard to its potential and the size of its production, but was also characterised by a very low-income population and by very particular institutional conditions. Thus, both Europe and Russia remained attractive, also due to the natural fluctuations on the domestic market. *McCormick* moved in the direction of directly controlled branches endowed with competent human capital and warehouses with inventories and spare parts, and controlled the regional selling networks. By 1902, offices of this kind could be found in the UK, Germany, Switzerland, Russia and Austria-Hungary. The same year, however, American companies in the harvester market became aware that the only way for them to survive abroad was to maintain their oligopolistic positions in distant markets through joint efforts. Accordingly, they decided to create a company, especially dedicated to the development of foreign markets. It was called the *International Harvester Company*. And, here again, the main, the potential gold mine was the Russian Empire.

For both *Singer* and *McCormick/International Harvester*, Russia had all the characteristics of an attractive bet. Before the 1890s, it was still an under-developed market, a backward society, and a very low-income country in which tribal structures prevailed in a rural society. This Turgenev-type society started to change at the end of the nineteenth century under a number of cultural, social and economic pressures, and rapidly acquired the status of a "developing" country, and the term "developing" meant "promising", not just in terms of household consumption but also in terms of capital investments in key activities, such as grain farming and harvesting.

Kompaniya Singer opened a plant in Podolsk, near Moscow, in 1902. A few years later, in 1909, under the urgency of the Russian government's changes in trade policy, which veered sharply towards protection of the manufacturing of machine tools for agriculture, it was *International Harvester* which bought an existing engine factory in Lubertzy, near Moscow, and secured itself its first operating nucleus to produce in the Russian Empire.

The first steps of both ventures went in two different directions. *International Harvester* had much trouble in developing a factory which could attain the same levels of efficiency attainable in the US. This was due to a mixture of different reasons, most of which were related to the mismanagement of relations with the Russian government: the American managers systematically ignored what was going on in the Russian government, as well as its attitudes towards trade policies and foreign investments. The early story of this Russian acquisition shows a series of misunderstandings and mistakes, which, added to the serious problems in managing manufacturing at local level, resulted in the Russian plant running with serious losses. The effective running of the sales network also created a series of problems. The Americans tried to replicate the same techniques in use in the US, not realising the differences in the Russian situation. In addition, they were selling expensive, non-standard products to non-standard consumers, something which affected the effectiveness of their marketing techniques. The situation only began to improve from the beginning of 1912, after a consistent turnover of management.

The history of *Kompanyia Singer* went very differently. When it came to Russia, it was already endowed with international experience and knowledge of this foreign market. It had been operating in Russia since 1865, albeit without a direct presence. It was also used to replicating production and marketing techniques, including its famous network sales organisation. Moreover, it had also learned how to adapt some of its main advantages and competences (in this case, in marketing and selling), to markets which were somewhat different from the domestic one. Basically, one of the secrets of *Singer*'s success in Russia was that the local managers in charge of the investment enjoyed a considerable degree of flexibility in applying the marketing and working practices developed elsewhere to the new context.

Both companies concluded their Russian adventure with the market implosion provoked by the First World War and the October Revolution in 1917.

Source: Fred V. Carstensen, *American Enterprise in Foreign Markets.*
Studies of Singer and International Harvester in Imperial Russia,
Chapel Hill, NC and London: University of North Carolina Press, 1984.

★ ★ ★ ★ ★

The history of *Singer* – about which a remarkable amount of evidence is available – allows us to introduce another issue which is relevant from the perspective of this book. The general impression that one obtains when one examines the stories of the pioneering modern multinationals is that of recurrent traits and regularities. First, the decision to open a productive branch was the consequence, as stated above, of an enduring presence carried out through commercial branches and sales agencies, and was, in some respects, a step further when the existing practices revealed themselves to be insufficient to cope, for instance, with a sharp rise in demand. A second common trait is the presence of "entrepreneurial" agents or other kinds of individuals, such as company employees willing to act as foreign branch managers in charge of the establishment of operations and the connections with the headquarters in the country of origin of the investment. The presence of these people, often locally connected, was, in some sense, an indispensable pre-requisite for setting up the enterprise. Third (and connected with the previous point), even in the case of greenfield investments, the presence of local investors and even entrepreneurs in the share capital of the foreign branch was frequent.

According to some scholars, the minor degree of complexity and product diversification allowed these companies to cope reasonably with internationalisation even in the presence of a relatively poor (but existing) system of transport and communications. The obvious consequence of this situation was that subsidiaries tended in general to have a non-negligible degree of autonomy in their relationships with the mother company, in terms of marketing and commercial policies, and a part, of course, of the design of the product. Other cases mentioned in the literature reinforce this perspective. For instance, many investments in the US were made in the form of the acquisition of a stake in a licensee firm, which logically maintained its operational autonomy.

In this first phase, in sum, autonomy was still prevailing, reflecting the non-standard conditions that companies going abroad found in the targeted markets. The case of *Singer* in Russia (see Box 4.3) provides remarkable evidence of the opportunities derived from domestic headquarters leaving local branches the freedom to do things as they saw fit, acting as a mixture of commercial agencies, coordination devices for local sales networks, and, of course, production plants. This autonomy and overall flexibility in managing local subsidiaries was, in this phase, a pre-requisite that was essential for surviving in markets characterised by a high degree of uncertainty, as was the case in most of the markets which were emerging at the time.

8. Varieties of multinationals

The early phase of multinational activity was a period of experimentation in the internationalisation practices of companies, and it is not easy to identify general patterns or the prevailing models of internationalisation. Scholars have, however, identified some general archetypes of internationalisation which were in place from the beginning. These archetypes reflect, in their turn, the particular patterns of development adopted by different capitalist models, or at least the differences in the nature of industrial capitalism among Western countries. In this perspective, the history of the internationalisation process and of the rise of the modern multinational is, in a sense, another way of looking at two broader issues: the debate about the "varieties of capitalism", and the development of national competitive advantages in modern industrial capitalism. In addition, the present section is important because it allows us to stress once more how the history of international business is a way of looking at the more general issue of the "great divergence" between the West and the rest introduced by the First Industrial Revolution. By 1914, the total stock of the estimated foreign investments by country of destination (or, technically, *inward* foreign direct investments) was around 14 billion dollars; Asia (China and India included) accounted for less than 3 billion. In terms of the total stock of *outward* investments – which is a very rough indicator of the capability of actively engaging in the global economy – Western Europe and the US accounted for more than 99 per cent of the total at the time. Thus, by the end of the nineteenth century, Europe and its Western offshoots had concentrated not only the largest share of the riches of the world, and not only the most relevant part of international trade, but also almost the totality of international business activity in active terms, as they were also important recipients of outward investments. To put it another way, from the point of view of international investments, it becomes even more straightforward the marginality to which the industrial revolutions of the nineteenth century had relegated those areas which had once been the main repositories of the riches of the world. In sum, and in contrast to what happens today, companies investing abroad came from, and went to, countries that were characterised by a relatively high level of economic development much more than those that were marginal in terms of income level and growth prospects.

As noted, the largest share of foreign investments came from Europe and from the US. According to the data mentioned above, by 1914, the UK was by far the largest investor in the world with more than 8 billion dollars in outward foreign investments, followed by the US (2.6 billion), Germany (2.6 billion), France (1.7 billion) and the rest of Europe. Apart from size, behind this ranking lie very different patterns of the international presence between European and American companies. The basic idea here is that multinationals coming from different countries enjoyed different competitive advantages from others, advantages that they subsequently enjoyed in the international arena. This is a key concept that we will find again in the following chapters, and which clearly originated in this phase.

Given that it was the first industrial nation, Britain accounted for the largest stake of foreign investments in the period preceding the First World War. The reason for this pre-eminence has been investigated by several scholars, some of whom stress the fact that, differently from the US, European countries, and the UK in particular, were short of inputs, and foreign investments in natural resources were a necessity. This is, of course, true, but it is only one part of the whole picture. As the data clearly show, foreign investments in production inputs in the primary sector were relevant, but they were accompanied by an equally relevant amount of investment in the secondary sector and in services, even from and towards European nations.

It is, however, important to assess the differences between the different areas that were home to foreign investments in a systematic way. A first important area in which Europe and America were different concerned the incentives to foreign investment activity. These were the conditions present in the domestic market, which influenced the propensity, or the relative cost, of investing abroad in general, but not the specialisation of domestic companies in terms of the sector targeted. This is a very important distinction. Countries can, in fact, vary their propensity to multinational activity according to the advantage developed in some industries or in others, but also according to other more general advantages, which are country-specific, and not industry-specific. In this respect, the available literature focuses on some aspects which include the size and structure of the domestic market, the quality of the management and the ownership, and other determinants of an institutional nature. The following part of this section will illustrate this relevant issue with some examples drawn from the existing literature.

The first relevant point to discuss is the influence of the domestic market on the propensity of companies to engage in international activity. From this point of view, the US and European cases are quite interesting to analyse. Companies headquartered in the US had developed a series of advantages linked to the nature of the domestic market. First of all, for them, the pressure of the scarcity of domestic demand was far less relevant than for European firms. In the US, demand was continental in size, clearly playing a key role in shaping the capabilities of the American companies, used to managing multi-plant operations over long distances. The situation was very different in Europe. The smallest countries, such as Switzerland, Belgium and the Netherlands, are, quite remarkably, present in the list of countries which were home to multinational corporations, along with Sweden. In these cases, it is quite clear that internationalisation on the Continent, both commercial and post-production, was a necessary condition for the survival of companies based in small nations from the very beginning. An important corollary of this point, which is less investigated by the literature, is the nature of foreign, but geographically close, markets. An example can help to clarify this point. After 1870 (or, rather, after the customs unification of 1834), German companies in electro-mechanics had before them a domestic market whose size and potential was anything but negligible. However, they systematically also targeted markets in Southern Europe and in the Balkans, both areas which were quickly developing and in which competition was weak or completely absent. In the expansion strategy of leaders such as *Siemens* and *AEG*, the potential of close markets played a relevant role in incentivising international mobility.

Another relevant point concerns the nature of domestic demand. American companies had before them a country in which the large bulk of demand came from low-income immigrants, a situation very different from the one that European companies faced. As we will see shortly, this had the consequence of shaping both product specialisation and, in the medium to long term, also the internationalisation patterns of companies. Americans were, by nature, more inclined towards the low-cost standardisation of global products, while Europeans had a more pronounced propensity towards specialised, and customisable, products.

A second important country-specific factor shaping the internationalisation process, only superficially investigated by the available international business history research, is that of ownership and management. American companies accelerated their multinational activity in coincidence with a major transformation in their ownership and managerial structures. By the end of the nineteenth century, the majority of large US firms were in a quite advanced process of separation between ownership and management, and the result was that even strategic geographic diversification in foreign countries was undertaken by professionals who were internally trained or hired on purpose. In the case of European countries, the prevalence and persistence of concentrated ownership and family control may have had some impact on the internationalisation patterns of European companies, which tended to be more prudent and to rely on the internal resources available to the family itself. Historians of European multinationals also stress the tendency of Europeans to expand abroad by privileging partnerships and joint ventures, while Americans were more inclined to expand through fully controlled subsidiaries. There is, however, no systematic evidence on this issue. Clearly, past history mattered: Europe (and, in particular, the UK) had established almost all the free-standing companies that existed at the end of the nineteenth century (Chapter 3), and the trading companies, particularly those active in Asia, which would evolve into diversified multinationals. This meant that Europe was home to a wider variety in types of international business, ranging from free-standing firms to trading companies, to mercantile ventures and modern multinationals shaped on the American model.

A third element that contributed to shape the form of modern multinationals was the attitude of institutions at home, which will be further analysed in the next chapter. However, it must be noted at this point that, according to many business historians, the presence of antitrust legislation from the end of the 1880s incentivised US companies to go abroad, replicating and expanding abroad the oligopolistic position that they enjoyed at home. In contrast, European companies were allowed (when not incentivised) to take part in cartels and, in particular, in international trade agreements, with the opposite effect on their propensity to put aggressive practices of investment in place in other countries.

As shown in the previous sections, country-specific advantages tended to play a role in shaping the process of the internationalisation of companies from different areas of the world. One has, of course, to bear in mind that differences can also be found in the industrial specialisation of companies originating in different countries and endowed with different advantages.

At first glance, the European and the American multinationals were different in terms of the sectors targeted, in which both had competitive advantages which determined the difference. The first, relevant difference lay in the different endowment of production inputs. US companies tended to be more competitive in capital-intensive and scale-intensive industries; after all, the process innovations of the Second Industrial Revolution were particularly well suited to a country characterised by a permanent shortage of labour. Steel production, oil refining, food and beverages, tobacco and the automotive industry, are all examples in which US entrepreneurs developed a permanent competitive advantage at home, which was then deployed abroad. *Vice versa*, European – and British in particular – companies performed better in those areas in which labour intensity was high – labour was not an issue even in an emigrating, but still crowded, Europe – and capital was cheap. The second important difference was in the endowment of natural resources; US companies were, in this respect, better positioned than European ones in general on the domestic market. America was a huge, quite well-endowed continental market – and, when necessary, it was relatively easy to expand into very close areas, such as Canada, or Mexico or the Caribbean, which were certainly not lacking in natural resources. For Germany, France and Britain, but also for other European countries, things were very different. During the nineteenth century, for instance, British companies expanded in some Mediterranean areas – for instance, Sicily, Sardinia and even Spain, in search of natural resources. The stories narrated in Chapter 3 of *Rio Tinto* and *Peñarroya* are examples of this. However, the European endowment of natural resources was always limited (and in the case of coal, even at the origin of harsh conflicts), and justified an early expansion abroad, first in Eastern Europe (e.g. the Balkans were always attractive in this respect), then on a global scale.

In addition, historical and structural patterns maintained some kind of long-term relevance. British foreign direct investments, for instance, tended to cluster in high added-value consumer goods, textiles (mainly cotton) and related machinery. Belgian firms specialised (in part with French firms) in utilities, mainly transport, particularly through the instrument of the free-standing company. Germans specialised in technology-intensive and science-intensive industries, also thanks to the high level of the technical human capital made available through a sophisticated system of professional education.

★ ★ ★ ★ ★

During the last quarter of the nineteenth century, a new industrial revolution radically transformed a number of industries. Companies in activities related to the chemical transformation of materials and in the production of goods composed of several standardised and interchangeable parts became larger in order to achieve economies of scale and scope. The necessity of obtaining continuity in production flow lay at the origin of strategic investments whose purpose was basically to achieve vertical backward and forward integration. All this had a radical impact on the world of international business. Companies started to invest abroad permanently both in order to pursue the above-mentioned process of vertical integration, and in order to secure access to the necessary inputs and to maintain the oligopolistic positions that they had achieved domestically, while at the same time benefiting from additional demand in distant markets. This process created a completely new type of internationally active firm, one which was radically different from – even if not an alternative to – those which already populated the arena of the global economy (free-standing companies, trading companies, international merchants, etc.). These firms were motivated, as demonstrated above, by strategic purposes and by ends that were very different from those of the others, and had before them challenges and opportunities of a very different nature than those faced by international entrepreneurs in the past. These challenges ranged from the identification of the appropriate location for investing in production plants, to that of the proper way of making the investment. This chapter has also shown how not only the entry strategies, but also the countries and the sectors targeted, varied according to the geographic origin of the company investing abroad. The birth and diffusion of the "new multinationals" also stress once again, and from a very particular point of view, the radical transformation which occurred in the world economy within just two centuries, marked by the "great divergence" between Europe (and its Western offshoots) and the East (basically Africa and China), which became increasingly marginal in terms of its contribution to the global economic growth, trade and development. The new multinationals were no longer traders connecting distant parts of the world and providing exotic (even necessary) products. They were also no longer effective ways of internalising capital markets, or of providing technically trained human capital to invest in developing areas. In contrast to merchants, traders and even to free-standing companies, the new multinationals were permanently investing in production facilities abroad, and often in more than one country, on the basis of the experience and knowledge gained in their respective home countries, with the purpose not only of making profits, but also of safeguarding their position in oligopolistic international markets.

The story told in this chapter took place in a relatively short span of time, to wit, the more or less fifty years preceding the First World War. This was a period characterised by unusual openness to trade and input mobility, by relative political stability and peace, and by the presence of institutional arrangements which were favourable to globalisation, whatever its meaning. The modern multinationals benefited from this situation fully. Foreign direct investments moved around in the same way that financial capital did. Less developed countries generally welcomed foreign capital and technology, while, in developed nations, foreign firms were free to compete with domestic ones for the consumers' preferences. Some countries deliberately established barriers to imports, in order to incentivise foreigners to invest directly in production facilities. Others encouraged national firms to associate with foreign firms in order to gain access to knowledge and competences. For some governments, direct investments had the same nature as capital imports, or as foreign purchases of domestic bonds: they demonstrated a favourable attitude towards the country's general outlook.

This (in many aspects, unique) situation became to an abrupt end on 28 June 1914. The First World War brought the global economy of the nineteenth century to a dramatic collapse. In public opinion, in political rhetoric, in newspapers, books and pamphlets, foreign capital and foreign investments had transformed their nature, turning from opportunities into threats. Francesco Saverio Nitti, an eminent Italian politician and economist, wrote (explicitly referring to German investments in Italy), in 1915, a sentence which could surely have been written by many of his contemporaries, both in Italy and abroad:

> No foreigners have to dominate in our financial, banking and industrial system. One cannot deny to foreign investment a warm welcome, when they are invested in production effort. However, we must avoid all the organizations which do create constraints, exert control and provide directions, which end up being a dangerous limit to the country's own political life.[5]

The disintegration of the world order did not spare the basic building blocks of the international economy. Some simply vanished, extinguished by the transformations in the external environment. Others, which were too strong or too necessary to disappear, transformed or adapted, thereby creating new varieties of international entrepreneurship. This will be the focus of the next chapter.

Notes

1 Alfred D. Chandler, "The Competitive Performance of U.S. Industrial Enterprises since the Second World War", *The Business History Review*, Vol. 68, No. 1 (Spring, 1994), pp. 1–72.
2 John H. Dunning, "Changes in the Level and Structure of International Production: The Last One Hundred Years", in: Mark Casson (ed.), *The Growth of International Business*, London: Allen & Unwin, 1983, pp. 84–139, at p. 85.
3 Andrew Godley, "Selling the Sewing Machine Around the World: Singer's International Marketing Strategies, 1850–1920", *Enterprise and Society*, 7 (2), 2006, pp. 266–314, at p. 266.
4 Mira Wilkins, "Comparative Hosts", *Business History*, 36 (1), 1994, pp. 18–50.
5 Francesco Saverio Nitti, *Il capitale straniero in Italia*, Naples: Sangiovanni, 1915, p. 32.

Bibliography

Casson, Mark, (ed.) *The Growth of International Business*, London: George Allen & Unwin, 1983.

Chandler, Alfred D. *Scale and Scope: The Dynamics of Industrial Capitalism*. Cambridge, MA: Harvard University Press, 1990.

Dunning, John and Lundan, Sarianna M., *Multinational Enterprises and the Global Economy*, second revised edition, Cheltenham: Edward Elgar Publishing Ltd., 2008.

Wilkins, Mira, "European and North American Multinationals, 1870–1914: Comparisons and contrast", *Business History*, 30, 1988.

5 International entrepreneurship between crisis and rebirth (1914–1945)

1 The clay pot breaks[1]

I was born in 1881 in the great and mighty empire of the Habsburg Monarchy, but you would look for it in vain on the map today; it has vanished without trace. I grew up in Vienna, an international metropolis for two thousand years, and had to steal away from it like a thief in the night before it was demoted to the status of a provincial German town. [...] Whenever, in conversation with younger friends, I mentioned something that happened before the First World War, their startled questions make me realise how much of what I still take for granted as reality has become either past history or unimaginable to them. [...] All the bridges are broken between today, yesterday, and the day before yesterday. [...] Both my father and my grandfather lived their lives in a single, direct way – it was one and the same life from beginning to end, without many vicissitudes, without upheaval and danger, a life of small tensions, imperceptible transitions, always lived in the same easy, comfortable rhythm as the wave of time carried them from the cradle to the grave. [...] There was probably a war of some kind in progress somewhere in their time, but only a little one compared to the dimensions of modern warfare, and waged far away from their borders. [...] But as for those of us who are now sixty years old, [...] what have we *not* seen, *not* suffered, *not* experienced? We have made our way through the catalogue of all imaginable catastrophes from beginning to end, and we have not reached the last page of it yet. [...]

If I try to find some useful phrase to sum up the time of my childhood and youth before the First World War, I hope I can put it most succinctly by calling it the Golden Age of Security. Everything in our Austrian Monarchy, then almost a thousand years old, seemed built to last, and the state itself was the ultimate guarantor of durability. The rights it gave its citizens were affirmed by our parliament, a freely elected assembly representing the people, and every duty was precisely defined. Our currency, the Austrian Crown, circulated in the form of shiny gold coins [...]. Everyone knew how much he owned and what his income was, what was allowed and what was not. Everything had its norm, its correct measurement and weight. [...]

Then, on 28 June 1914, a shot was fired in Sarajevo, the shot that in a single second was to shatter the world of security and creative reason in which we had been reared, where we had grown up and were at home, as if it were a hollow clay pot breaking into a thousand pieces. [...] After the defeat of Germany and Austria, [my country] was now only a grey, lifeless, shadow of the old Austro-Hungarian Monarchy. Its new outline on the map was uncertain. [...] The factories that used to bring wealth to the country were now in foreign territory, the railway network was a mere remnant of its former self, the national bank's reserves of gold had been seized, and it still had to pay off the huge burden of the war loan. [...] There was no bread, no coal, no oil. Revolution or some other catastrophic outcome appeared inevitable. [...].

This long quotation by Stefan Zweig, one of the most tormented and reflective novelists of the generation which had had their personal, everyday lives radically displaced by the dramatic events following the assassination in Sarajevo, clearly testifies to the idea of the revolutionary changes introduced by the First World War. The words of a Jew, a middle-class intellectual, who overnight saw his own existence completely changed by the conflict, vividly demonstrate how the years of the Great War introduced a new order which revolutionised everything, from the existence of individuals to the international political order which had been established after the Napoleonic wars and the Restoration period which followed them. It is no exaggeration to say that the war years constituted an invisible, but effective, watershed between two very different periods. The first period, labelled as "the first global economy", which coincided with the rise and consolidation of the transport and communication revolutions, and the diffusion of the new organisational forms generated by the second technological paradigm described in the previous chapter; and the second period, in which the technological achievements had to cope with a political and institutional (and even cultural) transformation, which resulted in the fragmentation of a previously cohesive world economy.

In his autobiography, Zweig described the disintegration of the Habsburg Empire, one of the most "honourable" European institutions of the time. Although it was largely fought in Europe, the war was by no means just a European phenomenon. More or less directly, its effects were felt all over the world. First of all, almost all the European nations involved in the war (starting with Britain and France, the countries which had by far the two largest colonial possessions in the world) were also powerful imperial powers (as were Austria-Hungary, Belgium, Germany, Italy, Russia and Turkey (Ottoman Empire)). The Russian Empire, which participated in the first phase of the war before its collapse during the Communist Revolution of 1917, extended from Europe to the Pacific Ocean, from the Baltic to the Black Sea. Colonies were thus, by definition, not excluded from the conflict, as witnessed by the Commonwealth casualties lying on the European battlefields. Consequently, hostilities were also extended to the distant territories in which the Western powers had established their colonial presence: to Africa, the Pacific and the Middle East, albeit with less intensity and frequency. The Far East, too, was not immune. Japan, in full militaristic swing, had immediately declared war on Germany in August 1914, and had seized the main German outpost of Tsingtao (Qingdao), which was strategically located on the Shantung (Shandong) peninsula in China.

This brought a reaction from a weak and politically divided China, which entered the war against Germany in 1917. By this time, almost all the advanced nations in Europe, Asia and America were, in some way or other, taking part in the conflict, with all the consequences that this involved. Looking at the same phenomenon from another point of view, the disruptions and perturbations of the Great War involved, with few exceptions, all the nations which had previously taken part in the great mosaic of the global economic, social, and, to some extent, political integration that had characterised the First Industrial Revolution at its height and the emergence of the first global economy. And just as the economy was truly global, so too was the Great War which brought to a halt this process of integration.

A global reach was only one of the characteristics of such a large-scale conflict. For the purposes of this book, we will emphasise the characteristics which had a more direct effect on the general shape of the global economy and on the choices of the internationally active enterprises and entrepreneurs, even if it is impossible to disentangle completely these effects from those taking place on a wider scale.

2 The War: stimulating internationalisation

The First World War had both positive and negative effects both on the dynamics of international business and on the strategies of internationally active entrepreneurs. Even if it is not easy to disentangle these effects from the more general transformations introduced by the conflict, including those of a social and political nature, it is nonetheless beyond all doubt that the conflict deeply transformed the general scenario in which international business took place. This transformation was, in its turn, the consequence of the new general rules of international competition, which were, if not completely created, at least emphasised by the new and particular nature of the Great War. If, as this section will show, the turmoil of the war seriously damaged the existing equilibrium in the world economy which had matured in the decades of the First and the Second Industrial Revolutions described in the previous chapters, it certainly did not stop the technological transformations initiated by the new technological paradigm of mass production based upon economies of scale in capital-intensive industries. The process of technological convergence among the most advanced nations (for which international investments were largely responsible) became now both mandatory and mainly domestic, i.e. managed by domestic firms. This, of course, also had some deferred effects on the international competitiveness of national leaders, and in general on the scenario of global entrepreneurship in which new competitors started to be aggressively present. Even though it is almost impossible to disentangle the contribution of the First World War to the development of the technologies that later impacted on international investment activity, some kind of effect was nevertheless present: many national leaders (or champions, as they were later called) developed during the hostilities and, in fact, it was a high degree of international competitiveness that to a large extent determined their future positions as international investors.

The war was, in a sense, the first real occasion in which the new technologies of the Second Industrial Revolution were applied for military purposes. The war was an effort which was based upon the products of industrialisation. Thus, and probably for the very first time to such an extent, the offensive capacity of the belligerents was not only based upon the availability of efficient armies composed of enormous masses of troops, but also upon a technological component, which was to prove necessary both in logistic terms (in order to maintain the troops in efficient fighting condition and able to reach the assigned objectives quickly) and in terms of offensive capacity. As became clear from the very first days of the conflict, this was a new kind of war, fought on the battlefield but in a completely different way from the past, and in which the consolidated strategies developed throughout centuries of direct clashes in open fields between subsequent waves of infantry supported by cavalry proved to be *de facto* useless. This was a war fought by human beings who had amplified their offensive capacity through the use of a vast array of weapons, all of a sophisticated technological nature (given the times). The war effort was, thus, an unprecedented global industrial effort, which involved all the manufacturing sectors which, in all the belligerent nations, were forced necessity to achieve mass production standards as quickly as possible. Even in the most labour-intensive industries, scale-intensive production techniques and the organisation of the production process in high volumes had to be introduced almost everywhere. Clearly, the sectors most affected were those in which mass production was an absolute necessity, and which were more functional to the offensive engagement strategy. Heavy and light mechanics, energy, iron and steel, chemicals, transportation means of all kinds, all became a must-have condition in order to have the minimum chance of success in the conflict. And what could once be imported had, in many cases, now to be produced domestically, since the countries involved in the war tried to maintain both the production and the usage of the inputs necessary to the military effort under strict control. In some countries, the war quickly consolidated an industrial basis which had only started to develop quite recently. Italy, for instance, definitively consolidated its endowment in capital-intensive industries such as steel, the production of electric energy, automotives, chemicals, mechanics and shipbuilding, thanks to the wartime effort, when (also thanks to the resources made available through the huge profits derived from war procurement) some industrial leaders completed the concentration process and both vertical and horizontal integration. Two further consequences of this acceleration in the diffusion of the technologies of the Second Industrial Revolution should be mentioned here.

The first was a general expansion in the productive capacity of firms, both in the countries directly involved in the war and in those, such as Canada and, for most of the conflict, the United States, which remained neutral but adjusted their national economies in order to meet the needs of the belligerent nations. This had no immediate effects on their process of internationalisation, but constituted a relevant premise for the changes that affected the geographic diversification strategies of many companies after the war. While the overall trend after the conflict was towards a general scaling down of volumes of production, the expansion of productive capacity also led to attempts to increase international trade. On the other hand, the barriers to trade flows, which followed the war, led, as we will see, to a wave of international agreements which were set up in order to allocate the production surpluses as best as possible. Thus, the existing capacity was largely saturated through strategies of related diversification, which, in their turn, increased the competitive range of companies also outside national borders.

Growing demand and input shortages squeezed companies in the non-belligerent and neutral countries. These companies thus found incentives to increase their productive capacity abroad. The Swiss-based *Nestlé*, for instance, doubled its production between 1914 and 1918, thanks to the orders coming from the European armies involved in the conflict. Shortages of cattle and milk in its factories (most of which were located in areas affected by the fighting), however, incentivised *Nestlé* to invest outside Europe, and, in particular, in the US, where it acquired production facilities. By 1917, *Nestlé*'s production plants numbered almost forty, most of which were located outside Europe (where most of the production was sold). This "internationalisation by necessity" provided *Nestlé* with the skills and competences (and, of course, the resources) to pursue a further push towards production in foreign markets. According to the company's official figures, by 1921, *Nestlé* had about eighty plants under its control, plus a dozen subsidiaries and affiliates, and its geographical diffusion ranged from the US to South America and Australia. *Svenska Kullagerfabriken*, or SKF, the Swedish producer of ball bearings founded in Gothenburg in 1907, had already developed an international sales network, plus some direct investments across Europe, the United States and South America. A direct investment was almost immediately established in the UK in 1910. Swedish neutrality coupled with the sharp rise in the demand for roller bearings generated by the "mechanisation of mass killing" allowed SKF not only to consolidate its market position by selling to all the countries involved, but also pushed the company towards a policy of expansion through direct investments during the war years. In 1916, SKF acquired an important competitor in Philadelphia; in 1917, a factory was established in France; and sales agencies continued to be opened everywhere. Subsidiaries – particularly those opened in the US and South America – functioned as buffers against price fluctuations in Europe.

A second, not irrelevant, effect was the consolidation and increasing importance of technology in the generation of international competitive advantages. The war served to emphasise beyond any doubt the role of scientific progress (in this case, for destructive purposes), which, in many cases, generated superior competences which companies could exploit as competitive tools in international trade, and served as drivers of geographic diversification of production. The Great War contributed to the generation, in sum, of competitive advantages (later, commonly referred to as *ownership advantages*), which were largely at the basis of the dynamics of global entrepreneurships during the decades to come. To put things differently, the war, as a technological effort, generated national leaders who mastered production technologies as the basis of successful future internationalisation strategies. These advantages were purely technological, and were not based, as they had been in the past, upon superior or idiosyncratic knowledge of (distant) markets, or on the availability of capital to be invested in infrastructural projects or natural resources. More than ever before, technology was the main driver of the internationalisation process. This trend, which began during the First World War, was to gain further momentum in the course of the interwar years, when the possession of superior advantages became one of the main elements in determining the internationalisation process of firms. There are numerous examples of this, some of which are illuminating, particularly in the case of industries characterised by a high degree of technological intensity, such as aircraft production, which, at the beginning of the hostilities, was still in its infancy. Aircraft technology developed very quickly after the first experiments, and, by 1911, the new means of transport was already being adopted by armies for operative patrolling purposes. Aircraft production began almost simultaneously in various European countries (the UK, France and Germany), thanks to the efforts of pioneers such as Anton Fokker or Louis Blériot, and expanded mainly through licensing and, in some cases, joint ventures. For instance, the French manufacturer *Nieuport* entered the Italian market – to which it already exported – directly through a joint venture with an Italian producer of coach chassis, *Macchi*. The *Nieuport-Macchi* company, created in 1913, was soon able to develop autonomous technology in aircraft production. Other companies, such as the above-mentioned *Fokker*, established in Germany by a Dutch inventor who, in 1919, repatriated his business (in order to circumvent the ban on the production of aircraft in Germany imposed by the Treaty of Versailles), had developed a solid technological advantage (and a strong brand image) during the war, which was of paramount importance when the company began civil aircraft production and established a production branch in the US in 1923.

A third effect was induced by war requisitions, shortages and the control, in particular, of raw materials. The contraction in the architecture of the global markets generated by the war had an immediate effect on the procurement strategies of companies which had an absolute need for certain inputs for their production processes. The case of *Pirelli*, introduced in the previous chapter, which had acquired natural rubber plantations in the Far East, is an outstanding example of vertical integration through foreign investment induced by the wartime shortages and by the necessity of guaranteeing the supply of a strategic input. And the *Pirelli* case was by no means unique: in sum, the conflict created new incentives for companies, which were forced to invest abroad in order to secure the inputs that they needed, find new markets, and exploit abroad the technological competences that they had developed or had had to develop during the war.

3 The War: the negative effects

Notwithstanding a number of positive (direct and indirect, and often delayed in time) effects, the available research on international business is unanimous in emphasising the devastating impact of the Great War on the general framework of the global economy and on international entrepreneurship.

Despite the fact that, in some cases (notably, Canada, the US and Japan), the war coincided with an increasing degree of commercial openness, in particular due to the demand coming from Europe, the data show beyond any doubt the disruption in international trade flows, which had been characterised by smoothness in the second part of the nineteenth century (see previous chapters), and which constituted one of the most evident signals of the ongoing economic globalisation. As a result of, first and foremost, trade restrictions (the technological side of the war was mainly about keeping inputs and resources under control), and of blockades and counter-blockades, which affected not only the countries in conflict, but also the neutral states, and also because of the submarine war, global trade sharply contracted. According to the data available (which are, in any case, fairly uncertain and inaccurate), the total volume of world trade fell by approximately 20 per cent during the war years, only attaining pre-war levels in 1924. The global reach of the conflict, which, as depicted in Map 5.1, involved the majority of the nations of the world, meant that both the potential and the real effects on trade flows were amplified on a general scale.

The disintegration of world trade was, however, a multi-faceted phenomenon, and, even though this book is primarily concerned with the evolution in the organisational structures and strategies of international companies, is worthy of our consideration, albeit only generally.

The most striking feature was, of course, the decline in trade volume in absolute terms, as mentioned above. However, the geographic distribution of the contraction was not homogeneous across countries.

Among the major European belligerents, for instance, exports fell (in order to keep resources under control), and imports rose (for the same reason), provoking a permanent situation of trade imbalance. Neutral countries experienced a very different situation,

Map 5.1 Participants in the First World War
Note: light grey: the Triple Alliance; black: the Entente; grey: neutral
Source: http://en.wikipedia.org/wiki/Participants_in_World_War_I.

particularly those that had recently industrialised or were richly endowed with natural resources. As we saw above, this also happened, to some extent, in the case of foreign investment activity.

Another component of trade disruption was the sharp reversal in the process of price convergence, which had characterised the decades preceding the war. Differences in prices between the sources of commodities and their principal markets rose considerably. In contrast to the past, however, this was not due to asymmetric information, but to another element, namely freight costs, which, according to some calculations, almost tripled during the conflict. In sum, transporting and shipping goods, in general, had become more expensive (and dangerous) during the war.

And, of course, the Great War dramatically affected another key component of the globalisation process, i.e. the international capital market. The "symbol", to some extent, of globalisation, the transparent, smooth, integrated and frictionless international financial market based upon the gold standard, symbolically collapsed in August 1914, when all the continent's major stock exchanges simultaneously closed down, only to be re-opened some months later under strictly regulated system of price caps, in order to facilitate the trading of government bonds. The re-opening of European (and US) stock exchanges dramatically highlighted the transformation in the nature of European (and, indeed, the world's) financial markets, now largely non-integrated, and domestically oriented towards the trading of bonds issued to finance the war effort.

Another immediate impact of the Great War on the state of the international economy affected direct investments more closely, albeit in a less global, more limited way, but with potentially dramatic consequences. The "age of security", in Zweig's words, had coincided – as stressed in the previous chapter – with an unprecedented wave of cross-border investments which involved both multinationals *strictu sensu,* and, more often, free-standing companies. Capital flowed unrestricted, carrying with it the other main component of the phenomenon, namely technological expertise. Where trading barriers hindered exports, or where the dynamics of local markets made it convenient (as in the case of *Singer* in Russia; see Chapter 4), companies decided to invest their resources directly in local assets. Foreign capital was present almost everywhere, particularly, although not exclusively, in the peripheries. The outbreak of war put an end to this favourable situation overnight. Foreign direct investments were, technically, assets which belonged to foreigners, who suddenly acquired – in many cases – the status of "being the enemy". The effects of these changes on the general status of multinationals and of free-standing companies were both immediate and hard-hitting. One of the first effects, one which is often underestimated, was the repatriation of human capital, generally skilled labour. The phenomenon was common to both enemies and allies; technicians and managers left, causing an immediate disruption in the daily operations of subsidiaries; otherwise, they became "alien civilians of enemy nationality", that is, *de facto*, prisoners of war or interned aliens. The major belligerents included, Britain, Belgium, Germany and Austria-Hungary, that is – the US apart – the main sources of foreign investments across both Europe and the rest of the world in capital-intensive and technology-intensive industries, such as chemicals, electricity, electro-mechanics, steel and transport equipment, and the impact of the human-capital loss was certainly felt. When the war broke out the Russian Empire was a country whose process of industrial development was greatly of exogenous origin, and particularly German and French. According to some calculations, immediately before the war, one manager out of three was not of Russian origin, and so was one out of ten of the technicians and skilled professionals.

A second relevant disruption came from the requisition of foreign assets (in the case of enemies) or their involvement in war-related production, something that completely severed the links with the mother companies, often without any kind of compensation. Expropriations, seizures and their more "democratic" version, i.e. "forced liquidations" of foreign-owned assets in the countries involved in the conflict, all impacted on the realm of international business. The case of Italy which, as a latecomer country, was intensely crowded by foreign investors in technology-intensive and capital-intensive industries is particularly relevant. According to the data available, by the beginning of 1917, more than 1,200 German-owned firms of different size and type were expropriated or put under the control of the government. In France, seizures of foreign enterprises amounted to around 3,000 by the end of 1915. In Russia, by November 1917, there were approximately 2,000 seizures. Even before Red October, Russia was pushing for the liquidation of foreign assets and their nationalisation, even of the subsidiaries of large firms such as *Siemens* and *General Electric*. *Singer*'s Russian subsidiary, which was considered to be very close to Germany, was already under a sort of "siege" from nationalistic factions by the end of 1914 and became fully nationalised after the October Revolution.

4 The end of globalisation

Physical destruction, seizures, liquidations, and haemorrhages of skilled human capital, deep market contractions, and capital shortages: in the course of few years, the Great War devastated the foundations of the global economy. The conflict, however, accelerated and exacerbated some contradictions which were deeply embedded in the process of globalisation analysed in the previous chapter. These contradictions concerned the structural pillars of the economic, social and cultural integration which had characterised the years before the conflict itself. At the end of the hostilities, they emerged in all their dramatic intensity as ghosts of a tragedy in which millions had perished. These ghosts would affect the future of the international economy (and of the world in general) in a decisive way, and thus it is worth examining them in greater depth.

First, the war had definitely killed the "universalistic" attitude that had characterised the integrated and progressive first global economy. Huge masses of men had squeezed into muddy trenches, killing each other in hundreds of thousands, internationalist attitudes had disappeared, and nationalist sentiments had strengthened everywhere. The Socialist International had melted down in August 1914, and the war had definitively extinguished the effervescence of some truly cosmopolitan cities, such as Vienna. In this case, it was the cultural component of the first globalisation that revealed its fragility: in the years following the conflict, the concept of national identities, of nationalism, of protection against the enemy, of the alien, gained much more significance than in the decades before. After all, the Great War had disintegrated three secular empires in Europe: the German *Reich*, the Ottoman Empire and the Habsburg Empire, the latter, in some sense, the symbol of the contradictions of this age, an empire in which almost all European nationalities and several religions peacefully co-existed, but which was, at the same time, under strong nationalistic pressure.

Universalism is a general concept, which can, however, be useful to capture the propensity towards openness, towards the idea of "foreign" being perceived as an opportunity more than as a threat. Clearly, this can be applied to everything, from culture to more concrete things such as production inputs, capital and labour, as well as goods and merchandise of all sorts. As stressed in the previous chapter, all of these circulated relatively freely, even though, particularly in the most recently industrialised countries, this process had already begun to raise controversial sentiments before the war, which the post-war years further exacerbated.

One of the most evident phenomena of the first period of globalisation, and one which was palpable in everyday life, was, as stressed above, that of mass migration. The massive population outflows from Europe and Asia directed towards America and Oceania, which had characterised the second half of the nineteenth century, started to be perceived with growing hostility long before the war, due to the effects that the over-supply of labour had on wages and hence on living standards. The (probably) most effective examples of the change in attitudes towards migration were countries, such as Australia and the US, whose prosperity had been based on human capital inflows, but in which un-restricted migration also started to be increasingly considered as the origin of lower growth rates. Starting from 1897, and in a progressively more and more restrictive way, America started to select immigrants, reducing their flows and applying severe rules of admission. The backlash against migration increased everywhere in the years after the Great War, both at transcontinental level and in a Europe which had been ravaged by the war, in which almost all countries had become selective towards both incoming and outgoing migration flows. During the post-war years, and especially right through the Great Depression, migration played an ambiguous role. In some cases (and in some countries more than in others, such as France), it was a way to restore the loss of human capital that the conflict had inflicted, and this explains the rise in the percentage of European continental migration in the world total. In other cases, and especially in the years of the Great Depression, the more or less permanent flows of human beings across borders were increasingly perceived as a necessary but problematical evil, which had to be either strictly regulated or carefully managed. Colonies thus became a necessity, whose creation was "justified", as occurred in the case of Italy with Abyssinia, or with the Japanese invasion of Manchuria in 1931, by the search for "vital space". Internal migrations were also subject to regulation, as again was the case in Fascist Italy, where agricultural labourers were "relocated" across different regions.

In sum, whatever the situation, the interwar years were characterised by a reversal of the general cosmopolitan attitude towards migration and foreign labour which had characterised the world economy before the war.

The second pillar of the international order which had preceded the Great War that was destroyed by the conflict and by the years of the economic depression was that of international trade.

As suggested in the previous chapter, the first period of globalisation created what was, under many aspects, a seamless world, but it also simultaneously created the conditions for the reactions against it – reactions which were destined to undergo further intensification in the following decades. One example can be found in the reaction of European agrarian nations against the expansion of the international grain trade during the last quarter of the nineteenth century, which resulted in a wave of protectionist tariffs in the primary sector.

As suggested above, the war years were disruptive, and relatively ambiguous, with some countries even increasing their international trade levels. Despite the general willingness to recreate the pre-war free-trade conditions, the post-war years that both preceded and followed the Great Depression were characterised by a steady and sharp rise in tariffs, which *de facto* restricted international trade. Table 5.1 provides a snapshot of the situation in European countries between 1913 and the early 1930s for different macro sectors.

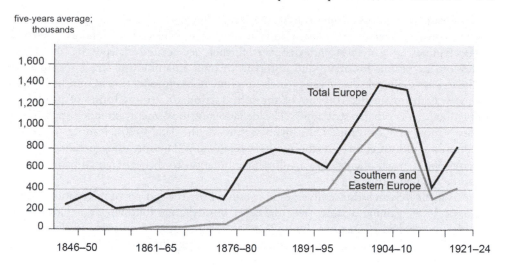

Figure 5.1 European Migrations 1850s–1920s

Table 5.1 Tariffs across Europe, 1913–1931, %, *ad valorem*

(b) Liepmann indices

	Foodstuffs			Semi-manufactured goods			Industrial manufactured goods		
	1913	*1927*	*1931*	*1913*	*1927*	*1931*	*1913*	*1927*	*1931*
Austria	29.1	16.5	59.5	20	15.2	20.7	19.3	21	27.7
Belgium	25.5	11.8	23.7	7.6	10.5	15.5	9.5	11.6	13
Bulgaria	24.7	79	133	24.2	49.5	65	19.5	75	90
Czechoslovakia	29.1	36.3	84	20	21.7	29.5	19.3	35.8	36.5
Finland	49	57.5	102	18.8	20.2	20	37.9	17.8	22.7
France	29.2	19.1	53	25.3	24.3	31.8	16.3	25.8	29
Germany	21.8	27.4	82.5	15.3	14.5	23.4	10	19	18.3
Hungary	29.1	31.5	60	20	26.5	32.5	19.3	31.8	42.6
Italy	22	24.5	66	25	28.6	49.5	14.6	28.3	41.8
Poland	69.4	72	110	63.5	33.2	40	85	55.6	52
Romania	34.7	45.6	87.5	30	32.6	46.3	25.5	48.5	55
Spain	41.5	45.2	80.5	26	39.2	49.5	42.5	62.7	75.5
Sweden	24.2	21.5	39	25.3	18	18	24.5	20.8	23.5
Switzerland	14.7	21.5	42.2	7.3	11.5	15.2	9.2	17.6	22
Yugoslavia	31.6	43.7	77	17.2	24.7	30.5	18	28	32.8

Source: Findlay O'Rourke, p. 445.

The persistence, and even increase, in the level of protection had many determinants, even though the overall effect was clearly to emphasise the general tendency towards *autarkic* regimes, a general trend that was further accelerated sharply by the Great Depression. Economic historians and historians of trade unanimously stress, for instance, that the steady fall in agricultural prices (in its turn, due to overproduction in non-belligerent nations) was the main determinant of the introduction of various forms of protection (tariffs, quotas and other restrictions). The deflationary movement extended outside the primary sector, and constituted the main feature of the late 1920s, leading to further protectionism and, of course, to the resultant retaliation. The spreading nationalistic and anti-cosmopolitan sentiments gave a cultural legitimation to this generalised path towards economic fragmentation.

The available research thus converges in stressing how the indices of international trade rose until 1929, gaining a third over the level immediately following the Great War, dramatically dropped again until the mid-1930s, before rising again prior to the Second World War. This oscillating trend, however, cannot hide the overall decline in trading activity, particularly among the advanced nations (see Table 5.2).

The overall decline in international trade due to contingent determinants also coincided with the transformation of some structural elements. As suggested above, one effect of the war was to accelerate the industrialisation process in the peripheries, particularly in first-industrial-revolution industries, mainly textiles. This was what happened, for instance, in India, Japan and Latin America, where a process of industrialisation through import substitution took place, largely at the expense of Britain. Industrialised countries thus lost quotas in the international trade of staple goods, but increased their relevance in more technology-intensive industries, such as machinery and machine tools, something that could also have incentivised the establishment of subsidiaries abroad. In the interwar

Table 5.2 World trade in the years of the Great Depression

	1929	1932	1937	1929	1932	1937
(a) Regional export and import values (gold dollars, 1929 = 100)						
	Exports			Imports		
Europe including U.S.S.R	100.0	40.8	43.8	100.0	42.8	45.9
North America	100.0	32.6	40.9	100.0	30.5	40.0
Latin America	100.0	37.2	50.1	100.0	27.7	42.8
Africa	100.0	58.5	71.3	100.0	47.4	59.6
Asia	100.0	35.8	52.0	100.0	40.7	49.7
Australasia	100.0	44.8	59.6	100.0	28.5	45.9
World	100.0	39.0	46,7	100.0	39.2	45.9
(a) Regional export import quantities (1929 = 100)						
	Exports			Imports		
Europe including U.S.S.R	100.0	68.5	83.0	100.0	82.0	90.5
	100.0	58.5	˙84.5	100.0	61.0	95.0
	100.0	95.5	127.0	100.0	62.5	106.0

Source: Findlay O'Rourke, p. 450.

years, in sum, together with a general contraction in trade and a progression towards *autarky* in many countries, a general reshuffle of the distribution of "comparative advantages" across the different regions of the world also took place. New industrialisers accelerated their process of import substitution, temporarily filling the technological gap through the acquisition (under the form of imported goods but also of direct investments) of technology-intensive goods from some of the old industrialisers.

Another relevant structural transformation is linked to the fact that a relevant section of Europe (and an increasingly privileged destination of foreign activity, both in terms of trade and in terms of direct investments) had suddenly become largely "off-limits" for global entrepreneurship. The legacy of the Soviet Revolution was that, around the mid-1920s, the foreign trade of the (now) Union of Soviet Socialist Republics was only one-third of its pre-war level, and was largely aiming at the importation of the capital goods necessary for its industrialisation efforts. The self-sufficiency implied by the Communist vision was clearly not stimulating an active involvement in the framework of the international economy, while requisitions (without compensation) had definitely discouraged the activity of foreign investors.

The third broad area upon which the war had a disruptive effect is the one concerning monetary stability and, in general, of capital markets. Monetary stability (granted by the widespread gold standard system) and high capital mobility had unambiguously characterised the phase preceding the conflict, with clear, beneficial effects on international trade, and, of course, on the circulation of capital, in whatever form. The hostilities abruptly, and, much more importantly, permanently, interrupted this virtuous trend. It is, unfortunately, beyond the purposes of this book to examine in depth the complexity of the interwar monetary, banking and fiscal policies undertaken by the most advanced countries. In general, however, the evolution of the international financial order had an obvious impact on the trends of international business and of international entrepreneurship. It is thus worth examining some of the main dynamics that were in play. The monetary equilibrium introduced by the gold standard could clearly not be maintained during the Great War, a war that was largely financed by creating inflation. The years following the war were thus characterised by huge efforts to recreate the pre-war equilibrium, and to strengthen the international financial system. In comparison to the period preceding 1914, the interwar years were characterised by much higher regulatory efforts on the part of national governments (in terms of the independency of central banks and fiscal policy discipline), which occurred on an international scale (the introduction of cooperation among central banks). In general terms, however, it can be said that:"the international financial system of the interwar period was more ordered and regulated than the nostalgically celebrated prewar gold standard."[2]

Monetary control in order to fight inflation and restrictive fiscal policies (fostering deflation) went, however, hand in hand with something that had a much stronger impact on foreign investment activity, particularly on cross-border capital flows. The IMF-designed capital mobility index (CMI)[3] depicts an unequivocal trend. Measured in percentage of GDP, the index went from 3 to 5.5 per cent between 1870 and 1913 to a relatively steady decline during the interwar period, touching a minimum of 1.5 per cent in the first half of the 1930s. Thus, the 1914 level was never reached again until 1989, the beginning of the present phase of globalisation. International finance was, in sum, substantially depressed in the interwar period, notwithstanding some positive signals before the Great Crash (Wall Street) of 1929.

A complex phenomenon in itself, the Great Depression added further emphasis to this already deteriorated scenario. There is general agreement that the origins of what was probably the worst crisis (also in terms of length and mismanagement) of capitalism are largely to be found in the tightening up of monetary policies in the US and in Germany, a move which, in its turn, was undertaken to prevent an excess of speculation on the respective stock markets. The move was successful, even too successful. In Germany immediately after the war (1918–19) and in the US in 1929, the stock market contracted. At the same time, deflationary policies spread to other countries, which were trying to maintain the gold parity of their currencies. Deflationary policies also implied a further contraction of imports, rising levels of protection everywhere and the imposition of quotas (see above), which led to the crisis spreading on a world scale (see Table 5.2). This, in its turn, was followed by deteriorations in the conditions of many domestic economies, in particular in the manufacturing sector, which also suffered from a series of failures in the banking sector. GDP, industrial output and external trade all contracted dramatically almost everywhere. The crisis of Western economies, in which unemployment levels reached 25 per cent in the US and over 30 per cent in many European countries, extended to the exporters of natural resources and primary commodities, in particular in South America, Africa and South-East Asia.

Another side – maybe the worst – of the collapse of the first global economy and of the cosmopolitan, universalistic pre-war international order was a widespread decline in liberalism, or, to put it more bluntly, the rise of nationalism first across the former belligerent nations, and then on a world scale.

The interwar period also introduced major political transformations, which had significant institutional effects. From the 1920s (as a response to the social turmoil following the Great War) to the 1930s (as a clear outcome of the Great Depression), dictatorships "rolled like waves"[4] not only across, but also outside, Europe. Italy was among the first, together with Hungary, at the beginning of the 1920s, Greece and Spain came later in the decade, but, in the meantime, authoritarianism had spread to almost all European countries, from the South to the North of Europe. And when it was not an openly fascist (or socialist, if we include the newly born Soviet Union in the argument) dictatorship, it was some form of totalitarianism, normally enjoying the active or at least passive support of the majority of the population. Authoritarian regimes spread in Asia, too, including the increasingly imperialistic Japan.

The turn to authoritarian regimes went hand in hand with other "keywords", sometimes openly used by dictators as slogans in their public speeches. One, often abused, was *autarky*, a loose concept in which many ideas were included, from the exploitation of internal markets, to rigid control of imports, to the intensification – when possible – of exports in order to keep a positive trade balance. *Autarky* meant the emphasis on the consumption of domestically produced items, and the maximisation of domestic production both in the primary and, above all, the secondary sector. All this coagulated into a sort of inward-looking version of economic nationalism, aiming at fostering the domestic economy, which was, in its turn, perfectly suited to the general framework of depressed international trade.

Autarkic policies meant also, in one way or another, careful control of prices in order to maintain the economic equilibrium within national borders, which included labour costs and, more in general, employment. Internal competition had thus to be disciplined, and it comes as no surprise that the interwar period in Europe was characterised by a generalised consolidation of cartels, more or less formalised agreements among companies about prices, quantities and regional markets and even concerning the exchange of technical information. Co-operative agreements between domestic firms had existed well before the Great War, but their diffusion was incentivised by economic policies which aimed at seeking and enforcing internal equilibrium. By the 1920s, domestic cartels could be numbered in their thousands. Cartels were so important for interwar *autarkic* policies that governments often directly fostered their creation and even regulated their functioning. To some extent, cartels were an efficient alternative to, or even a complement of, planning, a strategy that was increasingly attractive to European policy-makers. Clearly, as we will see in the following sections, cartels prevalently, albeit not exclusively, involved domestic companies cooperating among themselves; in some cases, cartels not only involved domestic and foreign companies, but were also composed of internationally active companies.

A further legacy of *autarky*, authoritarian governments and inward-looking economic and industrial policies, was the increasingly invasive state intervention into the economy. Governments, from Europe to Asia to South America, all enlarged their sets of interventionist policies, from procurement to subsidies to favourable tax treatment for domestic companies. An extreme – but frequent – form of intervention was the creation of state-owned enterprises, or even the nationalisation of the existing national champions. In extreme cases, such as Italy, state intervention – which was already pervasive, just as it had been since the political unification of the country in 1861, but which had accelerated during the Great Crisis of the early 1930s when the banking system was on the verge of default – took the form of the creation, in the early 1930s, of a government-controlled super-holding, the *Istituto per la Ricostruzione Industriale*, or IRI, which directly supervised the activity of state-controlled enterprises in a large number of industries, included the country's largest banks. States, and not just Italy, quickly realised that direct control of production gave them a powerful regulatory instrument, and the possibility of managing a key component of *autarky* policies, and of the industrial modernisation itself, in particular for the peripheries.

Clearly, the trend described here is, in some way, an extreme example of a range of industrial policies which swept through both the industrialised and the less industrialised countries. The alternative to *autarkic* dictatorship, developed in part of Western Europe and North America, was social democracy, which was itself based upon a mixture of interventionist economic policies and government intervention, even in a country such as the US, which traditionally refrained from forms of direct involvement of the government in the economy.

To summarise, in synthesis the Great War accelerated and brought to light some of the contradictions which were already both present and embedded in the pre-war decades, particularly with regard to international trade and migration flows. The years following the conflict saw the attempt to restore some of the components of the first period of globalisation, in particular in the area of trade, international finance and monetary policies, but with scarce results. The Great Depression reinforced the trend of progressive contraction in the international economy which had started as a sort of natural reaction to the full swing of the first global economy and precipitated into a war of world proportions. The sunset of the liberal age in Europe, the emergence of dictatorships and authoritarianism, together with the consolidation of Communism in Russia, the interwar instability in East Asia – once one of the key nodes of the international economy – built the political and institutional framework in which the first global economy quietly but inexorably collapsed.

5 Global entrepreneurship in the interwar years

The general framework faced by internationally active companies and global entrepreneurs in the interwar years was, thus, completely different from that which had characterised the years of cosmopolitanism, liberalism and, in general, the first global economy. The situation, which took its form – for the most part, but not exclusively – in Europe (which was by far the most attractive market for multinational and international firms) was, at least, ambiguous. Clearly, while doing business in the Communist area was a very risky choice, and while other areas, both inside and outside Europe, were suffering from political instability which discouraged foreign investors, dictatorships and nationalist authoritarian governments guaranteed a stability which was much appreciated by foreign investors in an overall framework characterised by much greater uncertainty than in the previous years. Not surprisingly, for instance, for an American company such as *Standard Oil*, willing to establish some kind of investment abroad, the political climate in Italy in the 1930s was probably far more promising or reassuring than that in Mexico, where nationalist sentiments were quickly pushing in the direction of a nationalisation of the domestic oil industry. US direct investments in manufacturing during the 1930s declined by 48 per cent in France, but doubled in Nazi Germany during the same period of time. If, in some cases, the turn towards authoritarian governments was very welcome to investors, in others the outcome of nationalism was that foreign investors found themselves heavily penalised *vis-à-vis* domestic competitors. This was going to occur, of course, more frequently in some industries than others, where national interests were under threat, and where potential negative consequences, particularly in political terms, were highly probable. One telling example from the interwar years involves the largest car manufacturer in the world, a powerful European dictator and a big domestic family company: *Ford* had chosen the free port of Trieste, on the Adriatic Sea, as a basis for its operations in the Mediterranean area, the Balkans and the Middle East. The *Ford Motor Company d'Italia* plant, opened in 1922, to complete semi-assembled cars and tractors.[5] Initially, the attitude of the Fascist government, which was beginning to consolidate its power, was more than favourable, and even culminated in an explicit invitation made to *Ford* in 1925 to make more ambitious investments in the country. *Fiat*, the main domestic manufacturer, did not have a very good relationship with the regime at that time, even though the domestic market was heavily protected. However, when *Ford*, after due deliberation, decided in 1929 to take up the invitation of the Italian government, which offered very generous conditions that would have configured the investment fundamentally as a joint venture with the involvement of domestic investors and managers, the attitude of the government had profoundly changed. Given the crisis in the domestic market, *Fiat* was able to increase its pressure on the Fascist regime in order to request more protection (it was one of the largest employers in the country). The Italian car producer lobbied the government, which, for reasons of national security, imposed severe restrictions on all foreign presence in the industry. By the end of 1929, together with the new laws concerning strategic industries, additional protection was applied to the automotive sector, following *Fiat*'s wishes. *Ford*'s attempts to penetrate the still poor, yet promising, Italian market was wrecked, in sum, by the ability of the local manufacturer to mobilise the national government, which was, in its turn, motivated towards the protection of the national industry and able to take effective counter measures quickly.

The *Fiat–Ford* case clearly demonstrates one of the contradictory situations of the interwar years, during which multinational companies found themselves between the search for stable market outlets and the rising protectionist stances being adopted by the governments of the most advanced countries in Europe.

The period between the two world wars, in sum, coincided with a dramatic change in the general framework of international business, for both economic and political reasons. Such a transformation, as would be expected, had an impact on the "ecology" of global entrepreneurship. In the following part of this section, the most important strategies will be discussed, although the reader should bear in mind that the range of policies put in place was, of course, much wider.

The first relevant transformation has to do with the fading presence of free-standing companies, once among the most diffused forms of foreign direct investment activity. Free-standing companies, which, according to some calculations, accounted for nearly half of the total of global FDIs by 1914, very quickly declined as a form of investment abroad. By the 1930s, classic foreign investments abroad made by a company head-quartered in one country had become *the* most frequent way in which capital was invested abroad, and very few new free-standing companies were created, while many evolved into standard multinationals. The determinants of this phenomenon are, of course, far from being univocal. A large number of free-standing companies engaged in investments in quickly developing areas, for instance, in the European periphery. During the 1920s and 1930s, however, these were no longer "developing areas", and the intermediaries of foreign capital were thus much less necessary. In some cases, when free-standing companies operated in local services, the investment was taken over by companies controlled by municipalities at the end of the concession period. Nationalisation of public services was a fairly common practice in Europe after the Great War, and this resulted in a decreasing number of free-standing companies. In addition, this particular type of foreign investment activity was structurally suitable in the early phases of an investment, but less appropriate in the subsequent phases. By the interwar period, many free-standing companies in the peripheries had transformed into stable investments, and standard multinationals had replaced free-standing companies almost everywhere. The second determinant of the reduced presence of free-standing companies clearly had to do with the general crisis in the international market of primary products and natural resources in the interwar years. Many free-standing companies were in fact (see Chapter 3) active in sectors that had been heavily hit by the decline in international market prices, and entered into a serious period of crisis. Finally, another determinant that has to be mentioned has to do with the general situation affecting the international capital market. Free-standing companies were intermediaries of capital between developed and developing areas. Capital was invested in free-standing companies by investors wishing to obtain a reasonable return on their investments. These companies started to feel seriously uncomfortable in a world in which exchange controls seriously hindered the possibility of an easy remittance of profits, and in which restrictions on cross-border capital transfer were increasingly taking place. Not by chance, most of the few free-standing companies created in the interwar period were active in areas – such as the British Empire, for example – in which the negative effects of capital-transfer regulations were felt in a less intensive way.

Many investors abroad – not only free-standing companies, but also traditional and standard multinationals, based in one home country and investing abroad in a search for markets or resources – decided to leave, abandoning their foreign investment activities, and directing their investments at home. In such a complex framework, disinvestment decisions were frequent, and exit options were frequently exerted. *DuPont*, one of the world's largest players in the chemical industry at the beginning of the 1930s, liquidated its main interests in Europe, significantly selling its shares in its main continental competitor, *I.G. Farben*. *DuPont* sold its shares not just for reasons relating to the difficulties on the international market and in capital markets, but also because investments in an unstable, and increasingly politically complex, environment needed to be handled with serious care.

Other companies, however, decided to remain, their motivations for so doing differing on a case-by-case basis. Some even increased their assets: in some countries, in fact, the repatriation of profits was so difficult that subsidiaries started to invest locally, even in alternative assets such as real estate, in order to "freeze" the available resources.

For the stubborn ones, however, it was, in many cases, necessary to find the best way of coping with nationalistic and protectionist stances both abroad and in the home market. One (quite intuitive) form of behaviour was for firms to disguise themselves. This became necessary in foreign markets, where aliens were now perceived as a serious threat to national interests. US companies found themselves under attack in Europe (in Nazi Germany, they had to produce certificates of "pureness", while, in Fascist Italy, a common form of behaviour was to "Italianise" names, and thereby erase or disguise the traces of foreignness), as well as in South and Central America. A good practice was to create, or increase the power of, subsidiaries in neutral countries, such as Switzerland, the Netherlands or Sweden, transforming them into holdings for the mother company's international investments. This was the way in which, for instance, the above-mentioned *I.G. Farben* handled its investments on the other side of the Atlantic. In order to avoid problems relating to its government's policy – accentuated by the political sensitiveness of the chemical industry, in which the German giant showed a high degree of technological superiority – *I.G. Farben* empowered its Swiss-based subsidiary, entrusting it with the control of its North American subsidiaries and *de facto* hiding their German ownership. Similar behaviour was common to other German companies, some of which additionally transferred the ownership of their holdings in neutral companies to trustees. Camouflage techniques also included joint ventures and other techniques of disguise, which implied the involvement of capital and even human resources in the host country, and were also common in order to avoid information asymmetry and to exploit political connections.

Camouflaging (or, as it has also been called, cloaking) has been extensively (and understandably) studied by historians of international business with reference to German firms, which, during the 1930s, had to cope both with the appetites of the Nazis at home, and with the hostility of both public opinion *and* governments in the host countries. For many of them, managing operations both abroad and at home became seriously difficult, even if the presence of foreign subsidiaries allowed them legally to continue to employ a non-negligible number of Jewish employees, dispatched abroad for the most disparate purposes. Companies with a high Jewish presence, both in the ownership and among the top management and technical staff, such as *Schering* in pharmaceuticals or *Beiersdorf* in cosmetics, were, in fact, facing issues that bore political risks under many aspects: abroad, because of their nationality, at home, because they were investing abroad and not in Germany, and because they were run by "national enemies".

Techniques which aimed to disguise a company's "foreignness" were thus spreading in a world which was becoming increasingly closed, nationalistic and *autarkic*, and had to be quickly developed by companies that wished to remain internationally active – a strategy that bore little or no resemblance to international investors and global entrepreneurs during the first global economy. Political risk, in sum, had become a major issue for companies that were active abroad, and being a "foreigner" was increasingly becoming a "liability". Thus, obtaining or captivating the sympathy of the political and economic élites of the host countries increasingly became a requisite skill in order for internationally active companies to increase their own legitimacy.

Box 5.1: Foreigners at home, nationals abroad: German companies in India in the interwar years

The difficulties of international business during the interwar period emphasise one important topic labelled in the literature as the "liability of foreignness", that is, the burden that a company doing business abroad faces in terms of information asymmetries, discrimination, ignorance of local rules and institutional arrangements, and other difficulties which translate into additional costs implicit to being a foreign presence in a more or less unknown environment.

Clearly, the liability of "foreignness" is dependent on a firm's specific characteristics and capabilities, but it is also dependent on its external conditions, first of all in the market hosting the investment. This may stimulate a series of strategies aiming at counterbalancing the problems brought by asymmetric information and, more in general, by "foreign" status.

The revolution in the global economy brought about by the Great War further emphasised problems of this kind. Almost overnight, a friendly framework became relatively hostile. Companies that were used to doing business even in distant locations suddenly found themselves facing problems, relating both to the targeted location (which, for instance, became increasingly protective and restrictive) and also to their own origin, which, at worst, was sometimes transformed from neutral status into a handicap – particularly when nationalist stances, moulded by local culture and perceptions, came to the fore. This has been called the "liability of home", a concept which summarises the liabilities connected to a multinational's home country.

An effective example of this situation is provided by the case of two multinational companies of German origin between the First and Second World Wars in British imperial India. Both *Bayer*, the chemical leader founded in 1863 and the electrical and electro-mechanical company *Siemens* (founded in 1847) had been running some kind of business in India since the "official" inception of British domination in 1858. *Bayer* had transformed its sales agency into a wholly owned subsidiary in 1896; in 1903, *Siemens* did almost the same thing, co-founding a sales agency in Calcutta. India was regarded by both companies as a promising, expanding and developing market, both *per se* and as access to other markets in Asia. Moreover, the favourable conditions of the First Global Economy made it accessible at virtually no cost (apart from transport, of course). This proved to be a successful strategy, and British firms started to be increasingly displaced in the Indian market by the German competition. To some extent, being German turned out to be a sort of asset in this phase: many Indian consumers, tended to prefer non-British products, purely for nationalistic and anti-colonial motives, and as a way to damage Britain's interests. The situation went further, even becoming paradoxical: there were cases in which British goods were sold as fake "Made in Germany" in order to make them more attractive to Indian customers who wanted to support the cause of Indian independence from Britain. The war completely revolutionised this situation. As a British colony under imperial rule, India was at war with Germany, and thus all German assets were expropriated. Overnight, former competitors and fellow businessmen became "hostile foreigners", or "alien enemies". Firms related to the enemy were either liquidated or could only trade under strict control. Their German, Austrian and in general "enemy" employees were interned in camps surrounded by barbed wire. Both *Siemens* and *Bayer*, as well as other German companies present in India, were heavily hit by the situation.

After the end of the hostilities, it was not easy for German companies to restore their previous reputations. For years after, Germans could not travel to India, something that heavily hindered the possibility of returning to business as usual, that is, to the position that they had occupied in India prior to hostilities. And thus, since these restrictions applied to Germans and to German companies, strategies which aimed at "cloaking", that is to say, disguising the national identity of the companies, became increasingly necessary. Both *Bayer* and *Siemens*, for instance, leveraged the relationship with an Italian company, which had a branch in Bombay, and sent personnel with non-German passports in order to restart their business. When, at the end of 1925, *Bayer* became part of *I.G. Farben*, a new contract was set up with a Dutch trading company, which was put in charge of trading in India. *Siemens* incorporated its business in India, just as other famous German brands, such as *Krupp* and *Schering*, did during the second half of the 1920s. At the same time, German companies tried to set up and strengthen strategic alliances with local partners, and to network with Indian banks and other financial institutions. To a limited extent (albeit no less racist than the British culturally), German companies also made an effort to please Indian employees and distinguish themselves in this way from their British competitors. Furthermore, previous connections between German companies and Indian nationalist movements were at work, and Germans explicitly leveraged the Indian discontent towards British rule in order to regain relevance in the local market. Nationality was thus acting in quite an ambiguous way, both as a liability, but also as an advantage, where Indians counterparts were concerned. As foreigners in a foreign country, which was also a colonial possession of another major European nation, German companies and entrepreneurs had also to maintain friendly relations with the British, something that was not easy at all, particularly after 1933, when the Nazi party came to power in Germany.

At first, the Indian reaction to the "Nazification" of Germany was, at the very least, ambiguous. Racist attitudes were condemned, but, at the same time, Indian nationalists were not eager to break completely with Nazi Germans. German companies, on the other hand – including *Siemens* and *Bayer* – constantly increased their sales and profits, steadily exploiting their status of "non-British" (and, thus, friendly) companies and hiring Indian personnel.

For German companies, however, problems were to come not from the Indian, but, paradoxically, from the German government, and from its racial policies. Policies restricting the employment of Jews in national firms, even abroad, and the required monitoring of "politically undesirables", created permanent problems for German companies, which started to suffer from a shortage of qualified personnel. In this case, in sum, nationality resulted in another type of liability, that is the problem connected to the home government's interference in corporate affairs.

The Second World War – which began in 1939 – recreated or, in a sense, restored the situation that had already been in place twenty-five years before. The Germans became the "enemies" once more, and were again imprisoned in internment camps, their possessions seized and confiscated. The Germans, however, had learnt something from the past. Notwithstanding the difficulties brought about by the war, they attempted to maintain a good relationship with their local employees, compensating them for their loss of service, in an effort to preserve a good image as intangible capital to be used to their advantage upon the conclusion of the war, and through the careful avoidance of colonial attitudes, in order to leverage local nationalist sentiments.

Based upon Christina Lubinski, "Liability of Foreignness in Historical Context: German Business in Pre-independence India (1880–1940)", *Enterprise and Society* 15, no. 4 (2014): 722–58. The author is responsible for any errors and/or omissions.

★ ★ ★ ★ ★

Camouflaging or cloaking added further complexity to an already complex framework. As suggested above, companies had to accustom themselves to policies which aimed to take the general conditions in the host market into consideration, both in political and in cultural terms. While, for instance, free-standing firms, as the intermediaries of capital, were characterised by strategies which aimed at resource exploitation (as in the case of mining, for example) or provided goods and services in the peripheries, interwar multinationals had a much more complex life, becoming progressively familiar, for instance, with strategies of political risk management in order to cope with nationalistic and protectionist stances abroad. It is also important to note that this was a skill that was not just necessary for companies based in countries in which foreign policy could create difficulties for the top management (as in the case of German companies, particularly after 1933 (see Box 5.1)); it also applied to firms based in neutral countries, which had a strong track record of marketing their own products in association with positive images of their own home countries. The Swiss-based *Nestlé*, for instance, experienced serious difficulties in penetrating the Japanese market during the interwar period, due to the opposition of local producers – as was the case for many other multinationals which found themselves facing the increasingly hostile environment of mounting Japanese nationalism during the 1930s. *Nestlé* had mainly started to export condensed milk to Japan at the beginning of the twentieth century, and had encountered, from the very beginning, the open hostility of the local producers, who initiated aggressive forward integration policies, also lobbying the government for trade protection. As a counter move, *Nestlé* decided to open a production plant, a strategy which took the Swiss company more than twenty years to complete, with the opening of *Awaji Rennyu KK* (ARKK, or *Awaji Condensed Milk*) in 1934. However, given that nationality was the main issue, the "official" ownership of the Japanese company was in the hands of seven Japanese nationals, who were, however, acting as *Nestlé*'s "strawmen". At the same time, ARKK depended on both *Nestlé*'s technology and its financial loans, something which was kept relatively undisclosed.

The widespread policy of the creation of multiple holdings in neutral countries, so widespread among European companies, led to an increasingly complicated type of organisational design, and, to some extent, a complicated type of authority relationships, when compared to the high de-centralisation which characterised free-standing companies, or to the high centralisation which characterised other companies which based their internationalisation upon the opening of production facilities across borders, under the close centralised control of the mother company. To put it in another way, the unstable environment of the interwar period required international companies to invest in the direction of increasing flexibility and adaptation to local political conditions, more than in terms of consumption culture, as would subsequently happen. To rely on a flexible (also in terms of organisational design and authority channels), multi-domestic organisation thus became a condition for survival in the complicated framework of the interwar years. For the first time, the emphasis on the careful management of political relationships started, in many cases, if not in all, to make the relationship between the mother company and its subsidiaries less asymmetrical than it used to be.

More than a strategy, technological superiority was an asset which, to some extent, allowed an easier way in. Nationalist governments around the world were also in a relatively ambiguous situation. Closure meant the preservation of national wealth, but also isolation from the technological developments taking place abroad; and, as discussed in the previous chapters, multinational companies were already the intermediaries of both soft and hard knowledge. Clearly, the situation varied considerably from country to country, and even from company to company. To return to the Italian case, if the relationship between the Fascist government and *Ford* was, to say the least, ambiguous, *IBM* had a much easier life. The absence of local companies able to compete to the same technological standards made life much easier for *IBM*. In addition, the obsession of authoritarian governments with counting and measuring made *IBM* technology and products very popular, which, to some extent, had a positive effect on the company's strategic freedom in a world which was very much under government (and party) control. In other cases, compromises were necessary. Mira Wilkins reports the case of *Norton*, an international leader in abrasives, a well-established multinational, which used to manufacture abroad, albeit by exporting some crucial components form the US. Import restrictions during the interwar period meant that *Norton* had to start manufacturing these materials abroad, thereby being forced to disclose essential product and process technologies.[6] Thus, the presence of restrictions of a more or less authoritarian nature emphasised the strategic relevance of some characteristics which had already made a difference in the past, thereby incentivising companies to cross borders, notwithstanding the problems embedded in the strategy of industrialisation of the company. In sum, companies controlling superior, idiosyncratic technologies perceived this ability as their most relevant and effective competitive tool. They actually *owned* advantages over competitors, which, most importantly, exceeded the implicit costs of internationalisation. Again, such a situation challenged the relations between the national subsidiaries and their home headquarters, not just formally, but, in some cases, also in substance, the latter being forced to transfer part of their authority. It has, in fact, been noted that the rise of nationalism and protective policies provided incentives for local subsidiaries to increase their level of local embeddedness – with local production networks, local companies, and host-nation governments – transforming the "radial" organisation typical of pre-war multinationals (based upon vertical relations between the home headquarters and the local subsidiaries) into a "polycentric" one, characterised by a higher administrative and organisational independence of the local branches.

To be global in the interwar period was, in sum, not an easy task at all. From the evolutionary theory perspective, it was the changes in the environmental conditions that determined the selection, and provoked the adaptation, but also, to some extent, led to the diffusion of the most flexible organisms. A hostile environment also resulted in a strong incentive towards co-operation, both at domestic and at international level. As effectively cited in a report by the British Board of Trade – published immediately after the Second World War, but drafted upon the basis of previously collected material:

> Periods of economic dislocation are favourable to the spread of cartels, and it is undoubtedly true that when conditions are unstable, manufacturers are disposed to consort together for purpose of defence.[7]

Second, these differences led to different behaviour in times of crisis. The First World War and, later, the Great Depression marked – for the first time, in fact – an unexpected interruption in the process of the (seemingly) monotonic economic integration incentivised by technological and institutional factors which had characterised the world economy during the preceding centuries. Multinational corporations were, to a large extent, "brought to life" by the specific set of conditions that characterised the first global economy. They were still relatively "recent" creations when a global crisis hit the world's economy, abruptly threatening their existence. They thus had to adapt to the changing environment through another set of strategies in order to survive internationally, until the world economy progressively started to integrate again.

The outcome of all this was an increasingly pervasive presence of a particular form of foreign business activity: that of international cartels.

6 International cartels and cooperative agreements

Definitions of cartels and international cartels are abundant. One, which is comprehensive enough to include a large variety of cases and types, considers cartels as a particular type of the even broader category of "agreements" among firms, agreements seen as alternatives to pure market competition. International cartels are thus considered as mutual agreements among companies (or among their national associations or national cartels) based in different countries, in order to coordinate – if not completely, at least in part – the market in which these companies were active. Clearly, international cartels can be seen as a sort of amplification, or expansion, of cartels which exclusively involved national companies that were active upon a domestic basis. Their cross-border nature made them more complex and, to some extent, provided them with more sophisticated structures, particularly in terms of organisation and governance.

As (maybe temporary) alternatives to competitive markets, some kind of collaborative settings had existed long before the Great War. Cartels, trusts and agreements were quite a natural stage in the evolution of capital-intensive industries characterised by high advantages in high, stable and planned volumes of production. As a way of regulating competition and of improving stability, cartels were particularly effective in the early stages of the evolution of an industry, when national producers had to consolidate themselves at national level. Trusts and cartels thus were diffused well before 1914, to such an extent that, in some cases, as with the US for example, they prompted a sort of institutional reaction to the artificial control of competition, and led to the establishment of antitrust laws. In other cases, however, and contrary to what is current common sense, there were also good reasons for the perfectly legal existence of such agreements, both at national and at international level. The validity of such reasons is confirmed by the diffusion of cartels, both domestic and cross-border, in the interwar years. Unfortunately, is not easy to collect reliable data on such a topic, which was, in part, undisclosed and, in part, impossible to regulate centrally. Some tentative statistics speak of around 350 such agreements in the 1930s, mainly involving European continental companies, a few Japanese and some American companies, managing to circumvent the hostilities of national institutions. According to contemporary research, in 1938, the percentage of exports falling under the umbrella of some kind of international agreement ranged from a relatively small 7 per cent, for instance, in cotton yarns or rubber products, to 85 per cent of iron and steel, and 88 per cent of coke. International cartelisation concerned, of course, industries in which monitoring was easier and in which product differentiation was low: oligopolistic, standardised, scale-intensive and technology-intensive industries, and in intermediate products and capital goods. Examples include iron and steel, chemicals, electrical and mechanical engineering, glass and non-ferrous metals. A report by the British Board of Trade reviewing the situation in the 1930s, analysed over 120 cartels in which British companies were involved.

Historians of global entrepreneurship agree, however, on the fact that the Great War further accelerated the creation of co-operative agreements, for a number of reasons which were, in part, generated by the exceptional conditions created by the conflict. The war, for instance, created such huge imbalances between production capacity and demand that, after the hostilities, some kind of regulation and rationalisation of production capacity became absolutely necessary, in particular where industries of strategic relevance were concerned. One example is reported in Box 5.2, which deals with nitrogen, a basic component in the explosives industry. The war over-expanded the production capacity of nitrogen and led to international regulation of both nitrogen export activity and of production – which was normally subject to domestic cartel agreements.

Box 5.2: The nitrogen cartel

The interwar period saw the peak of the cartel movement. In Europe and the European-dominated parts of the world, cartels were generally accepted and cartelisation was viewed as a positive force. Governments and firms alike resorted to international cartels as regulation mechanisms, which, they thought, could replace administrative measures, such as customs and import quotas. In the case of the chemical industry, national cartelisation regulated the home market while international agreements focused mostly on exports.

Both before and after the First World War, the chemical industry was at the forefront of international cartelisation. The nitrogen cartels (*Convention Internationale de l'Azote*, or CIA, 1930–31, 1932–39) were among the most influential cartels; in the chemical sector, only the international dyestuffs cartel was of a similar size in terms of turnover. Furthermore, given that nitrogen was the basic raw material for the production of fertilisers and explosives, it was regarded as being of strategic importance by national governments. Until 1900, two-thirds of world production of chemical nitrogen came from natural deposits of nitrates, principally those of sodium nitrate in Chile. The process for producing synthetic ammonia by the combination of nitrogen and hydrogen in the presence of a catalyst was invented in Germany between 1905 and 1913, and is known as the Haber-Bosch process. The great success of the synthetic ammonia process in Germany during the war stimulated worldwide research into this method of the fixation of atmospheric nitrogen. During the 1920s, many firms were drawn to the nitrogen industry by the expectations of high profits. In addition, for security reasons, a number of countries were concerned about their dependence on foreign supplies of nitrogen and wanted to produce the basic material for their industries. The creation of new synthetic nitrogen factories threatened the strong position of the major producers, which were Chile (for natural nitrogen), Germany, the UK and Norway. By 1926, these countries alone would have reached a worldwide level of over-production.

In order to cope with this situation, an international conference was held in Biarritz (France) at the end of April 1926. The representatives of about ten countries discussed both the current situation and the development of the nitrogen world market. At the conference, the British and German delegations brought attention to what would be the ultimate effect if nitrogen production continued to expand during a decline in the world prices of agricultural crops. On 26 June 1929, the first international nitrogen cartel was announced, consisting of three separate agreements between the German Nitrogen Syndicate, the British firm *Imperial Chemical Industries* and Chilean natural nitrate producers. The Norwegian firm *Norsk Hydro*, because of its affiliation with the German industry, was subsequently included. The duration of the pact was initially for one year, and it was renewed and enlarged for another year in August 1930. This second cartel included the so-called DEN group, which had founded the original pact (DEN being the initial letters of Deutschland, England and Norway), France, Belgium, Czechoslovakia, the Netherlands, Italy and Poland. It covered about 98 per cent of European and 80 per cent of the world nitrogen production (the United States and Japan did not participate). The agreements provided for cooperation regarding advertising, for price uniformity and for some allocation of production and export quotas. Each country remained in control of its domestic market, in so far as its national industry could satisfy its domestic needs. Exports to members of the cartel or to outsiders were regulated by means of special agreements that established the export quotas. Production restrictions were not uniform, but varied according to the country: 10 per cent for France; 30 per cent for Germany, Norway, Belgium, the Netherlands, Czechoslovakia and Italy; 40 per cent for Poland; and 50 per cent for the UK.

Germany and the UK, the largest producers, had to make a few sacrifices. For Germany, which had previously been able to export about one-third to one-half of its production, the advantages of the cartel were: the guarantee of stable prices, the avoidance of a price war between the European producers, and the hope that the cartel would discourage a further expansion of production capacity. For the UK, the only advantage was in the area of the prices: the European market was virtually closed and the domestic market accounted for about two-fifths of production as a result of the importation of Chilean nitrates. In order to carry out the quota provisions of the agreement, it would appear that the cartel must have had the official sanction and assistance of the governments of the countries represented by the producers. Carrying out the provision for administration, it was announced on 15 August 1930, that the *International Gesellschaft der Stickstoffindustrie* A.G. had been set up in Basel (Switzerland) with an initial capital of 6 million Swiss francs. Its shares were owned by members of the cartel. This organisation had to safeguard profitable and stable prices. It also served as a compensation fund to make up for losses due to production restrictions, to fight outsiders and to pay for the cartel's organisation costs.

The cartel fulfilled the purpose of preventing excess competition in a market where several years of over-production had led to a severe fall in prices. Under its rules, formal free trade could be maintained, while consumers, especially European farmers, retained some freedom in their purchasing power. However, it did not succeed in its struggle against the plummeting of world demand. When the negotiations to renew the cartel began in April 1931, it appears that several nitrogen producers asked for higher quotas in accordance with their capacity, which had now increased to 4 million tonnes of nitrogen, whereas consumption had decreased to 1.5 million tonnes. Conflicts of interest proved impossible to resolve, and there was a complete breakdown of the negotiations for a renewal of the pact in July 1931. Almost all countries responded by raising import duties or by imposing licence systems, quotas or embargoes to protect the domestic market. Duties were not raised on the importation of nitrogen to Germany, which, at this stage, was the largest exporter. However, after the collapse of the CIA, the German Nitrogen Syndicate wanted to prevent possible imports from being dumped on its territory. Consequently, it asked the government to impose high customs on nitrogen imports. The government proved to be cooperative, but it was already laid down in trade treaties with Belgium and France that no customs duties were to be imposed on imports of nitrogen. Thus, first, these states had to agree to declare the relevant treaty clauses to be invalid before the German government would be able to raise customs duties. The German syndicate approached their Belgian and French counterparts, both of which, in exchange for a special payment, agreed to cooperate and informed their governments that they were not interested in the respective clauses of the trade treaties. On this basis, the French and Belgian governments renounced their respective rights, thereby allowing Germany to raise customs duties. This process, which required only a few weeks to be brought to completion, was exemplary in highlighting the intensive co-operation that existed at various levels: between the firms which were member of the syndicates in Germany, France and Belgium, between the syndicates and their respective governments, and in the diplomacy of the states involved.

After being shrouded in mystery for many months, the formation of a new cartel became known in the autumn of 1932 following the signing of an agreement in London in July of the same year. A new element was the entry of Switzerland into the cartel. The French producers, on the other hand, withdrew under pressure from their government. The DEN group, as a unit, was responsible for the sales of export quotas, and, accordingly, entered into a series of contracts with each of the other countries, thus providing cooperation in the matter of price and production limitations. Another important feature was the continuation of compensation to certain producers for restricting production. Illustrative of this was the yearly payment of 4.5 million gold marks granted to the *Companie Néerlandaise de l'Azote*, a Belgian–Italian joint venture established in 1929, for the restriction of the output of its plant at Sluiskil in the Netherlands by two-thirds. The Sluiskil plant could produce at very low cost thanks to its advantageous geographical location and its state-of-the-art technical equipment, and thus represented a serious challenge to German producers in export markets.

A special agreement with Japan was signed in the spring of 1934. In the same year, the cartel was renewed, introducing for the first time a penalty clause for member countries exceeding their export quotas. Receipts for exports in excess of quotas were to be paid into a compensation fund, upon which European producers not fulfilling their export quota allowances were to have first claim. In July 1935, a new agreement was reached, extending the cartel over three years this time. The stipulation remained roughly the same. Equally, the renewal of the cartel in 1938, which was to last until late June 1941, did not show any fundamental change. After the Second World War, the American nitrogen producers gained a much stronger position and began to force European companies out of the principal export markets. In 1962, a new international nitrogen cartel – *Nitrogen Chemical Fertilizer Export Cartel* (NITREX) – was established in Zurich (Switzerland) by major West European nitrogen fertiliser producers.

This box was written by Mario Perugini.

International business research has largely focused on cartels as a particular – albeit pervasive – form of cross-border entrepreneurship in the interwar period. International cartels were, in fact, not only institutional arrangements which aimed at rationalising production and controlling both exports and international trade; they were also multi-purpose governance structures which allowed the companies belonging to them to pursue a different set of goals in a phase during which international business activity was dramatically stagnant. In addition to this, international cartels were also often characterised by centralised organisational bodies which functioned as common governance structures, and are quite often described as a sort of "intermediate" organisational form, neither market-like nor hierarchy-like. From this point of view, at least formally, international cartels resembled a sort of multinational structure, characterised by the presence of a headquarters, which dealt with coordination and administrative functions, and of production plants in different geographic locations. These structures were, by definition, based upon a centralised but nonetheless loose coordination of the individual companies participating in the agreement(s).

For the purpose of this book, we will mainly focus on the different types of international cartels, analysing some of the organisational arrangements put in place to coordinate their activity. International cartels were no different from domestic ones as far as their functions are concerned. Some taxonomies list various functions performed by cartels, many simultaneously. Agreements concerned caps on production quantities, on the quantity of sales in a domestic market – often left, fully or partially, exclusively to national producers – and export quotas for companies belonging to the cartel (in some cases, this even led to the creation of centrally coordinated bodies which oversaw sales in the international markets, and, of course, prices). There were even cartels which, alongside other agreements, also regulated and coordinated the exchange of technological information, through the exchange of patents (very common, for instance, in the chemical industry, a notable example being the hydrogenation process, in which a patent pool included, in the interwar years, the Germans of *I.G. Farben*, the Americans of *Standard Oil*, the British-Dutch of *Shell*, and the British of *ICI*), and even the creation of common research units. In some cases, these agreements were strengthened and enforced by interlocking financial interests or even interlocking directorates (the mutual exchange of board members), between firms from different countries.

Given these premises – that of the protection of internal markets and the preservation of the oligopolistic power of domestic producers, and simultaneously the maximisation of the export capacity of national firms – international cartels were also highly appreciated as instruments of economic and industrial policy by protectionist national governments which, at the same time, pushed national companies towards both exports and the acquisition of technological competences. The participation of national companies in international cartels was, thus, by no means neutral for governments during the interwar years, and this is relevant to explaining the general attitude towards this particular form of international business activity.

7 Governance and organisation of international cartels

Apart from their strategies and overall diffusion, a pertinent reason for emphasising the role of international cartels in this volume is the nature of their attributes in terms of organisation and governance. Cartels were, in fact, co-operative agreements that, to some extent, aimed to manipulate free-market competition. For this reason, their shape was continuously transforming according to changes in the external framework and market structures, which, in turn, had relevant effects on their internal cohesion and stability. In particular, international cartels added another kind of instability to this, that is, the instability derived from the fact that the companies belonging to them were subject to different national jurisdictions, which made the enforcement of the rules governing the cartel itself intrinsically weak. In some sense, the same causes of economic instability that determined the creation of a cartel could be at the basis of its crisis and decline. There could be the sudden devaluation of a currency, or the appearance of a new source of raw materials, or even a new, substitutive product. For instance, new sources of potash – a basic component of fertilisers, at the basis of a powerful international cartel created in the interwar period – disrupted, for some time, the existing agreements between the French and the German producers, to which those in Palestine, Poland and Spain were soon added. Cases are countless.

Governance and organisational structures were thus absolutely necessary in order to keep agreements stable and efficient, and the understanding of their design is particularly relevant for understanding the effectiveness of cartels as instruments for international business.

Box 5.3: The (tormented) governance of an international cartel: aluminium in the interwar years

Aluminium has often been considered a model of international interwar cartelisation. Both supporters and detractors of the international cartel movement have used the aluminium industry to show either the good or the evil of cartels. For instance, aluminium has often been presented as being able to embody the proposals to use cartels to restore cordial relationships between France and Germany after the Great War and to help the economic restoration of interwar Europe. Both the League of Nations and the International Chamber of Commerce praised the role of the cartel in the 1920s, as a powerful agent for economic rationalisation, and, in the 1930s, as an important tool to tackle the global market slump that followed the Wall Street Crash of 1929. In contrast, in the US, the aluminium cartel provoked infamous criticism during the Second World War and was taken to be an essential device of Adolf Hitler's "master plan", one which frustrated the Allied war production, thereby granting a decisive advantage to the Axis powers at the beginning of the war.

Aluminium was a new commodity in the landscape of non-ferrous metals. Even though the earth's crust consists of 8 per cent of aluminium, no deposits of pure aluminium are present and the lack of a viable technology to separate the metal from other elements delayed the creation of a modern industry until the late nineteenth century. In fact, the modern aluminium industry could only be developed after 1886, when Paul Toussaint Héroult in France and Charles Martin Hall in the US independently invented the modern process of electrolysis. Both inventors were linked to the creation of the first movers of this industry, *Aluminium Industry Aktien-Gesellschaft* (AIAG, successively *Alusuisse*) and the *Pittsburgh Reduction Company* (successively the *Aluminum Company of America* (ALCOA)) respectively, which were founded in Switzerland in 1887 and in the US in 1888. These firms were also the main actors of the transnational diffusion of aluminium technologies at the end of the nineteenth century: they both resorted to FDIs (AIAG invested in Austria in 1897 and in Germany in 1898, while ALCOA created a unit in Canada in 1900, which subsequently became

ALCAN), and licensed foreign companies (AIAG gave a licence to *Société Electro-métallurgique Française* (SEMF) in 1888 and to *British Aluminium Company* (BACO) in 1894, while ALCOA granted a licence to another French producer in 1895, which was absorbed by *Produits Chimiques d'Alais et de la Camargue* (PCAC) in 1897). Until the Great War, this small group of interconnected firms dominated the global aluminium scene. From 1901, an official cartel called the *Aluminium Association* was created and, during a short-lived crisis, it was able to set market quotas, to programme output expansion, and to set stable prices that accompanied a steady increase of consumption. In particular, the *Association* was able to share the greatest pre-war market, i.e. Germany, amongst its members, all of whom were looking for outlets in which to deploy their scale productions.

The Great War had a dramatic impact on the global market for aluminium. First, the war meant an impressive technological spin-off for aluminium. Military uses dramatically increased, reshaping aluminium into a key strategic material and spreading the use of what had hitherto been a rather new and relatively unknown material. Second, the war completely changed the patterns of the European market. Before 1914, Germany had been the biggest market for aluminium and the main commercial target for the group of producers. The heavy intervention of the German state led to the creation of a new national producer, *Vereinigte Aluminium Werke* (VAW), which saturated the home market, provoking a dislocation in the market strategies of the older firms. Third, the war enabled ALCOA to emerge as a giant firm which was able to control more than half of the global output on its own. The US also became the greatest market in the world for aluminium, since the demand from the automotive industry led to a spurt in this market during the first half of the 1920s. The legacy of the war was a general displacement of the fundamentals that had determined the aluminium market before 1914. While the global output had seen a three-fold increase during the hostilities, thanks to the war consumption, it was not taken for granted that this output could have found an outlet for civil use once the war was over. Issues regarding how to adapt a disproportionate output, designed for the war effort, to a downsized civil market situation again required cartels as a possible means of international economic governance.

From November 1918, the allied aluminium producers (SEMF-PCAC, ALCOA and BACO) debated the possibility of reviving the pre-war *Aluminium Association* and of helping the transition from a war economy to a peace economy without market disorder. They also discussed the possibility of institutionalising the cartel with a common R&D agency in order to foster the transition from the war uses of this metal to its civil application. However, the economic crisis postponed the creation of the cartel, and governmental policies continued to shield their national firms from international competition. In this environment, not only tariffs, but also trade licences, political control of prices, and the settlement of anti-dumping codes, such as the US "Antidumping Act of 1921", delayed the return to normal international trade. In 1922, the French executive of *Alais, Froges et Camargue* (AFC, which had been created in 1921 by the merger of SEMF and PCAC), Louis Marlio, undertook some vigorous action which, by newly establishing trust amongst the group of producers, was to prove sufficient to re-establish the cartel. He helped the Swiss producer AIAG, which had had its German interests confiscated by the French government during the war, to regain its investments in France. In addition, he initiated the first *rapprochements* with the new German producers and was able to combine the various patents that both ex-belligerent fronts owned with regard to aluminium-magnesium alloys. Finally, he was the main architect of some joint ventures in countries that were judged to be potentially critical for the international market, such as Norway, Italy and Spain, because their output was bigger than their domestic demand. In October 1923, the first "global" meeting of aluminium producers was organised in Zurich, and it was considered to be the first move towards the re-establishment of a world cartel.

In spite of its involvement in joint ventures and for the first post-war meetings, ALCOA dropped out of the network of producers in 1924, after procrastinating about a decision on the formal establishment of a cartel. Anti-trust fears were assumed to be the main explanation for its behaviour, but, in fact, ALCOA was procrastinating about its entering into a cartel scheme because it was deciding on a robust strategy of internationalisation, which demanded a global re-positioning of the firm. In 1925, ALCOA succeeded in blocking the construction of a new unit in Canada that was ventured by *General Electric, Ford* and *Duke & Price*. By taking over this unit, not only did ALCOA obtain a new major source of output that reversed the supply/demand situation in the North American market, it also provoked the slowdown of aluminium use in the automotive industry. While the new Canadian smelter came on stream at the end of the 1920s, when the international economic situation was also moving into recession, the new output of ALCOA required additional outlets in the international market. This strategy also provoked the creation, in 1928, of an autonomous Canadian firm to manage the FDIs of ALCOA, *Aluminum Limited* – the forerunner of ALCAN. Fearing that a disorganised evolution of output would have disrupted the international market for aluminium after the trade liberalisation that followed the reshaping of the international monetary system, the European firms established a new cartel in 1926, again called the *Aluminium-Association*. While the new association failed to obtain the participation of the American company, this cartel proved to be unable to control the expansion programmes of its members, which continued to invest during the euphoria of the 1920s in order to improve their market quotas while waiting for ALCOA to join the association. However, without coordination between the Europeans and the North Americans, the global recession that followed the expansion at the end of the 1920s meant harsh competition for outlets in the aluminium market, which, in some distant markets, such as Japan and India, resulted in cut-throat price reduction, while, at a global level, it produced a severe accumulation of unsold inventories, which were estimated to be equal to eighteen months of global output.

In 1931, the Canadian firm proposed the creation of a new global cartel scheme to the Europeans. Instead of a "proper" cartel, the creation of a Swiss finance company to handle the unsold inventories was proposed. At the same time, the *Alliance Aluminium Compagnie*, as this company was called, had imposed some output restrictions, while the inventories were liquidated on the market. A compromise was also found with ALCOA: the US market was cut off from the cartel regulation, but ALCOA agreed to avoid any operations outside its national market and to allow imports from the members of *Alliance*. Operating as a private "stock buffering scheme", *Alliance* differed greatly from the former Association that had imposed market quotas in order to manage the global balance between supply and demand. Without any national differences, *Alliance* imposed a global reduction in the output of firms, organising a system of swaps among the warehouses of each individual member. However, the mechanism of *Alliance*, in spite of its effectiveness in keeping international prices stable during the recession, became contrary to the military re-armament programmes of many governments during the second half of the 1930s. At the same time, the disruption to the international monetary order made it particularly difficult to continue the swap system that they had invented to manage the buffering of the unsold stocks. In particular, the output restriction became one of the main threats to Hermann Göring's Four-Year Plan in Germany (1936–40), which led the German group to ask for derogations to the scheme that ended up excluding the German output from the cartel regulation. At the same time, the emergence of new strategic policies in other states, such as the UK and Italy, led the international scheme to be seriously questioned. The emergence of new producing countries, such as Japan and many Eastern European nations, also called into question the ability of *Alliance* to operate an effective buffering of the unsold inventories. In 1937, the opening of a huge anti-trust case against ALCOA led its Canadian sister company to put the cartel on hold. During the last phase of the Second World War, the US authorities, using the threat of the pending anti-trust case against ALCOA, forced ALTED (*Aluminium Co. Ltd. of Canada*) to ask for the dissolution of *Alliance* as soon as the war in the European theatre had ended, which it did on 15 May 1945.

This box was written by Marco Bertilorenzi.

★ ★ ★ ★ ★

The huge variety of cartels and agreements makes it difficult to generalise about their organisation and governance attributes; however, some general characteristics can be summarised here.

To a certain extent, in sum, international cartels were efficient responses to the need to preserve national monopolies, simultaneously allocating production surpluses abroad and avoiding excess competition. Structures such as that depicted in Figure 5.2 resemble those of multinational companies, which were at that time characterised by the presence of a mother company controlling various production sites in different countries. The world's largest producers of electric lamps (including *International General Electric*, the British/European subsidiary of the US giant, which played a major role) created *Phoebus S.A. Compagnie Industrielle pour le Developpement de l'Eclairage*, in the mid-1920s in order to oversee the administration of production, quotas and price, as well as to coordinate the exchange of technical information. *Phoebus* was based in Switzerland and also had an internal board which was to settle disputes between the members of the cartel. Members could trade among themselves, and could impose production quotas in cases of necessity.

The purpose of the cartel was to grant the participants control of their respective internal markets, also allowing those which had surpluses to allocate them to "common" markets through a system of quotas.

However, differences from multinationals are also evident. International cartels are thus probably to be considered as relatively "loose" governance structures regulating international trade and production in some industries. Loose, but with some particular traits. Broadly speaking, cartels can be divided into two categories: those governed by a central body, independent from the individual companies within them, and those whose governance was entrusted to the assembly of the representatives of the participants to the agreement. In the latter case, based upon regular general meetings, the nature of the governance processes was much simpler than in the first, and the independence of the

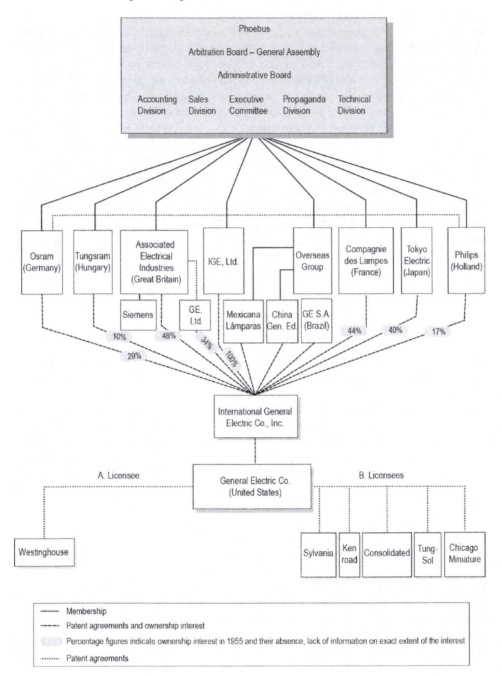

Figure 5.2 The world cartel in electric lamps

individual companies much more pronounced. When cartels became more complex in their organisation, they started to adopt more formalised structures, often corporatised in the form of a holding located in neutral countries, which often coincided with those characterised by more attractive fiscal regimes, such as Belgium, the Netherlands and, of course, Switzerland. These bodies were in charge of overseeing and administering all the issues relating to the cartel's operations, from quotas to prices, to the exchange of technical information among the participants. They also had arbitration roles in cases of litigation among the members; in some cases, such as that of the world cartel among electric lamp producers described above in Figure 5.2, the central body was also supposed to provide some forms of general services, of both an administrative and a technical nature.

International cartels, to some extent, resembled multinational corporations based upon holdings which centrally governed their production plants which were located in different countries. In the case of cartels regulating production quotas, for instance, local "branches" (the companies associated with the cartel, and their plants) first of all saturated the internal market, then allocated their eventual surpluses to other markets through exports. Central coordination bodies took care of some crucial functions – the administration of the agreement – but left basically intact the independence of the participants, which were free to pursue the strategies of their choice within the limits of the cartel framework. For instance, in the case of price cartels, the incentive for the individual company was to improve production efficiency in order to obtain higher profits at the same price level – which was, in part, also true for cartels that limited quotas and quantities. Managers were thus prevented from using some of the traditional competitive tools, but could resort to leverage on others, at the same time, in a general frame of relative competitive stability, and, in some cases, benefiting from commonly developed or mutually exchanged knowledge.

Conclusion

The period between the two world wars marked a particular phase in the history of global entrepreneurship, which radically challenged the equilibrium of the first global economy and urged international companies to face new problems and challenges. They had, for instance, to become much more versatile to adaptation to the local environment than before. "Foreignness" became a liability that, in some cases, offset all of the other assets upon which a company could count. Asymmetries grew considerably, notwithstanding the fact that the improvements in transport and communications technologies acted in the opposite direction. The Great War destroyed the fragile equilibrium of the first period of globalisation, in which the multinational corporation – as the dominant organisational form in international business – diffused itself pervasively. In many respects, the interwar years were characterised by conditions which were the complete opposite to those of the decades which had preceded the conflict: openings turned into barriers, free trade into protection. As a result of the previous phase of globalisation, these conditions were common, albeit with different degrees of intensity, to both industrialised economies and developing countries, and were further intensified by the global financial crisis that spread from the end of the 1920s. All this clearly affected the way in which international entrepreneurship actively pursued opportunities for profit. This chapter has focused on three aspects: the adaptation of companies to hostile environments through cloaking and camouflage techniques; the exploitation of technological competences superior enough to overcome hostile environments; and, finally, the creation of cooperative agreements in the form of international cartels. These strategies – and others put in place by international companies in this very specific phase – allowed international business activity to persist and even expand, notwithstanding the (objectively) problematical framework of the interwar years. The ability of global enterprises to adapt was undoubtedly great, as witnessed by the relative prosperity of internationalisation activities in the period under consideration. According to some aggregate calculations, the aggregate FDIs rose (at constant prices) by around 50 per cent during the period between 1914 and 1938. International cartels played a major role in keeping the international activity of companies alive. Even though they were very different from standard multinationals in many respects, to some extent they were centrally able to coordinate multi-plant production across borders in a wide number of industries. The mutual agreements nature of international cartels, however, meant that loose coordination prevailed, and that the participants maintained a substantial degree of autonomy – albeit within a strictly regulated framework.

After the Second World War, however, the general conditions had changed again, and consequently global companies found themselves not only with new opportunities in front of them, but also with new challenges to face. Again, new species appeared, and a selection was made among the existing ones. As noted by theorists, for instance, international cartels had begun to become less diffused and even to disappear after the Second World War, generally for reasons relating to the fact that they were less economically efficient when compared to other organisational forms, and not relating to the diffusion of institutional constraints. For instance, the cost of setting up a multinational activity became, in other words, inferior to the cost of creating, maintaining, enforcing and monitoring a cartel, in sharp contrast to what had prevailed in the interwar years.

The next chapter will investigate both the changes in the general framework of the global economy, and their effects on the forms of international business activity in the decades preceding the restart of the globalisation process on a global scale.

Notes

1 From Stefan Zweig, *The World of Yesterday*, (first published in German: Zurich: Williams Verlag, 1942). Stefan Zweig was born in 1881 in Vienna, into a wealthy Austrian-Jewish family. He studied in Austria, France and Germany, and was first known as a poet and translator, then as a biographer. In 1934, with the rise of Nazism, he moved to London and finally, after a long peregrination, to Brazil. He committed suicide in 1942.
2 Harold James, *The End of Globalization: Lessons from the Great Depression*, Cambridge, MA: Harvard University Press, 2001, p. 33.
3 Available at: www.imf.org/external/pubs/ft/icm/97icm/pdf/file14.pdf. The index is defined "as the average of the absolute values of current accounts relative to GDP for major capital-importing and capital exporting countries. The countries include Argentina, Australia, Canada, Denmark, France, Germany, Italy, Japan, Norway, Sweden, the United Kingdom, and the United States".
4 The definition is from Jeffry A. Frieden, *Global Capitalism: Its Fall and Rise in the Twentieth Century*, (paperback edition), New York: Norton, 2007, p. 209.
5 The story is narrated in detail by Pier Angelo Toninelli, "Between Agnelli and Mussolini: Ford's Unsuccessful Attempts to Penetrate the Italian Automobile Market in the Interwar Period", *Enterprise and Society*, 10(2), 2009, pp. 335–77.
6 This example is quoted by Mira Wilkins, "Multinationals and Dictatorship: Europe in the 1930s and early 1940s", in: Christopher Kobrak and Per H. Hansen (eds), *European Business, Dictatorship and Political Risk 1920–1945*, New York and Oxford: Berghahn Books, 2004, pp. 22–40.

7   Board of Trade, *Survey of International Cartels and Internal Cartels*, Board of Trade, London 1946, p. 29.

Bibliography

Fear, Jeffrey, Cartels, in Jones, G. and Zeitlin, J. (eds) *The Oxford Handbook of Business History*. Series: Oxford handbooks in business and management. Oxford: Oxford University Press, pp. 268–292.

James, Harold, *The End of Globalization: Lessons from the Great Depression*, Cambridge, MA: Harvard University Press, 2001.

Jones, G. (ed.) *Coalitions and Collaboration in International Business*. Cheltenham: Edward Elgar Publishing, 1993.

Jones, G. and Schroter, Harm, (eds) *The Rise of Multinationals in Continental Europe*. Cheltenham: Edward Elgar Publishing, 1993.

Kobrak, Christopher and Hansen, Per H. (eds), *European Business, Dictatorship and Political Risk 1920–1945*, New York and Oxford: Berghahn Books, 2004.

6   International entrepreneurship in a new global economy (1945–1990)

In 1962, a few months after the erection of the Berlin Wall, and seventeen years after the conclusion of the Second World War, the world was once again on the precipice of a global conflict. For a couple of weeks in October that year, the Americans and the Russians had been on the brink of war because of the Soviet Union's decision to accede to Cuba's request to position a battery of nuclear missiles on its territory, a stone's throw from the United States, as a deterrent to US aggression following the failed US invasion at the Bay of Pigs the previous year. The island's revolutionary Marxist government, which had seized power a few years before, (in 1959), overthrowing the corrupt regime of President Fulgencio Batista, had been heavily supported by the Soviet Union, and Cuba was thus a natural location for the military installations that aimed at counter-balancing a similar threat that the Soviet Union was facing from the American Jupiter nuclear missiles located in Italy and Turkey.

1. Rebuilding the global economy: opportunities and threats

The episode is authoritatively recognised as the one that brought the world to the verge of a third (and, probably, last) world war. It has inspired a flow of tales, memoirs, works of fiction and a number of scientific analyses in the fields of diplomacy and international political strategy. Beyond this, it has additional meanings which can help to shed some light on the conditions faced by global entrepreneurs in the period following the Second World War.

    The first is that the military confrontation was basically between the two political, but also economic, powers which emerged as dominant in the aftermath of the war. The United States of America (US) and the Union of Soviet Socialist Republics (USSR), came into confrontation immediately after the defeat of the Nazis. They did so on the basis of their respective leadership of powerful military alliances (the NATO Pact and the Warsaw Pact), but also on the more or less implicit "moral" leadership of the capitalist and the Communist world respectively. This East–West rivalry also took place in economic and industrial terms. The Soviet Union had fought much of the war on its own territory, which had been devastated, but, notwithstanding its huge manpower shortage, it succeeded in achieving a quick recovery through large investments in the capital-intensive industries, thanks also to the intensive use of central planning (the Fourth and Fifth Five-Year Plans (1945–1955)). The US had fought in Europe as well as the in Pacific theatre, and its war effort had been made possible by the superior efficiency of its manufacturing sector, which was almost unique in the world. At the same time, the two main competitors of the US, Europe – mainly Germany – in the West and Japan in the

East had both been destroyed and were exhausted. The war had thus had the notable effect of strengthening the industrial power of the US as the leading nation (and, in part, of its antagonist in the Communist area) at the same time as seriously weakening some of its most aggressive competitors for industrial and economic leadership. The Cuban confrontation was clearly a game with two players, to which the rest of the world's nations were looking on as increasingly worried spectators – supporting one team or the other. More importantly for the perspective of this volume, one of these two actors was a technological and industrial leader, ahead of the other by far, whose competitors had been neutralised, for a long time to come, by the tragedy of the war. To put it another way, the US economic and industrial leadership, which was already becoming ever more apparent during the interwar period, was definitively consolidated, beyond any doubt, by the war and its aftermath.

Another relevant element in the Cuban crisis was its technological side. The Russians were installing nuclear missiles which were unmanned, electronically powered and technologically sophisticated; they were detected and monitored by the Americans through a system of satellite spying and aerial photography. Computers were absolutely essential in decrypting coded communications. The Soviets were doing the same in Europe, where the even more technologically advanced US installations were also under surveillance. All the technological advancements developed during the Second World War were thus deployed in the first years of the "Cold War". The new, undeclared war was, in fact, the first hyper-technological conflict, in which high-tech industries – aerospace, electronics, related to physics and, in general, to the manipulation of matter – all played a major part, based upon high efficiency in transport and communications. And here again, America was the undisputed leader. The early history of the computer industry is undoubtedly American, and it was physicists at AT&T's Bell Lab in the US who developed the first industrial version of the basic building block of the computer industry, the transistor.

American technological leadership and dominance in the global economy was immediately mirrored by the expansion of its international presence. In 1962, the same year as the Cuban Missile Crisis, the list of the world's fifty largest multinationals – a list which is almost a facsimile of the list of the world's largest enterprises – was, in all honesty, quite monotonous. Among the companies listed, one could, in fact, find two companies of mixed nationality (*Unilever* and *Shell*, headquartered both in the UK and in the Netherlands), three British (*Imperial Chemical Industries, British Petroleum* and the *National Coal Board*), one Swiss (*Nestlé*), four German (*Daimler-Benz, Bayer, Volkswagen* and *Siemens*), one Italian (*Fiat*), one Dutch (*Philips*). The rest (thirty-eight) were all American, all world leaders in their respective industries.

It was, sometimes, a controversial presence among the largest multinationals, there was *International Telephone and Telegraph*, or *ITT*, founded in the 1920s. The leader in the communications industry, it had already established operations abroad before the war, and was present in Asia, Europe and Central and Southern America. After the Second World War, *ITT* started to refocus on domestic businesses, after expropriations in China or disinvestments in the politically unstable environment of South America. One of the investments it did maintain, incidentally, was in Cuba, where, before the revolution (1953–1959), *ITT* had enjoyed a sort of unchallengeable monopoly, a situation that was made even more attractive by the very favourable tariffs granted to it by the military dictatorship. Indeed, the dictator Batista pleased the American company so much that they presented him with a golden telephone in recognition of the outstanding treatment that the company had received (Batista had granted it an "excessive telephone rate increase") after the US government had applied pressure on the Cuban government in order to advance the interests and increase the profits of private American companies. This golden present was, however, also the symbol of the corrupt relationship and collusion among the local politicians, the American government and US multinational companies. One of the major driving forces behind the Cuban Revolution was the struggle against the corrupt practices of foreign (mainly American) multinationals. The identification between their presence and the despicable behaviour of colonial powers was almost immediate, and the outcome was strong opposition to multinationals as the drivers of exploitation and deprivation. (On 22 December 1946, the historic meeting known as the Havana Conference had taken place at the *Hotel Nacional* (Batista was a silent partner in the hotel) between the United States Mafia and the local Cuban *Cosa Nostra* leaders: the dark side – illegal – of an already dark – but legal – Cuban dictatorship–US relationship). Even though Cuba was not officially a colony, or an American protectorate, the Cuban Revolution was thus seen as one episode in the decolonisation process that took place after the war on a world scale.

2. The unstable framework after the Second World War

The Cuban episode is full of different meanings, but also emphasises the contrasting framework in which global entrepreneurs found themselves in the years following the Second World War. The first immediate contrast was the willingness to rebuild the "institutional facilitators" for the global economy in the face of the multiple, structural features which had prevented the restoration of a really global environment. In the end, the world (both developing and developed) had experienced the constant instability of global institutions from the outbreak of the Great War (1914–1918) and throughout the entire period of the interwar years, and the attempts to restore some sort of "gold standard" equilibrium during the 1920s had all come to grief, first in the years of the Great Depression and subsequently in the light of the widespread protectionism and *autarky* that preceded the Second World War, during which the League of Nations – the Geneva-based organisation established after the Great War with the purpose of maintaining world peace – had proved to be so ineffective. Thus, after the Second World War, attempts to restore a sort of shared, general equilibrium immediately took place under the strong leadership of the winning nations and, in particular, of the US, for the reasons stressed above.

Among the other reasons, it is worth mentioning at least four elements here, all of which influenced, in one way or another, the realm of international business.

The first is the attempt to restore some kind of monetary stability through a shared agreement about fixed exchange rates based upon the dollar and its full convertibility into gold – the US was controlling two thirds of the world's gold reserves in 1944, when a conference to design the future world international monetary and financial order took place in Bretton Woods, New Hampshire. The agreement was made possible through the creation of the second element, that is, supra-national financial institutions which guaranteed the stability of the system (thus avoiding the *autarkic* strategies put in place in the interwar period) by permitting the temporary adjustment of the trade imbalances of the countries participating in the agreement. The Bretton Woods Agreement thus established the International Monetary Fund (IMF) – which started to operate in 1945 – and the International Bank for Reconstruction and Development (IBRD) (now the World Bank), which began operating in 1946. The IBRD was the first building block of what is known today as the World Bank Group. The IMF thus aimed to grant stability in the balance of payments system, while the IBRD had the primary purpose of fostering domestic economies, initially of the countries involved in the process of post-war reconstruction and then of the developing nations. A third pillar of the restoration of a sort of global equilibrium concerned trade, and essentially the establishment of multilateral agreements among countries in order to rebuild the general confidence which had been crumbling for at least two decades before the Second World War. The basic idea was to set up a sort of International Trade Organization (ITO), in the end substituted by the General Agreement on Tariffs and Trade (GATT) after the US had refused to ratify the Havana Charter (formally the Final Act of the United Nations Conference on Trade and Employment) in 1950, which was set up in Geneva in 1947 and was initially signed by over twenty nations. These "institutional facilitators" were clearly aiming at the restoration of one of the components of nineteenth-century globalisation, that is, the Atlantic exchange system that had been in place for centuries. A fourth element was the deliberate decision by the US to foster the European recovery through a systematic programme of "aid in kind" which aimed at accelerating the restoration of the productive potential of continental Europe after the war. The European Recovery Programme (ERP) (commonly known as the Marshall Plan), which basically restarted domestic economies and multilateral exchanges among the former belligerents in Western Europe, is often seen as the first driver of the process of European integration, which formally took place from the second half of the 1950s with the creation of the European Common Market as the first nucleus of the European Community. The European case is an outstanding example of the attempts to rebuild a global economy through the creation of a system of multiple "macro-regional" free-trade areas characterised by structural conditions similar to those in place during the first period of globalisation, a process later common to other areas of the world economy (Table 6.1). The overall effect was a progressive decline in the average protection level throughout the world (Fig. 6.1); the average tariff steadily contracted by almost 1 per cent every ten years throughout the world.

Broadly speaking, however, the efforts to recreate a global economy contrasted with some general conditions that went in the opposite direction, by restraining the opportunities for global entrepreneurship in many areas of the world.

The first was the presence of non-capitalist, planned economies in a relevant section of the world economy. A major part of Asia fell, in fact, under Communist regimes, including the Asian Soviet Republics, China (where Communism triumphed after the Second World War), Korea, Vietnam and a number of smaller South East Asian countries gravitating toward the Communist world. Communist rule included Eastern European countries and Cuba. Clearly, political divergence, Cold War tensions and a radically different economic structure meant a sharp reduction of trade flows between the East and the West, or, rather, between the Communist and the capitalist worlds. The extent of the reduction can be easily understood if one looks at the contraction of the percentage of trade from the Eastern *bloc* directed to the West, which fell from nearly 73 per cent in 1938 to less than 15 per cent in 1953. The realms of Communism and capitalism, in sum, became increasingly two distinctly separate (trading) blocks. Clearly, the hiatus also concerned foreign direct investments. With very few exceptions (and under exceptional conditions), Western companies were unable to invest on the other side of the "iron curtain", and *vice versa*. Thus, exchanges remained largely limited to trade relations (subject to strict controls, strategic embargoes and other restrictions – the intensity of which varied according to the degree of neutrality of the Western countries trading with the Soviet bloc) and to "technical assistance". On the other hand, the deterioration of political

Table 6.1 Tariffs on manufactured goods (unweighted average, % *ad valorem*)

	1902	1913	1925	1931	1950	Early 1960s	1976	Mid 1980s	1900	2000
Argentina	(28)	28	29			(141)			14.1	16
Austria	(35)	18	16	27.7	17		11.7	9		4.3
Belgium	(13)	9	15	13	11.2	13.1	9.1	7	8.4	4.3
Canada	(17)	26	23				12.6		10.5	4.8
China	(5)	4.5						(41)	43	16.2
Denmark	(18)	14	10		3.4		9.1	7	8.4	4.3
France	(24)	20	21	29	17.9	13.1	9.1	7	8.4	4.3
Germany	(25)	13	20	18.3	26.4	13.1	9.1	7	8.4	4.3
Greece	(19)							7	8.4	4.3
India	(3)	4	16					(80)	83.7	31.6
Italy	(27)	18	22	41.8	25.3	13.1	9.1	7	19	4.3
Netherlands	(3)	4	6		11.2	13.1	9.1	7	8.4	4.3
Norway	(12)				10.8		8.6		6.8	2.5
Portugal	(71)				18				8.4	4.3
Spain	(76)	41	41	75.5					8.4	4.3
Switzerland	(7)	9	14	22			3.8	3		

Source: Findlay and O'Rourke, p. 494, Table 9.1.

relations between Communist China and the Soviet Union at the beginning of the 1960s did not signify any re-opening of market and investment opportunities for foreign investors, who remained almost excluded from the markets of the area.

The second general condition which prevented a full restoration of global exchanges and direct investments, is to be found in the astonishingly quick dissolution of Western colonial rule in both Africa and Asia. A symbolic event, in this respect, can be found in the nationalisation – after months of rising political tensions, and under the threat of a military confrontation – of the Anglo-French *Suez Canal Company* (see Chapter 3), proclaimed by the Egyptian president Nasser in 1956. The Egyptians reacted harshly to the Western protests, stressing the fact that the asset nationalised was a vestige of a colonial past, which was to be wiped out. Israel – fearing rising Egyptian military power – invaded the Sinai Peninsula, causing France and Britain to intervene on the pretext of protecting a fundamental facility that was crucial for trade between Europe and Asia. Something happened, however, which served to make the story different from what used to happen in the past when a small developing nation confronted a major Western power. Fearing Soviet support for Egypt, the US forced France and the UK to back down and to accept a NATO ceasefire, which, *de facto*, legitimised the expropriation of the company. The new framework determined by the Cold War, in sum, revolutionised the relationships between the colonial world and the former colonisers.

The process of Western decolonisation (a term which includes a wide range of very different situations, in geographic, cultural, institutional and political terms) began immediately after the end of the Second World War. The ways in which the former

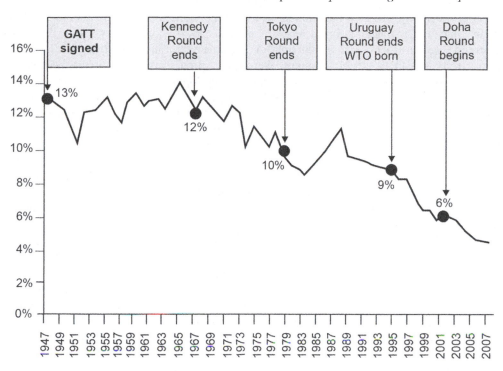

Figure 6.1 Tariff liberalisation (average incidence ad valorem) and main agreements

colonies obtained their independence varied from case to case, either through peaceful processes, such as the transition to independence that occurred in India in 1947, or, as happened in French Algeria, by means of a long and harsh conflict. Decolonisation peaked between the 1950s and 1960s, when large sections of Asia and Africa achieved independence from their former colonisers. The process, which, in many cases, ended colonial rule that had endured for centuries, had a number of effects. The political transformations in the former colonies had straightforward effects on the newly independent countries' domestic policies, and thus on their propensity to engage in the international economy. One of the most immediate consequences was a pervasive hostility, which included business activities, towards the former colonisers. Multinationals thus, almost immediately, had to come to terms with a radical change in their business environment, and in the level and nature of the political risk that they faced, especially when they were identified with the previous colonial governments. Hundreds of expropriations took place in the course of the decolonisation process, many with no compensation, or with painful disputes and settlements, which often resulted in a dramatic loss of efficiency. Furthermore, decolonisation, in some cases, was followed by long phases of political instability at local level, which affected the propensity of multinationals with regard to maintaining their presence or making new investments. Logically, changes in regimes meant a redistribution of the opportunities available to foreign investors. Companies able to apply leverage on these political transformations could transform risks into opportunities, especially when new rulers initiated policies of import substitution based upon the quick achievement of technology and expertise. As can be easily imagined, the situation turned out to be quite ambiguous for foreign companies, as they had to develop their ability to "manage" political relations with the local – often, very nationalistically oriented – governments and obtain political legitimacy among revolutionaries. In addition, the new leaders and governments were quite often, particularly at the beginning, oriented towards socialism, and made a great effort to develop their internal economies through a mixture of central planning and state-owned enterprises in sectors – such as natural resources, including oil, and/or natural monopolies – which had previously been dominated by foreign companies, and which now had to face either threats of nationalisation or the cumbersome presence of state-owned enterprises and governmental bodies.

This attitude was not only common to former colonies but also to other countries in which the post-war years brought a recrudescence of nationalism, independently of the government's political attitudes. For multinationals willing to accept these market conditions, this meant evolving to cope with the changes in the political scenario. For many, however, the rising level of risk meant simply a strong incentive to disinvest. Others faced the challenge through an acceleration of their geographic and strategic diversification in areas characterised by lower levels of risk. Others decided to adopt proactive forms of behaviour. American oil companies, for instance, started to apply in the Middle East the same profit-sharing agreements that they had developed in Latin America – particularly in Venezuela – during the Second World War. Others leveraged some kind of "political advantages" in order to overcome marginal market positions: *ENI*, the Italian Agency for oil, created by the Italian Government in 1953, successfully built close relationships with revolutionary post-colonial governments in North Africa and the Middle East, gaining a number of competitive advantages in these relatively unstable environments, by offering not only profit-sharing but also technical training and other forms of human-capital formation (see Box 6.2). Post-colonial environments, in sum, brought additional challenges for international entrepreneurs. Techniques of (successful) survival had, in fact, to be adapted in many contexts much more than in the past, and multinationals had to design and adopt collaborative attitudes which resulted in a new kind of core competence in dealing with domestic governments.

Box 6.1: Multinationals in post-colonial Africa: seeking legitimisation in unstable environments

In West Africa, British companies had begun to experience the rising level of political risk during the interwar period. After a long-lasting presence, dating back to the early phases of the colonisation period, British businessmen began to face growing criticism and hostility in some countries in the area of the Gold Coast, where imperial trading companies and merchant firms traditionally enjoyed favourable positions. After the Second World War, the situation deteriorated further with growing local nationalist attitudes coupled with anti-colonial sentiment spreading among the population, which resulted in open hostilities towards foreign investors in general. One symbolic target of local hostility was the *United Africa Company* (UAC), a trading company that was a subsidiary of *Unilever*, which had been created at the beginning of the 1930s by merging two already existing traders, the *Niger Company* and the *Africa and Eastern Trade Corporation*. For foreign investors, things also worsened because the British colonial administration was increasingly distancing itself from European companies, which were now perceived as personifying the worst aspects of exploitation. Companies such as the UAC were thus facing a clear alternative of adaptation or departure.

Adaptation meant, among other things, a strategy aiming at rebuilding political relations with the local élites in countries gaining independence, and policies aiming at rebuilding consensus and reshaping their corporate image. This was done by many means, including the provision of support to concrete initiatives aimed at fostering development and social progress. Despite their aggressiveness in public speeches, new local politicians were fully aware that foreign companies represented an important source of progress for accelerating local development.

One way that companies chose involved a deep restructuring of their communication strategies. Advertising campaigns were transformed to stress the new role that multinationals assigned to themselves in order to improve their public image, that of agents and supporters of local progress and modernisation. One telling example is provided by the way in which the above-mentioned UAC handled the situation in West Africa, and, in particular, in Ghana (which had been independent since 1957) and Nigeria (independent since 1960). The UAC created an advertising campaign under the evocative title "Men of Tomorrow", in which the concepts of progress and development – represented by agents of modernity such as telephones and typewriters – were stressed, emphasising the company's contribution to the achievement of these important goals. The advertising campaign targeted the middle class and West African political élites. This campaign, which began in the late 1950s, was in sharp contrast – or rather, it was a complete reversal – of previous ones, in which the UAC had emphasised its role as a trading company connecting Africa to Western customers – who bought traditional African goods as colonial customers had done. The new advertising instead emphasised the fact that the UAC was connecting African customers to the sources of the material goods necessary to foster local economic modernisation and political independence, in a period of progressive and "equal" economic relations.

A second wave of hostility towards the company (and foreign investors in general) started during the 1960s, due to internal tensions and political turmoil in both Ghana and Nigeria. In both countries, one military coup followed another, and this impacted heavily on foreign investments. For instance, in 1972, Nigeria issued a decree forcing foreigners to sell – either totally or partially – their ownership stakes to locals. A similar situation progressively took shape in Ghana in the first half of the 1970s. For companies like the UAC, which derived a significant part of their profits from their operations in West Africa, the ability to cope with this situation both quickly and effectively became a matter of life or death. To make this worse, the threat of expropriation was increasingly real, even if military juntas in both Ghana and Nigeria seemed to be collaborative and unwilling to attack foreign investors excessively. In its advertisements, the company reflected these growing concerns, trying to adjust its image in order to emphasise its contribution not only to modernisation and technological progress, but also to social welfare. The issue was increasingly one of inequality, and the problem for foreign companies – and even more so for former colonisers – was to be able to present and legitimise themselves as agents who were promoting equality rather than exploitation – the legacy of colonial attitudes, and, in general, the (perceived and widely criticised) attitude of foreign investors towards under-developed Third World countries.

This box is based upon Stephanie Decker's, "Corporate Legitimacy and Advertising: British Companies and the Rhetoric of Development in West Africa, 1950–1970", *Business History Review*, 81 (Spring 2007), pp. 59–86. The author is responsible for any errors and/or omissions.

To sum up, the years following the Second World War, in many respects, saw the emergence of a new era for foreign investment activity and global entrepreneurship. Here, three elements profoundly altered the framework of the global economy and prevented a full restoration of a "world economy". The first was the (temporary) destruction and fragmentation of Europe (and Japan) and the marginalisation of the once-flourishing international competitiveness of European multinationals. The second was the self-exclusion of the Communist countries, which maintained a very limited connection with the capitalist world – and, moreover, constituted a serious threat which threatened global entrepreneurs in many areas of the world. The third was the process of decolonisation. As stressed in the previous chapters, empires had offered generous conditions – in terms of transaction-cost reduction – to many entrepreneurs active abroad. In sharp contrast, the end of colonial rule meant that international companies needed to adapt to local conditions, which very often were quickly becoming both hostile and complicated owing to changes in political leadership and in the perceptions and expectations of local societies. This situation was, of course, not new. Companies investing abroad had had to take local factors into consideration as a relevant component of their "decisional" process before. Some countries were, for various reasons ranging from language, market prospects, resource endowments, cultural openness and stability, more attractive than others, and provided a set of advantages to companies locating their activities there instead of in other destinations. Decolonisation, however, stressed much more than in the past the relevance of local political conditions in determining the attractiveness of a country hosting an investment, and brought to the fore something which powerful companies had partly forgotten, particularly when they enjoyed the comfortable environment determined by a colonial empire: that "locality" (a wide concept, made by political, cultural and social attitudes) mattered a great deal, and could determine the success of an initiative, even more than technological superiority and the ability of entrepreneurs and managers to exploit the potentialities of the local market. In some cases, the ability of companies to build positive relations successfully with both local rulers and, more generally, with the population of the country in which they were investing, became *the* crucial asset.

Box 6.2: The decolonisation of states and economies

The following speech was to be delivered by Enrico Mattei, the chairman and founder of ENI – the Italian state-owned agency for oil – in Tunis on 10 June 1960. The speech (originally in French and today held in the company's archives) was postponed, since the refinery had not been completed, and the speech was subsequently delivered later. As a latecomer in a sector dominated by large and powerful incumbents, ENI was proactively pursuing a policy of expansion in Africa and the Middle East in order to gain access to oil fields. Two years after these events, Mattei died when the plane he was in crashed. Inquiries have recently ascertained that he was assassinated.

> I am here to answer to your call for investment and help you in your fight against under-development.
> I'm not afraid of the war in Algeria.
> I am not afraid of decolonisation.

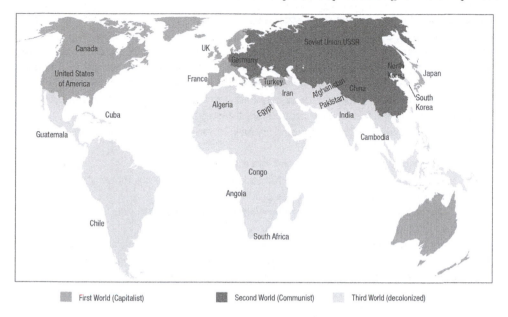

Map 6.1 The Three Worlds

I believe in decolonisation not only for moral reasons of human dignity but also for economic reasons of productivity.

Without decolonisation, it is not possible to stimulate in the Afro-Asian populations the energy and the enthusiasm necessary for adding value to Africa and Asia.

Now, the riches of Africa and Asia are immense.

The geography of hunger is a legend: it is connected only to passivity and inactivity created by colonialism in indigenous populations.

It was convenient for colonialism to encourage fatalism and resignation.

I always read your speeches and what has struck me most is your struggle against fatalism and resignation.

I, too, have struggled against the fixed idea that was deeply rooted in my own country: that Italy was condemned to be a poor country because of its lack of raw materials and energy sources.

I identified these energy sources, exploited them and got raw materials from them.

Before this, however, I had to fight for decolonisation myself, because many sectors of the Italian economy had been colonised; actually, I would go further: I would say that Southern Italy had been colonised by North Italy.

Colonisation is not only a political issue; it is, above all, an economic fact.

A colonial condition exists when the minimum of industrial infrastructure for processing raw materials is missing.

A colonial condition exists when the natural laws of demand and supply for an essential resource are altered by a hegemonic power, be it private, monopolistic or oligopolistic.

In the oil industry, this oligopolistic power is a cartel [*Mattei here refers to the oil majors*].

I am fighting against this cartel not because it is oligopolistic, but because it is Malthusian, and damages both producing countries and consumers.

The cartel is Anglo-Saxon, but I am not against the Anglo-Saxon world. Independent American producers are my friends, and have much weight in America and will have even more if there is a new administration in November.

I re-established the law of supply and demand because I cut all the Gordian knots, all the bottlenecks in production, transport, refining and distribution.

I have seen the price of petrol in Italy lowered to one hundred lire per litre, saving billions for consumers.

I wish others to save too if they join me.

By joining you, I bear in mind that today your interests are those of a consumer country, but tomorrow you will be producers.

The cartel may even build a refinery, but it will be a cyst in your economic body: it will not damage you, nor will it give you benefits.

I, however, in all cases, do not want to be a cyst in your economic body.

I want to create something more than a refinery: I want to create a centre of development in the South of Tunisia.

You asked me for Agip petrol stations. I have offered you a network of petrol stations and of motels, which will solve your tourism problem.

You asked me for a refinery, and I have offered you a petrochemical industry.

But I also offer you a market for your production surpluses, and I offer you, above all, equal treatment, co-management of production, and the training of a technological élite, so you will not be passive recipients of a foreign initiative; you will be the subject, and not the object of the economy.

I will be criticised in Italy (Why not a refinery in Sicily?), and you will be subject to pressure from the Anglo-Americans. Do not let yourselves be worried. I am not worried. Morocco is not worried. You should not be worried, either.

Source: *ENI Historical Archives*, fondo ENI/Segreteria del Presidente
Enrico Mattei, f64e b. 90.

★ ★ ★ ★ ★

A fourth element which characterised the immediate post-war period was thus a sort of consequence of the framework mentioned above. As anticipated, in 1962, of the world's largest multinationals, most were American: thirty-eight of the top fifty, sixty-eight of the top one hundred. American companies were unchallenged at home, and, immediately after the Second World War, benefited from the temporary decline of their potential European competitors. According to the data collected by a group of Harvard Business School researchers, out of 3,367 subsidiaries established by multinational companies around the world between 1946 and 1960, around 60 per cent were subsidiaries of US-based multinationals, 20 per cent of UK multinationals, 18 per cent were continental European and 2 per cent were subsidiaries of Japanese companies (in the interwar period these percentages were respectively 50 per cent, 18 per cent and 32 per cent, while no investments of Japanese origin are reported). According to Geoffrey Jones, between the end of the Second World War and the mid-1960s, the US accounted for the 85 per cent of the total flow of direct investments in the world.

3. The origin of American supremacy

Apart from the persisting European tendency to self-destruction, the sources of American superiority were mainly endogenous, and inherent to structural characteristics of the American model of industrial growth. First of all, these American companies were almost all technological leaders in their respective industries. The contribution of the war to the achievement of this technological superiority was, of course, highly relevant, in particular for companies active in industries characterised by high technological intensity (for instance, in aviation, electronics and the computer industry). Among the world's main multinationals, one could find the main American automobile companies, the oil majors, the top leaders in business machines (*IBM*) and in telecommunications (*ITT, Western Electric*), in aviation (*Boeing, Martin Marietta,* and *Lockheed*), in food and beverages (for instance, *Swift*), in steel (*US Steel, Armour,* and *Bethlehem*), in tyres (*Firestone,* and *Goodyear*) and basically in all the technology and capital-intensive industries, including chemicals, petrochemicals and pharmaceuticals. All these companies had started as national leaders, and after having consolidated on the domestic market, they expanded abroad in search of markets in which their technological superiority had no rivals. Thanks to robust investments in research and development, they introduced continuous product and process innovations which further consolidated their leadership: *IBM* did this when it diversified from business machines to computers, as did *AT&T* when it developed its leadership in transistors and then semiconductors. Technological leadership was at the basis of international expansion, since it was easier for these companies to start a directly controlled activity abroad (in order to exploit profit opportunities), than to resort to risky and difficult-to-monitor forms of licensing. Leadership in technology-intensive sectors meant, in sum, that internationalisation had to be pursued by investing abroad directly, and this was a strategy even more intensively adopted by US companies after the Second World War, for the reasons suggested above. The standard model followed by many of these companies has been analysed by Mira Wilkins: a company developed its technological competences at home, becoming a domestic leader and growing through a combination of mergers, acquisitions and investments. Thereafter, it replicated this model by investing abroad, by acquiring companies, but, more often, by opening new plants from scratch – and often, literally, in a "green field". Of course, since the source of leadership lay in technologies developed at home in research laboratories, the standard model mainly saw subsidiaries implement and market innovations developed and patented in the home country. Local subsidiaries were thus technologically dependent on the mother companies, even if they often enjoyed operative freedom in the host markets. According to John Dunning, they were functioning as "truncated replicas of their parent companies", all producing and marketing similar products in different geographic locations, in some cases even performing R&D, in others not. The home country's headquarters coordinated the whole organisation's architecture centrally, which was shaped, as the contemporary anti-multinational ideology frequently stressed, like an octopus, following a process which has been defined by Charles Wilson, one of the first historians to analyse the process, as "centrifugal".[1]

But these octopuses did not simply master technological competences that they then turned into solid competitive advantages. They were, in fact, basing their superiority on a number of other competences of non-technological nature, which they both owned and controlled, competences that were, in fact, synthetically labelled as "ownership advantages" – derived from the control of crucial assets – by scholars who started to study the phenomenon of the "international operations of national firms"[2] at the beginning of the 1960s. American companies went unchallenged in many areas: these included marketing, in which they had developed superior competences and scientific methods; distribution, where they had introduced innovative selling techniques; administration, accounting and finance. All these "advantages" were the heritage of the specific achievements of American capitalism during the first half of the twentieth century, and condensed into the superior competitiveness of the US companies abroad.

For many companies investing abroad, the availability of one fundamental organisational innovation, which had originated in the interwar period, was a crucial element in this process. Large US (and also some European) companies had, in fact, simultaneously started to manage the process of growth and diversification by separating the activity of strategic planning from that of day-to-day management. The device was an organisational structure based on a headquarters which coordinated administrative and financial divisions, which were autonomously managed by professionals. Each division has its own functions – from production to sales. The system allowed the top management to concentrate on long-term strategies while the divisions could concentrate on day-to-day operations. The multi-divisional structure, or M-Form, was based upon product divisions, but could easily be adapted to multi-geographic units, such as those which increasingly characterised the modern multinationals. Of course, not all the multinationals adopted the M-Form; it was, however, common among the largest, most powerful and dynamic, mostly American multinationals. The M-Form also allowed American companies to cope with another increasingly diffused tendency towards strategies of unrelated diversification. Conglomerates – that is, combinations of corporations engaged in entirely different business activities, and driven basically by the purpose of maximising the financial revenues from each individual business – expanded not only at home, but also spread abroad, whenever profitable acquisitions became possible. The main competitive advantage of many conglomerates, which made their acquisitions profitable, was actually the mastering of superior soft skills, for instance, in organisation, management, planning, and administration in general, which made them more efficient than their competitors abroad. A telling example is provided by *W.R. Grace & Co.*, a US conglomerate which in the early 1970s bought the majority control stake in *Barilla*, the Italian leader in pasta and baked products, and quickly consolidated the company's position on the Italian market by introducing a new organisational structure and modern marketing techniques.

The expansion of American multinationals was also facilitated by other elements. First, the post-war years were characterised by the beginning of a new transport and communications revolution. As suggested above, the Second World War was accompanied by an intensive wave of innovations, which were quickly transferred from military purposes to commercial ones, especially in the areas of transport and communications. The first jet aircraft passenger service across the Atlantic began in 1958, the same year in which the Americans launched and operated the first satellite for communications. During the 1950s, computers became increasingly common and started to revolutionise the world of business. The first commercial version of the fax machine was introduced in the mid-1960s. A major innovation in trade, the container, came into use in the 1950s. Technology was, in sum, pushing in the direction of making shipping, transport and communications easier, not only reducing the costs of trading, but also compressing the costs of control, and allowing the efficient management of long-distance operations. Owing to the spread of Communism, in sum, the capitalist world was shrinking in size, but, at the same time, becoming more interconnected. And the first movers in this process of technological intensification were, beyond any doubt, the Americans.

There were other advantages in being "American" (or "Americano", "Amerikanisch", as they were addressed by Europeans), advantages that explain the facility with which companies crossed the Atlantic eastward, locating themselves in Europe, or moving southward, where the attitude of local governments was favourable. In part as an emotional reaction to the gloomy interwar years, in part as a logical consequence of the immediate post-war starvation and of the relief brought by American intervention and by the Marshall Plan, and in part as the consequence of the cultural and political climate of the Cold War, American culture and American products quickly started to be diffused among European consumers, at a level markedly higher than in the past. This "irresistible empire",[3] which had already emerged in the interwar years, was further consolidated when Europeans – notwithstanding some resistance – started to look increasingly to American society and lifestyle as a source of inspiration. US companies benefited from this favourable climate, first of all increasing their exports to Europe, then directly producing abroad in order to save on transport costs. Their competitive strength was based, as stated above, upon superior technology, and on great ability in management, administration and organisation. They often found Europe (and Latin America) immediately receptive, for reasons which ranged from cultural similarity to a willingness or predisposition to imitate the successful American model. This, for instance, was very clear to management consulting companies, which started to sell their services abroad, becoming multinational themselves. One interesting case is provided by the cosmetic industry, itself a symbol of modernisation, emancipation and well-being, and in which American firms had gained an increasingly dominant position over their European competitors (the French and the Germans) immediately after the Second World War. Among the industry's main protagonists was the company *Avon*, which had been founded in 1886 as the *California Perfume Company*, which specialised in the door-to-door selling of cosmetics. After consolidating its position on the domestic market, immediately after the Second World War the company started to expand abroad, first targeting countries which were geographically close (e.g. Mexico and Venezuela, Brazil and Argentina) and then expanding to a booming Europe, where it opened facilities in the United Kingdom, Germany, France, Spain and Italy. By the early 1970s, *Avon* was the typical prototype of the US multinational, controlling subsidiaries in almost all the developed (and quickly developing) countries, and exploiting abroad the asset package developed at home. *Avon*'s penetration was facilitated by the replication of the selling techniques already in use in the home market, based upon a sales force made up of (female) representatives leveraging private networking in order to sell their products. The quickly changing Western (and South American) societies provided the right social environment in which cosmetics were transformed from an élite, superfluous product into a component of everyday life, and in which the emancipation process of women allowed the company both to find an expanding market and to build efficient sales networks easily and quickly. Similar cases can be found in almost all industries, including services, tourism and mass distribution.

The process of "Americanisation" which took place between, roughly, the 1950s and the 1960s, was clearly facilitated by the hegemonic role that the US was playing in the international political scenario (and also by the solidity of the dollar), even if this often turned out to be a constraint, in particular when – as suggested at the beginning of this chapter – local societies in ex-colonial countries tended to identify the actions of companies and governments negatively (see Map 6.2). The political economy of American

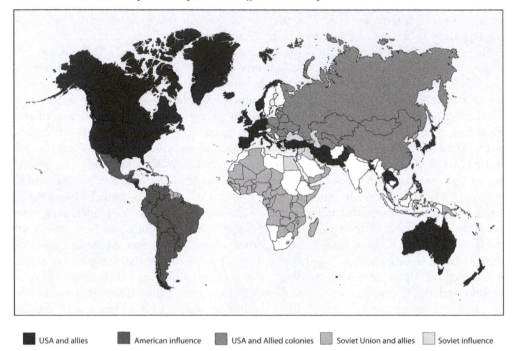

USA and allies   American influence   USA and Allied colonies   Soviet Union and allies   Soviet influence

Map 6.2 International alliances and spheres of influence, 1959

foreign investment activity has been a much-debated topic; undoubtedly, there was a connection between the American foreign economic reach and the hegemonic role played by the country at international level. However, the main element which determined the decision of US companies to expand abroad were the rapid changes taking place in European economies and societies. For instance, the creation of the European common market in 1957 – which *de facto* established a free-trade zone between Italy, France, West Germany, Belgium, Luxembourg and the Netherlands, some of the most dynamic and expanding markets in the world – incentivised US companies to tap into this promising area of free exchange, by opening facilities in the most convenient locations in order to sell on a continental scale. Within this framework, countries that were well positioned, for instance, in geographic terms, in terms of legal and institutional favourable conditions, or even in terms of cheaper labour costs, were targeted as the preferred locations. West Germany was particularly friendly towards foreign investors, while Italy offered oil companies a favourable geographic position for locating refineries and distributing their products throughout the continent. Italy also had an extraordinarily cheap cost of labour, but also had powerful national manufacturers in some industries, which were both state-owned and privately owned, as was happening in France and in the UK.

The situation was, in sum, a mixed one, with forces simultaneously attracting and repelling US investments. The same situation, with some nuances, could be found in Europe, in Canada, in South America, everywhere *le défi Américain*, or the American challenge – from the title of a famous book by a French journalist, Jean-Jacques Servan-Schreiber, published in 1967 – was brought through multinational investments. The sole country in which American penetration was successfully blocked and in which US multinationals were prevented from acquiring leadership positions was – paradoxically – the one which was under American military control and occupation for the longest period: Japan. Japanese companies were buying and adapting US technology and American management techniques (see below), but Japan rigidly prevented foreign takeovers of local companies, both through restrictive regulation but also thanks to the particular ownership system which characterised domestic business groups, the *keiretsu*, inside which companies mutually controlled (and thus protected) each other.

Until the beginning of the 1960s, in sum, the situation in the domain of global entrepreneurship was both quite simple and clear. Where possible, American companies dominated – after all, it has been calculated that, in 1950, nearly four-fifths of the total world output came from the US – thanks to superior technological competences and to a vast array of other soft skills, which made foreign investment activity more convenient, which was also made easier by technological innovations in transport and communications. The dynamism of the (mostly American) global economy, however, clashed with tensions in former colonised countries and with the self-exclusion of centrally-planned economies. The global economy was, in sum, successfully struggling to recover, but, still at the beginning of the 1960s, it was very far from reaching the level of integration that had characterised the world economy before it came tumbling down in 1914. But things were going to change very soon.

4. The recovery of the global economy

In 1981, one of the most influent scholars of international business, John Dunning, proposed an original interpretation of the diffusion of international entrepreneurship. Drawing on his profound knowledge of the domain of multinational activity, he introduced the concept of the Investment Development Path (IDP), which has since become quite influential. The IDP predicts, in a nutshell, that, during its process of economic development, a country passes progressively from a position of being a net recipient of foreign investments to that of being a net outward investor. The drivers of this process are largely foreign investors themselves, who foster the development of the country's domestic economy by encouraging the internationalisation of its firms. Clearly, this is a model which captures the dramatic variety of the historical reality only partially. In its elaboration, Dunning had, however, clearly in mind something that took place between the end of the 1960s and during the following decade, when the recovery of Europe and Japan, and the rise of South East Asian economies profoundly altered the framework of international business activity.

These changes can be detected simply by looking at the rankings of the world's largest multinationals. In 1972, among the top one hundred, fifty-four were headquartered in the US (there had been sixty-eight ten years before, and the rest had been Europeans, apart from two Japanese), thirty-seven were in Europe, and nine were in Japan. In 1983, "only" forty-five of the top one hundred multinationals were of US origin, thirty-four were headquartered in Europe, ten in Japan and the rest were in the new industrialisers, such as South Korea, South Africa, Brazil and even India. In two decades, the hierarchy of global companies had been dramatically transformed. US multinationals – which still remained the main protagonists in absolute number – were being progressively challenged by Europeans, and then by Japanese. By the end of the 1970s, "the rest" was rising, especially South Korea, whose *chaebols* (diversified, family controlled business groups) were increasingly expanding abroad.

5. The European challenge

Europeans first started to challenge US multinational leadership in the 1960s, and did so by increasing their foreign investment activity, in some cases even making investments across the Atlantic. The stock of European direct investments in the US rose from 2.7 billion dollars in 1962 to 6.6 billion dollars ten years later – figures much lower than the correspondent American investments in Europe, which, by 1973, amounted to 23.5 billion. This comparative weakness, however, co-existed with a series of reasons which explain both why, and how, some European companies successfully invested in the US. According to the data provided by Lawrence Franko, in a book published in 1976 (*The European Multinationals: A Renewed Challenge to American and British Big Business*), European large firms had, in 1971, around 230 subsidiaries in the US. Most of them were German, Dutch, French and Swiss. Clearly, European firms had invested in the US before, but it was mainly during the 1960s and 1970s that the European presence in the US expanded – even though it did not represent more than 10 per cent of the total European presence abroad. Europeans, in sum, increasingly targeted the US market, even though it never became absolutely significant. What is more interesting is the breakdown by industry of the European presence, in what was definitely the largest and most promising market of the world; the privileged areas of investments were those where European firms could display an enduring advantage, and thus included chemicals, electric machinery and, to a lesser extent, fabricated metals and pharmaceuticals. In these sectors, Europeans could successfully compete, and actually did so, even aggressively entering the home market of companies that were, in their turn, investing in Europe. European companies invested in America for several reasons, which are not mutually exclusive. The market, as stated above, was very attractive, and some European companies still had technological advantages, for instance in chemicals and pharmaceuticals. In several cases, tariffs and quotas played a role in the decision to expand to the US, particularly in industries in which US companies successfully obtained protection from their own government. There were, however, other drivers, which were probably less determinant but are no less interesting in order to understand the dynamics of international business strategy in general. In contrast to US companies – which internationalised their operations in order to exploit their ownership advantages – some European companies, such as the Dutch *AKU* and the Italian *Olivetti*, openly invested in the US in the 1960s in order to *acquire* knowledge and competences. This was the first time in the long story that we are recounting in this book, and certainly not the last, in which learning, and not technical knowledge, became the motivation and the main driver of investment abroad. This was particularly evident in industries characterised by a high degree of technological intensity (e.g. petrochemicals or electronics), where European firms invested in America in order to gain access to the expertise and human capital available there.

The story of European multinationals after the Second World War and during the period of intensive growth which characterised the Western capitalist world during the second half of the 1950s and the 1960s (in many countries remembered as the "Economic Miracle") has other general implications, which go beyond their relevance in terms of the total amount of direct investments.

First, from an organisational and structural point of view, European multinationals were characterised by two apparently contrasting features. On the one hand, beyond any doubt, they were the most sophisticated in organisational terms among their national counterparts. Often, they displayed an above-average propensity towards the adoption of the decentralised forms so diffused among US companies, so uncommon among the European corporations. In this case, "multinationality" meant quick modernisation, or rather, convergence, among organisational structures. On the other hand, European multinationals maintained some distinctive characteristics from their past history, in particular a strong heritage of the close connections which – particularly in family companies – characterised the relationships between the "mother" company and its foreign subsidiaries, or "daughters". In this organisational model, which was largely diffused among continental multinationals, family ties and personal relationships (which involved a low level of standardised procedures) between the presidents and the CEOs of both the parents and the subsidiaries played a much higher and more prominent role than in the case of their US counterparts, which were used to a more bureaucratic and rigid structure. Families, and, in general, concentrated ownership structures, in sum, still mattered a lot, and, to use the words of Mira Wilkins, they were clearly used to finding the "familiar in the unfamiliar", as a device for the reduction of uncertainty. The tradition, which dated far back in time (see the previous chapters), of recruiting managers from among the élites close to the controlling owners remained a distinctive characteristic of European capitalism even when it became internationalised. The rebirth of European global entrepreneurship after the Second World War, in sum, tells a very interesting story of organisational adaptation to the challenges of international expansion, but with the preservation of some distinctive characteristics – for instance, in terms of ownership – which heavily influenced the nature of the relationships between the parent and the subsidiaries. This, however, was not the only interesting takeaway from the history of European capitalism.

Another interesting (and often under-estimated) aspect is the fact that, among the largest European companies with operations abroad, a non-negligible number of enterprises under partial or full state control were included. The number of state-owned multinationals grew steadily during the 1960s and 1970s, the most intensive phase of nationalisation in Western countries. It has been calculated that, in the mid-1960s, there were only nineteen state-owned enterprises (SOEs) among the top 200 companies outside the US, of which three could be regarded as real multinationals, while a decade later there were twenty-nine SOEs (nine multinationals) and thirty-eight SOEs in 1985, of which eighteen could be regarded as real multinationals. *ENI* and *EFIM* in Italy, *CGE, Elf-Aquitaine, Pechiney, Aerospatiale, Saint-Gobain, Renault, Thomson* and *Rhone-Poulenc* in France, *British Leyland* in the UK, *DSM* in the Netherlands, *Voest-Alpine* in Austria, *Norsk-Hydro* in Norway, *Salzgitter* in Germany are just a few examples of state-owned enterprises which established and controlled more or less extended foreign operations abroad, some of them – as shown above in the case of *ENI* – displaying considerable ability, especially when it came to dealing with the newly established governments of former colonies. Independently of their overall relevance, it is important to note that these companies were basically a European phenomenon – quickly replicated in some of the emerging countries. Whether one likes it or not, these state-owned multinational enterprises – which sometimes resulted from the nationalisation of former private companies – benefited, in some cases, not only from the direct and indirect support of their governments during the process of their internationalisation (for instance, through tax exemptions and/or privileged access to credit sources), but also from host countries, in which state-owned enterprises could be privileged over private multinationals.

A third interesting aspect is that, according to many scholars, European companies tended to expand abroad in a particular way, directly influenced by their structural features. One example is the "mother–daughter" relationship discussed above. Another is a prudent strategy of progressive geographic expansion in "friendly" markets, geographically close and characterised by a high level of cultural familiarity and proximity. These strategies were so widespread that, in the second half of the 1970s, two Swedish scholars, Jan Johanson and Jan-Erik Vahlne, published an article with the telling title of "The Internationalization Process of the Firm: A Model of Knowledge Development and Increasing Foreign Market Commitments", which constituted the first step of the so-called "Uppsala model" which was, for many years, a very popular theoretical framework for the analysis of the drivers of the internationalisation of companies. The model was, like all good (and realistic) models, based upon the evidence provided by the process of internationalisation of Swedish companies in several industries, which included steel, pulp and paper, engineering and pharmaceuticals, during the 1970s. One of the basic assumptions in this conceptual framework was that companies internationalised progressively, first exporting, then investing directly, basically after a cautious process of learning which aimed at reducing the "psychological distance" between the home country conditions and those found in the host market.

The process of internationalisation of European companies after the Second World War contributed in a way which was anything but marginal to the rebirth of the international economy at least among capitalist countries. By the beginning of the 1980s, as shown above, the number of European-based multinationals was not negligible, and, in this period, the percentage of the world total of outward investment stock headquartered in the European Union was about 55 per cent, greatly exceeding that of the US (41 per cent). For the sake of comparison, fifteen years before, Europe had accounted for only 35 per cent against 50 per cent on the part of the US. Europe, in sum, performed well, also putting forward her own original model of internationalisation. But others, however, did even better.

6. The Japanese challenge

Toyota, Hitachi, Matsushita, Nissan, Mitsubishi, Toshiba, Honda: all these companies had a prominent place among the world's largest firms – and among the main multinational enterprises – by the beginning of the 1980s. As mentioned above, it had almost been impossible to find a Japanese brand in any single ranking only a few years before, at the end of the 1960s. By 1970, Japan had a stock of direct investments abroad of about 1.5 billion dollars, around 1 per cent of the world total. Fifteen years later, this percentage had risen to nearly 4 per cent – and would reach 11 per cent in 1990. In the US alone – which, during the 1980s had become the main target of the majority of the Japanese investments abroad – the direct investment stock of Japanese origin between 1980 and 1990 nearly doubled every year from around 11 billion dollars to 85 billion dollars, so that, at the end of the decade, one dollar out of five of foreign investment stock was of Japanese origin.

After an astonishingly fast recovery from the ashes of the Second World War and the loss of all its colonial possessions, the most dynamic capitalist market economy of East Asia was performing very well even in terms of internationalisation and global presence. It is not possible to investigate the reasons behind this success in depth in this chapter, which includes aspects relating to an efficient organisational structure, to a cohesive social system, a national culture which emphasised economic independence, a relatively harmonious system of industrial relations and an institutional system which was able to generate efficient policies for competitiveness – even without the direct involvement of the state in the economic sphere. However, even in the case of Japan, there are some elements which allow us to interpret the quick and successful internationalisation of Japanese enterprises – something which is even more striking when it is compared with the overall closure of Japan to foreign capital, which lasted until the end of the twentieth century.

Business and economic historians stress how there has rarely been any superior advantage of a technological nature which can be specifically cited as underlying the success of Japan in the manufacturing industry. The process of economic (and also social and cultural) modernisation of Japan which had begun immediately after the Meiji Restoration in 1868 was largely undertaken through the imitation of Western technology and institutions – while international commerce was already a flourishing activity, thanks to the consolidated experience of mercantile families and of their *shogo-shosha* (trading companies). The acceleration of the Japanese industrialisation process in heavy industries, particularly during the 1930s, again involved not only the importation, imitation, standardisation and adaptation of technological competences of Western origin, in chemicals, steel, heavy mechanics, electricity and electrical machinery, but also the direct presence of foreign investors who often created joint ventures with local producers, thereby contributing to the overall improvement of the technological endowment of the country.

As stressed above, however, until the Second World War the development of Japanese capitalism was basically domestic in nature; the level of international competitiveness of Japanese companies was extremely low, and only a strong protectionist attitude on the part of the government towards domestic companies preserved them from foreign superiority. Notwithstanding this, Japanese companies developed substantial competitive advantages in areas other than research and development and technological expertise, focusing mainly on process innovation and the internal organisation of the enterprise.

Box 6.3: Core competences and home country as "ownership advantages": *NEC Corporation of Japan*

In the early 1980s, Japanese multinationals emerged on the global market. Several of these firms shared common characteristics in terms of their internationalisation strategies, which ultimately led to the success of many Japanese multinationals. These included the influence of the environment in their home country and their corporate culture. *NEC Corporation* can be seen as a good example of a successful multinational Japanese business. NEC became competitive at an international level and expanded dramatically during the 1980s, thanks to its own internal resources. However, the Japanese environment in which the company acted played a crucial role. While the domestic culture significantly influenced the organisational structure of the corporation as well as the relationships between employees, the company and its competitors, NEC would not have been nearly so successful without the help of the Japanese government, which financed its development and protected it from early international competition. Both elements were interdependent and fundamental for the success of NEC.

The *Nippon Electric Company Limited*, as *NEC Corporation* was originally known, was founded in Tokyo in 1899 as a joint venture by a group of Japanese entrepreneurs and the US firm *Western Electric Company*. At the beginning, NEC's main business was selling telephone lines and equipment produced using the technology of its foreign partner. However, the company soon began to produce its own systems and to expand. With the aim of achieving technological self-sufficiency, the Japanese government supported the growth of the corporation from the very beginning and pushed it to develop new products. In the 1920s, *Western Electric*'s willingness to enter the electrical cables business led NEC to enter into an agreement with the *Sumitomo Group*. In 1925, *Western Electric* was sold to *International Telephone & Telegraph* (ITT), which renamed the division *International Standard Electric* (ISE). During the 1930s, nationalism spread throughout Japan and new laws against foreign companies were approved. ISE was first forced to transfer part of its ownership to NEC and to the *Sumitomo Group*, and subsequently it even lost all its remaining shares, which were confiscated by the government. In 1943, *Sumitomo* gained full control of NEC and renamed it *Sumitomo Communication Industries*. During the Second World War, the company worked on microwave communication, radar and sonar systems for the army and the navy. By the end of the war, sales to the Japanese Army accounted for 97 per cent of its total business. However, after the war, the Allied occupation authority ordered the break-up of Japanese *zaibatsu* enterprises (the giant family-owned business groups), such as the *Sumitomo Group*. *Sumitomo Communications* readopted the name *Nippon Electric*. Although NEC experienced some hard times, it was able to recover with the help of the Japanese government, which offered it public works projects. In the 1950s, NEC began research and development into computers and transistors. In 1953, it created a separate consumer-appliance subsidiary called the *New Nippon Electric Company*. During this decade, NEC also started to expand internationally by exporting communications equipment to other Asian countries. The international expansion proceeded throughout the 1960s. After a difficult period at the beginning of the 1970s, the president of NEC, Koji Kobayashi formulated the visionary concept of "C&C", a prediction of the future integration of Computers and Communications. He refocused the company on developing core capabilities in the technologies that were common to the different products of the company. By the 1980s, NEC had become the largest Japanese telecommunications equipment corporation, the world's largest supplier of satellite earth stations and microwave communications equipment, and the world leader in semiconductor sales. Moreover, NEC tripled its sales volume thanks to its international expansion, and NEC's stock was listed on several European stock exchanges.

NEC followed the same internationalisation process that many other Japanese companies followed. This can be divided into three steps. The first step was undertaken by foreign companies wishing to invest in Japan: these firms mainly created partnerships with local corporations in order to acquire business contacts and specific market knowledge. The Japanese companies, on the other hand, also benefited from these partnerships since they could learn more about foreign advanced technology as well as management, and thereby compete on a higher level with their own competitors. NEC's strategy was mainly based upon this approach: in 1899, in fact, NEC had, as already stated, been founded as a joint venture with the US firm *Western Electric Company*. The next step in the internationalisation process of most Japanese companies was their move first towards exporting products, shortly followed by foreign direct investment. NEC's own business grew steadily by relying on the domestic market, but it soon began to expand internationally. As an example, in 1951, NEC signed its first post-war major export contract with Korea for radio broadcast equipment. To sum up, through the investment of foreigners in Japan, Japanese companies gained useful insights into how foreigners do business, how to work with foreign employees and how to make use of technology. Then, they used this knowledge in order to invest successfully in foreign countries themselves. NEC first established a joint venture in Taiwan, before creating a subsidiary in the United States. It progressively extended its reach to other countries by setting up more branches from the 1960s onwards. In the following decades, the company established manufacturing subsidiaries in North America, Mexico, Korea, Brazil and Australia and entered the South American and European markets.

Competing in multiple business areas – semiconductors, telecommunications and computers – on a global level and excelling in all of them is a real challenge. However, NEC successfully met this challenge during the 1970s and 1980s, which was the period in which globalisation began to gain momentum. What were the reasons for NEC's success and how did it dominate the different product categories at the same time?

First of all, NEC was able to develop strong competitive advantages. In this period, the competitive advantage of Japanese companies was based upon three elements: excellence in operational logistics, a "culture of corporate governance" and a "community of fate" environment. While the concept of operational logistics is well known, a "culture of corporate governance" and a "community of fate" are concepts that have proved to be relatively new to Western companies. In brief, corporate governance in Japan relied on alliances and companies with interlocking business relationships, the so-called *keiretsu*. These kinds of informal relations helped to integrate knowledge, exchange information and foster teamwork. They also serve to create mutual trust between employees and the company and to establish good relationships with suppliers. Likewise, a "community of fate" is an environment based upon participatory management, job security and horizontal communication. Overall, these measures are used to create a closer relationship between the company and its employees. Workers displayed loyalty to their employers who, in turn, granted them job security. The result was the employees were well disciplined, more committed to their work and less reluctant to accept change.

Other interpretations, on the other hand, suggest that NEC's main competitive advantage was its focus on core competencies, namely, the company's deep knowledge of how to handle diverse production skills and technologies. Over time, the company was able to accumulate a broad array of core competencies by using collaborative arrangements to multiply internal resources. Core competencies can be defined as the ability to hold the organisation together by sharing knowledge and by coordinating and integrating multiple business units. How was NEC able to acquire these competencies? The company started to focus on acquiring core competencies in the 1970s. It thus adopted a special strategic architecture and communicated its new strategy not only to its employees but also to third parties, including the public. Coordination groups and committees were set up in order to link business units and facilitate communication. To obtain new capabilities, NEC entered into many collaborative agreements. This approach helped the firm to multiply internal capabilities at low cost and also to gain expertise in different sectors. It was the only company which simultaneously held knowledge in the areas of computing, communications and components, and, as a result, it was able to stay ahead of the competition. In general, the focus on core competencies fostered innovation and the exploitation of emerging markets. Similarly, it increased knowledge sharing and customer focus.

Finally, according to some research, the success of Japanese corporations is related to their skills and know-how in organisational knowledge creation, especially in accomplishing constant business innovation. In this interpretation, they are able to use the knowledge of individuals and transfer it to/within the whole organisation, enhancing in this way their competitive advantage. To summarise, the competitive advantage of Japanese companies, well represented in this case by NEC, is influenced by many factors, which include corporate governance and the "community of fate", core competencies, and the ability to create knowledge.

The second element to be considered when analysing the success of NEC and other Japanese multinationals abroad is the role played by the environment external to the company, namely, Japan itself. What is important to consider in the case of NEC, and many other Japanese companies, is the role that the government, in particular, played in its development. Japanese capitalism was based upon a comprehensive involvement of the government in economic as well as business matters. All governments in Japan have supported the growth and the internationalisation of companies incomparably. The Japanese companies could count on the help of the Ministry of International Trade and Industry (MITI), whose mission was to promote domestic industry and to protect it from international competition, thereby modifying, for example, the Japanese productive system so that it adapted to the variations in world demand. Indeed, Japanese capitalism strongly relied on the connections between the private and public sectors, and, in contrast to the United States, the Japanese state was actively involved in the internationalisation process of Japanese corporations. The public sector helped the private sector to develop its business nationally, making it strong enough to compete with foreign companies. For NEC, this help resulted in huge orders of technological materials both from and for the government, which helped it to remain viable by awarding it public works projects. Moreover, the Japanese government endeavoured to protect its national industry, by adopting foreign trade policies that helped Japanese companies to go global while ensuring that it remained difficult for foreign companies to enter the Japanese market. Both measures led to various scandals: Japan was often blamed for not respecting the rules of international free trade approved during the various rounds of the World Trade Organization (WTO). It also often had to deal with national scandals of bribery and corruption, and NEC is a good example of this: in 1998, it was involved in a defence procurement scandal. However, government support was crucial in order to allow these firms to become big and strong both at home and abroad.

This box is based upon a paper written by Monica Ermacora, Julia Gaekler, Francesco Marulo, Marina Minoli, Gaspard Revol, Federico Raggio, *NEC – Analysis of the Internationalisation Strategy*, in the course "International Economics and Business Dynamics – Module II: Evolution of International Business", Bocconi University, academic year 2009–2010. The author is responsible for any errors and/or omissions.

★ ★ ★ ★ ★

When the Japanese economy recovered after the Second World War and started a rapid process of growth, particularly from the 1960s onwards, the basic characteristics of the learning process, and of competitive advantages, of large companies remained very much the same. This largely influenced the way in which Japanese manufacturing firms internationalised, starting from the 1960s and during the 1970s. This is a point on which is worth focusing as a general takeaway. In more traditional industries, such as textiles or toys, and in mature industries – for example, some branches of consumer electronics – Japanese companies internationalised at the beginning in the traditional way, basically through a process that was largely resource-seeking in nature, in which the resource was low-cost labour. The privileged location was thus characterised by a pronounced geographic proximity, which was South East Asia. Some other investments abroad were undertaken for other purposes, as presented above. During the 1970s and 1980s, Japanese companies often invested in both Europe and the US in order to gain quick access to technological capabilities in high-tech industries such as electronics, pharmaceuticals, and computer software and hardware, but also fabricated metals and machine tools, a typical example of knowledge-seeking investment strategy. The technological nature of competitive advantages in some industries was clearly at the origin of these initiatives, which culminated in the acquisition of existing facilities. This was a facet of a more general phenomenon, which has marked the long history of global entrepreneurship as narrated in this volume. The 1980s, in fact, saw a shift (much sharper than in the past) in the motivations for investing abroad, from market- and resource-seeking to the acquisition of the strategic assets that were present abroad and a search for ever greater efficiency.

In the light of the above-described IDP theory, in sum, Japan quickly progressed from being a net receiver of foreign investments to being an outward net investor during the 1980s, through a mixture of different motivations and strategies. These include two important components of this increasing presence of Japanese multinationals abroad, which are worth discussing here. The first was the ability that Japanese companies displayed in transforming elements of an organisational nature into competitive advantages which enabled them to make a difference on international markets. The second was the role that the Japanese government played in the process of the internationalisation of Japanese companies after the Second World War, a role that has been labelled as a "holistic approach".

First of all, Japanese companies could rely on a particular type of corporate organisation, developed at home from the very beginning of the process of industrialisation. During the 1970s, when Japanese companies openly started to flaunt their superiority before their Western competitors, commentators stressed the role of the *keiretsu* network-like corporate structure in amplifying the competitive strength of individual companies. According to this interpretation, foreign subsidiaries continued to benefit from the advantages derived from this model of corporate organisation, which emphasised mutual support among the companies belonging to the same "family of companies".

A second organisational element, which played a relevant role as a competitive advantage for Japanese firms, pertained to some aspects of the management of the production process and of the relationships between capital and labour. One of the (much celebrated) key aspects of the Japanese model was the deep organisation of the production process, the management and circulation of knowledge within the organisation and, more generally, the architecture of the production methods, which allowed the introduction of practices which were subsequently adopted elsewhere in the world, such as "just in time" or "total quality management". In standardised production characterised by low levels of product adaptation to local needs, such as cars and consumer electronics, in which the Japanese were highly competitive with Western companies, Japanese companies invested abroad, opening greenfield assembling plants, in order to reduce transport costs (and circumvent trade barriers), leveraging the superior efficiency of their production methods, creating subsidiaries as "export enhancers" or – using an evocative metaphor – "screwdrivers". The replication of this behaviour brought scholars of international business to introduce a conceptual category which was different to that of the multinational. *Global companies* (embodied by the prototype of the Japanese multi-national of the 1980s) operated internationally producing standardised items, char-acterised by high economies of scale, exploiting ownership advantages that were mainly of an organisational and efficiency-enhancing nature. Compared to other multinationals, they displayed a far higher degree of standardisation and homogenisation of products and processes, and a much lower level of local adaptation.

A third element, not of organisational nature, but more "contextual", was the role played by the Japanese government in designing industrial policies aiming at the fast development of Japanese industry. In this framework, international trade – and the international activity of firms – played a key role; the maximisation of exports, the limitations to inward investments, together with the maximisation of outward investments, were of paramount importance. The prevailing model which characterised Japanese multi-nationals, described above, was to prove very functional to these policies for international competitiveness.

The 1970s and the 1980s, in sum, witnessed some major phenomena which con-tributed to shape the main aspects of the post-war global entrepreneurship. First, American supremacy started to be challenged by the Europeans, then, even more sensationally, by the Japanese. Crude numbers are straightforward. At the end of the 1960s – the peak of American dominance – the "Triad" (a label which indicated the major capitalist econo-mies, the US, Europe and Japan) accounted for 90 per cent of the total stock of foreign direct investments in the world. A quarter of a century later, by the 1990s, the three main capitalist macro regions had even increased their importance, reaching nearly 93 per cent of the total stock of foreign direct investments. What was profoundly challenged was the distribution of the slices of the pie among the "dinner guests". At the beginning, global entrepreneurship meant undoubtedly North America, as outlined above. By 1990, America accounted for less than one-third of the total stock of FDIs, the majority being concentrated in Europe. Japan accounted for half that of the US, being much smaller in terms of home market size and having started basically from scratch after the devastation of the Second World War – the sole country in the world to have experienced atomic bombing.

The European and Japanese challenges were brought about in many ways. Both Eur-opean and Japanese multinationals, like their American counterparts, made foreign investments, which were initially of a market-seeking nature. Europeans could, in some technology-intensive industries such as chemicals and machinery, count on technological competences, which translated into ownership advantages that were comparable (in quality, if not in quantity) with those of the Americans. Both Europe and Japan did not reject or exclude knowledge-seeking investments. As noted by many commentators (and formalised into popular theories), in this period, knowledge and competences started to be the most important asset in explaining the domestic and international competitiveness of firms, and these assets were at least as attractive for foreign investors as the most valuable natural resources. More importantly, the success of both Europe and Japan concretely demonstrated what scholars of international business were theorising, that is, that, in this period, the very *nature* of the global entrepreneurship strategies was changing, from a market- and resource-seeking nature, to the exploitation of competitive advan-tages of an organisational nature based upon internal efficiency. And, finally, in the cases of both Europe and Japan, most of the competitive advantages in international entre-preneurship were derived from structural elements (the role of families, of governments, of industrial relations) that had characterised the historical evolution of these capitalist systems.

★ ★ ★ ★ ★

The story narrated in this chapter reveals a very different image of the evolutionary process of the "modern multinational" than was depicted in the past, when companies had started a process of geographic diversification upon the basis of strategies which aimed at securing for themselves control both of resources – mainly strategic natural resources – and of markets, in order to maximise the advantages derived from superior capabilities which were mainly of a technological nature. Before the Second World War, radical changes in the deep structure of the world economy had already stimulated the birth of new forms of international entrepreneurship, which had included international cartels. The post-war decades analysed in this chapter once again bore witness to the capability of international companies to adapt to the changes that had taken place in the general environment. The period had started under American dominance, which was largely of a technological nature. The Second World War had strengthened it, and provided new technologies in terms of products, transport and communications, which considerably increased the reach of multinationals. The American dominance seemed – and actually was – unchallenged, owing also to the "marginalisation" (to express it optimistically) of the immediate competitors – Europe and Japan – and to the virtual isolation of the centrally-planned economies. However, the end of the war had, at the same time, created new national identities, expectations and, as a consequence, new contexts in which international entrepreneurs had to learn how to behave. Market-seeking strategies – and even more so, given the emotional meaning attached to the land, in particular in former colonies – resource-seeking strategies, had to be radically adapted to a situation in which former colonisers – and foreigners in general – were viewed with suspicion and even hostility. Suddenly, adaptation started to become a source of advantage, increasing the heterogeneity of approaches to international markets, something which, from that moment onwards, was to become a permanent feature of international entrepreneurship.

A second element of variation which emerged in these decades which were clearly dominated by monotone "yankee" multinationals comes from the story of the (successful) rebirth of international entrepreneurship in Europe and in Japan, which, in a few years, first challenged, and then almost outpaced, the US in terms of FDI stock. From these historical examples, further insights into the evolutionary process of multinationals can be derived.

The first one is the relevance of structural (or historical) elements in shaping the process of internationalisation of firms, as argued above. When approaching global diffusion, first European and then Japanese companies successfully achieved it on the basis of elements which were already in the "genetic code" which regulated the development of their own industrial structure. In the case of European companies, the "mother–daughter" model described above both resembled the way in which the continental capitalism geographically expanded throughout the nineteenth century, leveraging family relations in order to reduce uncertainty, but was also the logical consequence of the more "personal" and less bureaucratic orientation of most European companies. In the case of Japan, companies going abroad benefited from the presence, at home, of strong informal networks among domestic enterprises. In both cases, governments played a different, but equally supportive, role in the process of internationalisation.

A second and even more general lesson is that the case of Japan, in particular, confirmed the epochal shift in the nature of the competitive advantages of firms operating abroad. Ownership advantages were less and less of a technological nature, and increasingly involved the ability to coordinate resources, knowledge and capabilities across borders successfully. Investment strategies shifted from the search for inputs and the search for markets, to the search for opportunities to exploit these newly acquired capabilities to coordinate and improve efficiency in order to maximise returns.

By the end of the 1980s, there was little doubt left that the race for economic supremacy during the century to come was a "head to head"[4] competition between the US, Europe and Japan – with the latter being seen by many observers as the one with the most potential for the years to come. Most of this competition was, of course, to be fought on the battlefield of the international economy, a battlefield in which the three regions seemed to have no competitors. Multinational companies and "global" companies (see above) thus played an increasingly relevant role in this framework. It was, in sum, clearly a very "clubby" league, in which little or no space was left to outsiders. But, yet again, things were about to change in an unexpected way.

Notes

1 Charles Wilson, "The Multinational in Historical Perspective", in Keichiro Nagakawa, *Strategy and Structure of Big Business*, Tokyo, University of Tokyo Press, 1978, pp. 265–286. Quotation at p. 280.
2 This was actually the title of the PhD thesis submitted in 1960 by Stephen Hymer, a Canadian scholar who is unanimously considered the first to develop a systematic analysis of multinationals, of their strategies and behaviour.
3 This is the title of a book by the American historian Victoria De Grazia, *Irresistible Empire: America's Advance through 20th-Century Europe*, Cambridge, MA: Belknap Press, 2006.
4 This was the title of a bestseller by the American economist Lester C. Thurow, in which an explicit comparison among living standards and economic achievements and prospects of the US, Europe and Japan was discussed. The book was published in 1993 by Warner Books.

Bibliography

Beechler, Schon L. and Bird, Allan (eds), *Japanese Multinationals Abroad: Individual and Organizational Learning*, (Japan Business and Economics Series), New York: Oxford University Press, 1999.
Franko, Lawrence, *The European Multinationals: A Renewed Challenge to American and British Big Business*, London: Harper & Row, 1976.
Narula, Rajneesh, *Multinational Investment and Economic Structure: Globalisation and Competitiveness*, Oxford: Routledge, 2002.
Wilkins, Mira, *The Maturing of Multinational Enterprise: American Business Abroad from 1914 to 1970*, Cambridge, MA: Harvard University Press, 1974.

7 Epilogue
The last twenty-five years in the light of the past

Introduction

> Looking forward, the next half-century will be a competitive-cooperative three-way economic game among Japan, Europe, and the United States. In jockeying for competitive advantage, they will force each other to adjust. To mutually prosper, they will have to cooperate to create a world economy and a global environment that allows them to survive and to enjoy what they produce.
>
> Lester Thurow, *Head to Head*.[1]

The world order envisioned by Lester Thurow in the book mentioned at the end of the previous chapter was, in the end, a very "trivial" order.

First of all, it was a world in which there were three "contenders" that clearly and beyond any doubt displaced all the other players. As noted at the end of the previous chapter, the primary league was a very clubby élite. When, at the end of the 1980s – and symbolically on 9 November 1989 – the major part of the Second, Communist, world collapsed, the vast majority of the world's economic power was already firmly concentrated in or with the Triad, whichever indicator one may choose. From the perspective of international trade and entrepreneurship, as shown in the previous chapter, nearly 70 per cent of world trade, the absolute majority (80 per cent) of FDIs, and almost all of the headquarters of the world's largest multinationals were all concentrated in the US, Europe and Japan in 1990. The sole problem (and Thurow's book was almost all about this) was to establish who, among the members of the élite, was going to win the "economic battle" (as cited in the book's subtitle), and start the twenty-first century in the leadership position.

Second, Thurow's position is a very good example of Whig history and of Whig economics. In the end, the Triad's supremacy was the confirmation of the overall positivity of capitalism, of democracy and of the institutions that regulated capitalist societies. The fall of the Berlin Wall had clearly demonstrated the inefficiency of central planning and command economies *vis-à-vis* the forces of (more or less) the free market and free competition. It was thus natural that the losers were going to become marginal, quickly (at least implicitly) assuming the status of modern economic colonies. By the way, Thurow entitled the first chapter of his book, "The Bear in the Woods is Gone", in reference to the sudden vanishing of the Soviet Union and of the threat of a nuclear confrontation.

This Whig interpretation of the increasingly pervasive globalisation which took place in the last decade of the twentieth century rested on the solid and pervasive basis of the technological revolution in transport and communications that had characterised the whole of the twentieth century, which was further accelerated (as was stressed in the previous chapter) by the inventions and innovations developed during wartime (the First and Second World Wars). Thurow defined this as a "telecommunications-transportation-computer-logistics" revolution, with immeasurable effects on processes of global sourcing and, above all, on capital and financial markets. The last twenty-five years have thus been constantly characterised by technological improvements which reduced the cost of information, of control and monitoring, and of mobilising people, money and physical goods. Space and time, in sum, have shrunk at an exponential rate. Whichever indicator one takes, the impression is always the same: in the space of just a few years, the mobility of goods, people, information and capital all increased incredibly. The number of air passengers increased around 300 per cent between 1990 and 2010, more or less the same increase as in container port traffic – a fascinating proxy of the goods travelling around the world. The total goods unloaded in ports went from 4.1 billion metric tonnes in 1990 to 9.1 billion tonnes in 2013. The volume of the world export of goods and services rose by 500 per cent in the same period. World trade, in general, increased by 3.5 times, *vis-à-vis* real world GDP growth increasing by only 1.5 times. Workers' remittances as a proportion of world GDP increased from 0.4 to 0.8 per cent, not (only) because there was an increase in wages, but also because the stock of migrants increased by more than 60 per cent in twenty-five years, reaching and surpassing the level of 230 million. The number of fixed and mobile telecommunications connections per 100 people went from ten to eighty between 1990 and 2010. The list could be endless. Cross-border capital flows increased tenfold, from 1 to 11 trillion dollars between 1990 and 2007, the year preceding the global financial crisis – in which the sheer speed of contagion was the most self-evident signal of market integration. The overall financial integration, measured as a ratio of total assets plus liabilities as a proportion of GDP, nearly quadrupled between 1990 and 2010.

Box 7.1 describes some of the features of the globalisation process which had started by the end of the twentieth century, as summarised by the Organisation for Economic Co-operation and Development. As one can easily argue, looking back at Chapter 4, these features are anything but new. Even if the extent of the phenomenon had changed, the components were basically the same, probably with the sole exception of the political sphere, where, after the Second World War, one could no longer talk (at least formally) of colonial empires.

Box 7.1: Twenty-first-century globalisation: features. Anything new?

- a progressive reduction of trade barriers;
- the increasing integration of financial markets;
- foreign direct investment as a driver of re-structuring and of the diffusion of global industries;
- increasing connections between trade and foreign investments;
- the presence of multilateral agreements for trade and investment;
- globalisation of production;
- location strategies of multinational firms strongly influenced by the comparative advantages of countries and regions;
- increasing proportions of world trade take place inside a single company;
- international dissemination of technology and knowledge;

- simultaneous competition in markets between numerous new competitors from all over the world;
- high degree of integration of national economies, but also significant risks of contagion;
- compression of time and distance in international transactions and reduction of transaction costs.

Based upon OECD, *Economic Handbook on Economic Globalisation Indicators*, OECD: Paris 2005.

★ ★ ★ ★ ★

1. Foreign investments in the new global economy

Similarities, of course, cannot hide acute, structural differences, which it is possible to evaluate only through a longitudinal comparative analysis. One difference concerns the opportunities provided by marginal countries, and the degree of their involvement, in the process of integration. The first phase of globalisation, discussed in Chapter 4, was, in fact, an extraordinary phenomenon, but it was fundamentally unequal, in the sense that it privileged only Western countries. It generated a period of intense integration in terms of trade and investments, but it was characterised, in many ways, by persisting inequalities. The first global economy allowed the citizens of London described by Keynes to have access to exotic merchandise, but had little impact on the economic welfare of the humble peasants producing them in say, Burma. We have no reliable data, but it is quite certain that the first global economy did not coincide with a decline in the levels of inequality in the world. Certainly, it did not coincide with the enfranchisement of the peripheries, which remained, with very few exceptions, in a condition of passive marginality – something that, as previously argued, exacerbated their negative attitude towards their former colonisers.

The present global economy is, in this respect, different. It has given some peripheries (though not all) the opportunity to actively take part in the process of the consolidation of the world economy, in a way, and to an extent, that could not even have been imagined at the beginning of the 1990s, when the Second World, the antagonistic Soviet world, imploded and collapsed almost simultaneously and when significant sections of the Third World started a sudden process of growth. In this respect, the data are quite straightforward. According to the evidence collected by the United Nations Conference on Trade and Development (UNCTAD), during the last decades (and even more markedly after the 1990s), the developing and transition economies have assumed an indisputable, steadily increasing role as outward investors. Non-developed countries totalled 6.7 per cent of the world's outward investments stock in 1990, and about 24 per cent of the stock of inward investments. In 2000, these percentages were respectively 11 and 24 again, and, in 2013, they were 31 and 36. In sum, in terms of stocks of outward investments, progress has been steady and very intensive. The data are even more impressive if one looks at flows: in 1990, 4.6 per cent of total FDI outflows came from developing nations. In 2000, the amount was around 12 per cent, and it reached 39 per cent in 2013. The rise of developing nations as outward investors has, of course, been mirrored by a decline in the relevance of the developed nations, and particularly of the US. Clearly, developing nations have maintained their status as the increasingly privileged destinations of foreign investment from the developed – but increasingly also from the developing – countries. After decades in which developed countries were basically attracting the majority of foreign investment flows, developing nations have progressively gained the leadership, receiving more than 50 per cent of new FDI flows today.

This geography of foreign investments is, of course, something new, after centuries of asymmetric exchanges between the West and the East, and between the North and the South of the world.

2. Multinational strategies in the new global economy

Multinationals are the vehicle of foreign direct investments, and their role, during the last quarter of a century, has certainly expanded and strengthened. According to the data provided by UNCTAD in its yearly *World Investment Report*, today, the total sales of the foreign affiliates of multinational enterprises reach nearly 26 thousand billion dollars, against 5 thousand billion in 1990. The value of their total assets (nearly 87 thousand billion dollars) exceeds by far the total world GDP, against 4.6 billion dollars in 1990. They employ 71 million people (21.5 million in 1990). The number of foreign affiliates is impressive, and it has been calculated to be around 80,000. As happened in the course of the nineteenth century, in sum, the present period of globalisation also coincides with a steady expansion of foreign direct investments, in terms both of stock and of flows. And, similarly to the past phases of growth, according to the majority of commentators, multinationals are enjoying a growing generally positive consensus public opinion throughout the world, particularly in developing countries where they are both considered as agents of growth and convergence, and where internationalisation is now considered a possibility even for (and by) domestic companies.

The internationalisation of companies during the present period of globalisation still refers to the same mixture of strategies which have been recurrent throughout the past. John Dunning, among others, suggests six strategic drivers at work in explaining the internationalisation of companies: resource-seeking strategies, aiming at securing control of the sources of strategic raw materials; market seeking, in order to gain access to promising markets; efficiency-seeking investments, aiming at the rationalisation of production; strategic-asset seeking, in order to gain access to secure the control of crucial, and often immaterial, assets, such as knowledge-related assets; and, finally, political motivations. This book has retrospectively demonstrated that all these strategies co-exist, but that some tend to prevail according to particular conditions: in the age of companies and of the First Industrial Revolution, the driver of action was clearly the necessity to secure control of resources, basically natural resources. Later, companies went abroad not only in search of resources, but also of markets in which they could appropriate rents and benefit from their ability to fabricate, and sell in the most advantageous way, their products and services. The Second Industrial Revolution incentivised these tendencies considerably, since it not only increased the thirst for resources and markets enormously, but also generated a permanent search for efficiency in production processes. Thus, both before and after the Second World War, entrepreneurs started to invest abroad in order to improve the efficiency of their production processes. On top of this, the second industrial revolution emphasised something which already existed, namely, the overall relevance of immaterial knowledge, not only of a technological nature, but also concerning the way – as evolutionary economists put it – "to do things", that is, how to organise people, how to shape the production process, how to brand, pack, and sell, and how to do all the other things an enterprise has to master in order to be competitive on the market at all times. This kind of knowledge was scarcely available on the market, was idiosyncratic, and was progressively developed *inside* the organisation during its evolutionary process. It was, in sum, something embodied *within* the organisation: in order to appropriate it, it was much easier to obtain control of the organisation itself, instead of investing in order to develop this kind of knowledge. Cross-border appropriation of knowledge and immaterial assets is, intuitively, particularly relevant in the case of laggard firms in latecomer countries that promptly or quickly wish to start the process of catching up. Foreign investments often provide or offer the possibility of accelerating this process of the acquisition of critical assets in terms of knowledge and competences. Using foreign investments in order to acquire strategic assets has been an increasingly popular policy in firms in developing countries. Frequently, these are even state-controlled companies, something which brings once again into the picture the relationship between foreign investment activity and political economy issues. According to the current thinking in international business literature, political motives are another relevant strategic driver of international business, as they reveal a form of behaviour which is historically deeply rooted in the dynamics of international entrepreneurship, as narrated in the first chapters of this book.

Strategic asset-seeking and political motives are, in sum, increasingly popular policies among international business firms, even if there have been phases in the past in which they were even more relevant than they are today. Both emphasise the geographic dimension of international business and the relevance of a factor which, for some time, was considered relatively less important as a driver of multinational behaviour, to wit, the search for and the exploitation of the advantages derived from certain locations instead of others, what the literature defines as "location advantage".

The emphasis on the "L" (Location) in the already mentioned OLI paradigm is also justified by another major concept that has come back into use in the framework of international business, that is, the fact that many new investments are directed specifically at the acquisition of the control of natural resources, and are thus characterised by a clear distinctive location which determines both the direction and the extent of the investment. International investment in natural resources is, as shown by the analysis in the previous chapters, certainly not a novelty. What is new, in the present period of globalisation, is that, among the protagonists in the international acquisition of natural resources, there are more and more companies with their headquarters in emerging markets, China in particular.

Strategic asset-seeking and resource-seeking are, in sum, two relevant – albeit not new – components of international business activity in the present global economy. Other motivations do, of course, persist; however, the real novelty is the role that is being played in this process by the emerging economies.

This renewed emphasis on natural resources has several implications. As previously mentioned, the primary sector, and natural resources in particular, is a very sensitive area in which foreign investment activity has an impact on a number of emotional elements and aspects. Nationalism, broadly intended as the protection of national interests, has recently been re-emerging, and not just in developing peripheral countries. This book has already discussed the relationships between the emergence of nationalistic attitudes and the process of globalisation. The recreation of a global economy latently contains, in itself, all the premises for an intensification of nationalism, particularly among the countries more involved in this process.

3. Corporate architectures in the new global economy

A third conceptual area to explore in this conclusion refers to the issue of the corporate organisational structures which emerge in the current process of globalisation. And in the spirit of this conclusion, we will discuss the aspects of the evolution in corporate structures as part of a more general process that takes place very much in the long term.

A clear message that has been established in the previous chapters is that the organisational ecology of multinational firms emerges over time following the various processes of creative adjustment to the changes in technology, in the markets, in institutions and all the other aspects of the external framework. And this is what occurred anew during the re-globalisation period and what gave rise to the changes in the framework described above.

In 1989 – leveraging intense research activity carried out during the 1980s – two international business experts, Sumantra Ghoshal and Christopher Bartlett, published a book entitled *Managing Across Borders* which became a bestseller in the field of international strategy and was immediately ranked by the *Financial Times* as being among the top fifty most influential management books of the twentieth century. Through a huge variety of case studies, the two researchers demonstrated that, during the 1980s, multinationals had undergone significant changes in their strategic orientation, changes which mainly concerned the role played by the subsidiaries inside the multinational organisation. The framework of international business, characterised by increasing entropy, emphasised the strategic relevance of subsidiaries as the creators of value within the organisation itself. Subsidiaries, and, above all, the creative relationships between the subsidiaries in a multinational company, were the *loci* in which knowledge and competences were created and could be transferred and made to circulate inside the organisation. These capabilities originated from the simultaneous presence of the company in different markets, and "transcended" the national setting in which they were developed. Companies which were capable of both managing this complex network of subsidiaries – with each one creating knowledge and competences locally (local responsiveness) – and of diffusing these competences inside the organisation were thus defined as "transnationals". To sum up, transnational companies were able to perform simultaneously in the areas of global efficiency (as global companies did), able to create their own knowledge and competences locally (which was typical of multinationals), and, distinctively, transmitted worldwide learning and knowledge diffusion throughout the whole organisation.

The concept of the transnational firm was of absolute relevance in the field of international business studies, and clearly pointed in the direction of a new perspective on multinational organisations which were progressively more and more resembling networks of competences that the home headquarters had the responsibility of coordinating in an effective way. The changes in the external environment made local responsiveness a crucial capability inside the multinational organisation, not only because it allowed it to exploit advantages and make profits in the host market, but also because it generated valuable competences to be exploited at more general corporate level. The technological transformations described above, in terms of information and communications technologies, made this process of strategic re-orientation easier and smoother. As the history narrated in the previous chapters has made clear, once again it is changes in markets and technological improvements that have had an impact on the form of global entrepreneurship. International companies transformed themselves into networks of interrelated assets and capabilities. Functions such as research and development, finance and marketing, once characteristic of the organisation's headquarters, became geographically dispersed, and were no longer concentrated in the home countries. Clearly, all this had a considerable impact on the way in which multinational companies were shaped and governed. Many internationally active companies were increasingly resembling "communities of learning", characterised by horizontal, rather than vertical, authority relations. In this perspective, multinationals resemble geographically dispersed networks of production, in which subsidiaries are members of a partnership, and not of a bureaucratic organisation.

These transformations, depicted by Ghoshal and Bartlett in their seminal book, paved the way for further and even more radical changes. Once the organisational relevance started to shift from the centre to the periphery, through a sort of "centrifugal" process, a different set of organisational architectures started to become diffused. For instance, when local subsidiaries become independent, and are linked to the centre through loose forms of alliance, "transnational networks" come into existence, creating the necessity to achieve economies of scale at global level by maintaining flexibility and local responsiveness.

The evolution of multinational structures towards network-like agglomerations of competences also paved the way for another powerful concept, one which has been much in fashion in international business literature since the beginning of the new millennium, that of Global Value Chains (GVC) and of Global Commodity Chains (GCC). The fragmentation and globalisation of value chains (that is, according to the definition provided by the OECD, the organisation of international production, trade and investments in which "the different stages of the production process are located across different countries") is a prominent aspect of current global entrepreneurship. The possibility of restructuring the production process in this way is clearly connected to that of technological progress, which allows transport and communications across the globe to be performed at an increasingly reduced cost, and to the related possibility of coordinating and controlling activities at long distance. Many multinationals have consequently restructured their organisational architecture by increasingly using global value chains in order to put strategies of outsourcing and offshoring, that is, the relocation of processes and activities, into practice.

The possibility of fragmenting the production cycle into global value chains is clearly a product of the current period of globalisation. This is a phenomenon which has many effects, of which two appear to be particularly relevant from the perspective of this book.

The first effect again concerns organisational structures and, in particular, the relationships between the headquarters and the subsidiaries. According to the most recent research, headquarters are increasingly transforming their function into that of coordinators of dispersed activities across the globe, given that, as stated above, all the critical and strategic functions have been clustered into subsidiaries. Furthermore, global value chains, as networks of independent producers collaborating on specific projects through stable contractual agreements, require extensive effort in terms of design and coordination.

A second aspect connected to the emergence of global value chains as a privileged way of organising international production is again related to the issue of geography and location advantages. Global value chains function thanks to technology and globalisation, and benefit from the favourable conditions that can sometimes be found in emerging markets. This explains why emerging markets maintain – together with a growing prominence as outward investors – considerable relevance as the destinations of investments flows. This, of course, means a renewed interest in the advantages implicit in operating in specific locations, which is something fundamentally connected to the presence of comparative advantages across the developing and developed countries.

Clearly, global value chains and their intersections with international firms are a new organisational solution emerging both in a phase, and as a product, of intense re-globalisation processes. Notwithstanding this, in many industries, and in many geographical areas including emerging countries, traditional forms of multinational enterprises remain relevant.

★ ★ ★ ★ ★

The current phase of globalisation, and its most recent history since the early 1990s, has much in common with past episodes of economic and social integration. As in the past, technology and culture play a pivotal role in sustaining this process, also creating the institutions able to sustain it. As in the past, phases of global economic integration stimulate the energies of international entrepreneurs, who, in their turn, invest abroad in their search for business opportunities in distant markets. However, regarding the dynamics of the past which this volume has endeavoured to narrate, an acute difference can be detected at corporate level. Again, as happened in the past, technological progress and institutional elements are operating in the direction of enlarging the range of organisational types. Similarly to what is happening to many companies at domestic level, improvements in the technologies of transport and communications are apparently leading to a fragmentation of previously hierarchical and integrated structures, in the direction, as in the case of transnational companies, of transnational networks and global value chains which show an increasing dispersion of organisational authority relations. The first global economy – but, above all, the technologies of the Second Industrial Revolution – had created incentives to construct global integrated architectures, thereby transcending the network-oriented approach that was largely based upon decentralisation, which had characterised large sections of international entrepreneurship during the Middle Ages and the modern period. The current re-globalisation is apparently pushing back the pendulum in the direction of the decentralisation of authority relations, once again reorienting the action of global entrepreneurs, the opportunities provided to them, and the constraints that they face.

Note

1 Lester C. Thurow, *Head to Head: The Coming Economic Battle among Japan, Europe and America*, New York: Warner Books, 1992.

Bibliography

Cuervo-Cazurra, Alvaro and Ramamurti, Ravi (eds), *Understanding Multinationals from Emerging Markets*, Cambridge: Cambridge University Press, 2014.

Dicken, Peter, *Global Shift: Mapping the Changing Contours of the World Economy*, Thousand Oaks, CA: Sage Publications, 2011.

Ghoshal, Sumantra and Bartlett, Christopher A., *Managing Across Borders: The Transnational Solution*, Boston, MA: Harvard Business School Press, 1989.

OECD, *Interconnected Economies: Benefiting from Global Value Chains*, Paris: OECD, 2013.

Ohmae, Kenichi, *The Borderless World: Power and Strategy in the Interlinked Economy*, New York: Harper Collins, 1999.

Index